"This book is an engaging study o
and personal scams, so often tal
Written in an accessible style, the book combines the personal
scientific. Retelling everyday examples, it offers a captivating account of how
we fall victim to fraud and theft, and suffer their emotional consequences
because we fail to recognise the traps of deception. Dove dissects the
evidence, and rooting her account in scientific theory, she urges the reader
to learn and prepare to detect the fraud instead of succumbing to it."
– *Dr Andreas Cebulla, Associate Professor, Flinders University of South Australia*

"Dr Dove has produced a comprehensive but accessible text that summarizes the current social science research on frauds and scams. The chapters progress logically from defining fraud in all its variations, to describing the process by which victims are defrauded, to offering solutions and preventative measures. The case studies she presents are exceptional and provide the reader with real-world examples. As a professor and a public educator, I believe this book could be used in a classroom, by working professionals, and citizens who wish to protect themselves from frauds and scams."
– *Dr Roderick Graham, Associate Professor of Sociology and Criminal Justice, Old Dominion University*

"An exceptional piece of work that unpacks what it is to be a victim, an observer and even a perpetrator of different types of fraud. What Dr Dove has managed to do here is remarkable, giving astute academic analysis alongside practical advice, examples and explanations in a definitive resource on both the art and science of the scam."
– *Jenny Radcliffe, Director, Human Factor Security*

"A fabulously interesting read. Dr Martina Dove provides a window into the methods of criminals whilst giving a valuable insight into how criminals use our emotional responses to defraud. This is a book for all, fraud prevention professionals, academics and the public. This book could assist in stopping you and those around you from becoming a victim to this despicable crime."
– *Tony Murray, Former National Economic Crime and Fraud Protect Officer for National Lead Force, City of London Police*

The Psychology of Fraud, Persuasion and Scam Techniques

The Psychology of Fraud, Persuasion and Scam Techniques provides an in-depth explanation of not only why we fall for scams and how fraudsters use technology and other techniques to manipulate others, but also why fraud prevention advice is not always effective.

Starting with how fraud victimisation is perceived by society and why fraud is underreported, the book explores the different types of fraud and the human and demographic factors that make us vulnerable. It explains how fraud has become increasingly sophisticated and how fraudsters use communication, deception and theories of rationality, cognition and judgmental heuristics, as well as specific persuasion and scam techniques, to encourage compliance. Covering frauds including romance scams and phishing attacks such as advance fee frauds and so-called miracle cures, the book explores ways we can learn to spot scams and persuasive communication, with checklists and advice for reflection and protection.

Featuring a set of practical guidelines to reduce fraud vulnerability, advice on how to effectively report fraud and educative case studies and examples, this easy-to-read, instructive book is essential reading for fraud prevention specialists, fraud victims and academics and students interested in the psychology of fraud.

Martina Dove is a researcher with a fervent passion for fraud prevention, specialising in fraud vulnerability, individual characteristics that make people vulnerable to fraud and scam techniques used by fraudsters.

The Psychology of Fraud, Persuasion and Scam Techniques

Understanding What Makes Us Vulnerable

Martina Dove

Routledge
Taylor & Francis Group

LONDON AND NEW YORK

First published 2021
by Routledge
2 Park Square, Milton Park, Abingdon, Oxon OX14 4RN

and by Routledge
52 Vanderbilt Avenue, New York, NY 10017

Routledge is an imprint of the Taylor & Francis Group, an informa business

© 2021 Martina Dove

The right of Martina Dove to be identified as author of this work has been asserted by her in accordance with sections 77 and 78 of the Copyright, Designs and Patents Act 1988.

All rights reserved. No part of this book may be reprinted or reproduced or utilised in any form or by any electronic, mechanical, or other means, now known or hereafter invented, including photocopying and recording, or in any information storage or retrieval system, without permission in writing from the publishers.

Trademark notice: Product or corporate names may be trademarks or registered trademarks, and are used only for identification and explanation without intent to infringe.

British Library Cataloguing-in-Publication Data
A catalogue record for this book is available from the British Library

Library of Congress Cataloging-in-Publication Data
A catalog record has been requested for this book

ISBN: 978-0-367-85957-2 (hbk)
ISBN: 978-0-367-85956-5 (pbk)
ISBN: 978-1-003-01599-4 (ebk)

Typeset in Sabon
by Newgen Publishing UK

To fraud victims everywhere. It is not your fault, it is a crime. May you find your voice to tell your stories proudly.

Contents

List of figures	xii
Foreword	xiii
Acknowledgements	xv

1 Introduction   1
  My scam experience 1
  Anatomy of the scam experience 2
  Contents 3

2 What is fraud and who are the fraudsters?   5
  What is fraud? 5
  When is fraud a fraud? 6
  Who are the fraudsters? 8
  Fraud taxonomy 11
  Fraud reporting and sanctions 13
  Fraud victimisation from the victim's perspective 14

3 Different types of frauds and scams   16
  Nigerian or advance fee frauds 16
  Identity and synthetic fraud 18
  Romance scams 19
  Phishing and other social engineering attacks 20
  Psychic or clairvoyant scams and cold readings 21
  Miracle cures 21
  Charity scams and crowdfunding campaigns 22
  Lotteries, prize draws, sweepstakes and giveaways 23
  Investment or business opportunities and job scams 23
  Sextortion and extortion scams 24
  Mortgage fraud 26
  Food fraud 27
  Further reading 28

4 Deception and communication — 29
The process of communication 29
Deceptive communication 33
View of deception through cultural and societal conventions 35
Detecting deception 36
How fraudsters deceive 38
Deception and its role in fraud victimisation 40
Further reading 42

5 How we think and make decisions and why this matters in fraud situations — 43
System 1 and System 2 43
Elaboration Likelihood Model (ELM) of persuasion 45
Decision-making styles 46
Cognitive biases 47
Further reading 53

6 Persuasion and scamming techniques — 55
Evoking visceral influence 55
Liking and similarity 56
Credibility and legitimacy 57
Evoking social norms 58
Authority 58
Commitment and consistency 59
Scarcity and urgency 59
Social proof and social influence 61
Dishonesty and distraction 61
Priming 62
Altercasting 64
Grooming 65
Further reading 66

7 Human factors in fraud — 67
Impulsivity and self-control 68
Compliance and obedience to authority 69
Risk assessment and sensation seeking 70
Flattery and intimidation 71
Information processing and need for cognition 71
Trust and gullibility 72
Vigilance, delayed decisions, scam awareness and background knowledge 74
Demographics and circumstances 76
Behaviours and beliefs 78
Human factors and information security 79
Further reading 81

8 **Theories and models that could explain why we fall victim to fraud and scams**   82
 Errors in judgment 82
 The Model of Scamming Vulnerability 83
 Models of Gullible and Foolish Action 84
 Phishing susceptibility framework 85
 Suspicion, Cognition and Automacity Model of phishing susceptibility 87
 The Model of Fraud Susceptibility 88

9 **Learning to spot scams, fraud and persuasive communication**   91
 Scam situations and factors that contribute to compliance 91
 Spotting scam techniques in phishing correspondence 105

10 **SCAMS checklist: advice for reflection and protection**   120
 Scrutinise the correspondence 121
 Consider scam techniques 124
 Assess emotional state 125
 Moderate the response 127
 Share your experience with others 129

 References   132
 Index   151

Figures

1.1	Scam stages and relevant factors	2
3.1	Components of extortion and sextortion phishing correspondence identified by Dove (2019)	25
5.1	Illusion of control can make us think we have control over random events	52
6.1	Rational advice is often useless when one is in a visceral state	56
6.2	An example of a sextortion scam	63
8.1	The Model of Fraud Susceptibility by Dove (2018)	89
9.1	An example of a Nigerian/advance fee scam exploiting social norms	107
9.2	An example of a Nigerian/advance fee scam, adapted to reflect COVID-19 pandemic	108
9.3	An example of a classic Nigerian/advance fee scam	109
9.4	An example of a 'compromised account' scam	110
9.5	An example of a 'compromised account' scam that uses covert tactics	111
9.6	An example of a 'miracle cure' scam	112
9.7	An example of a scam targeting people's circumstances	114
9.8	An example of a job scam	115
9.9	An example of a 'refund' phishing scam for TV licence	116
9.10	An example of a 'refund' phishing scam for Amazon	117
9.11	A more sophisticated example of a 'renew your account' phishing scam	118
9.12	An example of a 'free giveaway' phishing scam	119
10.1	SCAMS checklist	121
10.2	Cross-referenced information and the warning signs revealed by the search	122

Foreword

It is my pleasure to introduce Martina Dove's excellent book. She was a celebrity in fraud and scam research even before she completed her PhD, being in regular contact with the main players in this field of study and active within the community for fraud advice. The book reflects both her scholarly knowledge and the rich repertoire of cases that she has come in contact with.

The book is a compact but exhaustive overview of different types of frauds and scams, from the famous Nigerian ones to romance scams to identity theft; it further covers the fraudsters manipulative techniques and the psychological processes that make us vulnerable. As such, it is not only a journey through this ever-growing criminal activity but also a crash course in social psychology: classic and novel studies are explained with accessible language illuminating fraud as a social and psychological phenomenon, making for a fascinating excursion into communication, trust and deception, decision-making and different personality characteristics that can play a role in fraud victimisation.

The sheer number of successful frauds and scams tells us that this is by no means something that the average person easily avoids. Such deceptions can be highly complicated machineries and there are many different factors involved in the different phases, from preparation to aftermath. This innovative book follows the fraud process in all its stages, explores the different practical and psychological aspects for each stage, and proposes a model that illustrates how for each stage that are conditions that favour resistance or vulnerability to a fraudulent offer or opportunity.

In the last part of the book, all the different parts come together in the presentation of real-life cases from different type of scams, with the inclusion of illustrations of fraudulent material such as emails or website pages. This vivid and memorable collection of stories and examples is accompanied by a commentary showing how different factors, identified by the research, come into play. For example, a credible enough email can grab a person in a hurry or people out or their comfort zone can be predated by a scammer who projects just the right type of character, be it an elegant broker or the modest local mechanic.

This book is a pocket guide to fraud, scams and deception useful for practitioners as well as for the lay person and for researchers and students. It has a captivating, personal style and the reader will learn effortlessly about the topic, acquiring expertise on a global phenomenon with enormous resonance in economic, social and psychological terms, and will strengthen their immunity to fraud as they go along.

The motivation for this book springs from Martina Dove's passion for, as she says, "sharing stories, raising awareness and destroying stigma attached to fraud victimisation", and as a contribution to all three goals the book is unbeatable.

Alessandra Fasulo PhD
University of Portsmouth
July 2020

Acknowledgements

From the moment I did my first research study with victims of fraud, I knew I would one day write this book. The stories touched me deeply and I know, for many, their experiences were extremely upsetting and not easy to recount. Therefore, this book would not be here without the people who shared their stories with me to help me understand how scams happen. Thank you all for contributing to this understanding and experience.

I want to thank my editor, Eleanor Taylor, who from the moment I emailed her the idea, showed an enthusiasm for this book and was supportive throughout. I would not be here without you. Thank you for believing in me. I also want to thank, in no particular order, Dr Andreas Cebulla, Dr Roderick Graham, Jenny Radcliffe and Tony Murray for reading an early draft of this book and liking it. Additionally, my wonderful PhD supervisor Alessandra Fasulo, for all the enthusiasm and support over the course of my research, and for writing the foreword. Thank you so much for your time and your encouragement. I also want to say that I truly admire each one of you. Additionally, I want to thank Prof. Stephen Lea and Darren Hodder, for giving me great pointers and ideas for this book.

On a personal note, huge thank you to my dear friend Joanna Lawrie Harrison, who helped me navigate my first book deal and offered encouragement. Thank you so much. Also, my husband for enduring many lonely weekends while I was writing this book. I want to say thank you to my talented friend Dubravko Kastrapeli for making custom made illustrations for this book and my friend Lidija Paradinovic Nagulov, who designed the book cover.

Finally, huge thank you to all my friends and colleagues, who showed enthusiasm for this book and offered encouragement along the way.

Chapter 1

Introduction

My scam experience

About five or six years ago, I was defrauded on eBay. I wanted to buy a mobile phone and since I had some money in my PayPal account, I decided to see if I could buy a new mobile phone on eBay. I purchased the phone (which was not a 'too good to be true' deal, only cheaper by a tiny amount than retail) and when it did not arrive when it was supposed to, I got a slightly unsettling feeling in my stomach, but I emailed the seller hoping for the best. When two of my emails went unanswered, I knew I had been scammed. I reported it to eBay and had to wait ten days for a resolution. In those ten days, I obsessively tried to find out as much information as possible about my seller. I found out that, on the same night that I purchased the phone, they advertised the same phone several times, as well as other types of phones. They also purchased camping gear on the same night. Their feedback prior to that was good and someone has even picked up things from their address. Perhaps they were just amateur scammers, thinking they could defraud a few people at the same time, to get some camping gear for their holiday. Or they had their eBay and PayPal account compromised by someone who used it for fraud. But I blamed myself for not checking what else they were selling, as I was convinced that this would have made me more suspicious. I was angry, disappointed in human nature and I imagined scenarios in which my scammers suddenly realise the money is taken out of their account by PayPal (as it frequently is when there is a dispute and goods are not sent), leaving them stranded without money while they camp in the wilderness. Or where police visit them and they get arrested, fined or shamed in front of their neighbours. I knew I would get my money refunded by eBay but I still felt angry and I felt taken advantage of and, until I got a refund, I had no closure. Even after I received a refund, purchased a phone and moved on, I would periodically have flashbacks of the incident and it made me question motivations of anyone I did not know. I simultaneously felt ashamed that I was not more mature and able to move on from this relatively benign fraud experience that did not even result in a loss of funds, and extremely angry that this happened to me. This is a struggle most fraud victims have long after they were defrauded, coupled with a sense of injustice. Many fraud victims are not as lucky as I was; they are never able to recoup funds lost to fraud. Often, the perpetrator is not punished. This, too, can have an effect on fraud victims. For many victims, the loss is significant too: a pension or entire life savings, money needed to live comfortably, money needed to survive. But fraud is not just about the money that is lost. It is also about the anger, sadness, humiliation, stress, disappointment, loss of trust, lack of sleep and loss of self-esteem, etc. It is about losing a sense of security that comes from knowing that certain societal and cultural norms forbid this type of behaviour. And, as such, it is extremely harmful.

Anatomy of the scam experience

My fraud was not even that sophisticated. Many people go through frauds that are socially engineered to enhance compliance, in which a scammer may pretend to be a friend over a course of many months, building trust and creating plausible scenarios. Or they may engineer highly effective and believable phishing emails. And all the time they are getting better at creating scams that target what makes us human: social norms, personality characteristics, behaviours and circumstances.

As such, scam experience can be extremely complex. Talking to fraud victims allowed me to configure a map of a typical stages and factors that come into it. I identified three stages: precursors, commitment and aftermath (see Figure 1.1).

Precursors can be situational or personal circumstances that can influence engagement with fraudulent offers. These can include lack of time to consider the information before a decision is made, existential problems, such as lack of funds, which can make fraud offers seem less risky and more appealing. Also, the backing of other people can make the offer appear legitimate and

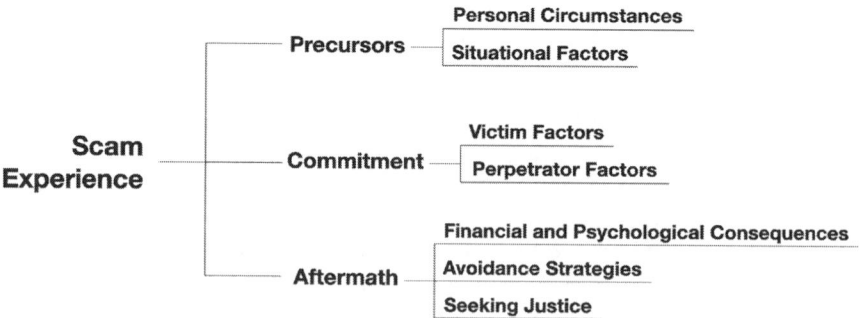

Figure 1.1 Scam stages and relevant factors.

influence our decisions. In the commitment stage, the victim is engaged with the fraudulent offer, either by clicking links and following instructions or by talking to the scammer. In this stage two, different types of factors come into play: those pertaining to the perpetrator and those pertaining to the victim. Perpetrator factors include tricks used by scammers, which encourage compliance, such as appearing likeable and trustworthy, producing legitimate-looking communications and manipulating our decision-making processes by limiting the time offers are valid for. Victim factors include emotional reactions evoked by scam offers (e.g. excitement at the prospect of money or a job), inadequate information processing and compliance with social norms, which are exploited by scammers. Finally, the aftermath stage comes after the victim is defrauded, and includes different struggles victims might encounter including financial hardship and psychological distress suffered as a result of the fraud, such as loss of self-esteem and anger. Or it may include difficulties in reporting fraud and getting justice, or attaining a sense of closure. These difficulties often lead to a loss of trust in society as a whole. Victims often alter their behaviour or try coming up with different strategies to avoid being defrauded in the future. Some reported having less empathy for others as a part of a strategy, to not let this happen again (Dove, 2018).

Seeing the scam experience dissected in this way, it becomes clear that scams can be highly orchestrated and contain very persuasive elements that encourage compliance. These elements synchronise with victims' own circumstances and vulnerability factors, increasing the likelihood of compliance further. Fraud warnings often forget to consider these complexities, concentrating instead on 'dos and don'ts'. This can be counterproductive, as there is so much fraud advice online that users do not know what to listen to anymore. It leads to fatigue, which can result in non-compliance and less caution (Furnell & Thomson, 2009). For example, researchers found that warnings that give a detailed explanation of why malware is harmful and what it does, are received better than vague warnings (Modic & Anderson, 2014).

Instead of simple and authoritarian fraud warnings that generally lead to resignation, we could look deeper and consider the psychology behind fraud, and make warnings more people friendly, more personal. People often want to know more; they want to know how to protect themselves and understand the intricacies that make them vulnerable to fraudulent attacks, but often this information is just not there. In this book I want to address how scammers persuade us and how; what makes us human is often what makes us vulnerable to different frauds.

Contents

Chapter 2 explains what fraud is, how it might be different to unethical practices, what are typical characteristics of the fraudsters, problems with underreporting and sanctions and what fraud victimisation looks like from the victim's perspective. Additionally, this chapter outlines suggested fraud taxonomy, which may be of interest to fraud prevention and fraud reporting specialists.

Chapter 3 describes common and enduring frauds, their variants, where appropriate and whom they may target.

Chapter 4 and Chapter 5 describe some of the processes that facilitate fraud, such as the process of communication, deception, how we think and make decisions and how scammers may utilise or exploit these processes.

Chapter 6 outlines persuasion and scamming techniques, designed to cloud judgment and influence decisions, which are frequently used by scammers to evoke compliance.

Chapter 7 outlines human factors in fraud, such as individual characteristics that make us vulnerable to fraud and Chapter 8 explains how and why fraud happens by reflecting on different models and theories that aim to explain fraud vulnerability.

Chapter 9 offers a variety of real scam examples and case studies, broken down to help illustrate scam techniques and individual vulnerabilities targeted by scams.

Finally, Chapter 10 gives a 'SCAMS' checklist, which can be used as a handy guide when one is not sure about potential scam situations or correspondence, or generally as a way of minimising fraud vulnerability.

Chapter 2

What is fraud and who are the fraudsters?

What is fraud?

Fraud is an act of deception resulting in personal or financial gain and can be committed in several ways. It can be committed by false representation (e.g. pretending to be a police officer to gain trust), by abuse of position (e.g. where someone occupies a position of a guardian, safeguarding someone's finances, but they are not acting in their best interest) and by failing to disclose information that might be important (Fraud Act, 2006). Fraud can be perpetrated in many ways and against many different sectors, such as public (e.g. government), private (e.g. financial services, technology, construction, etc.) and the charity sector. Public sector fraud includes fraud perpetrated against local and central government, tax and benefits, the National Health Service and State Pension. Private sector fraud includes financial services, consumer goods, manufacturing, technology, media and telecoms, construction, retail and wholesale, travel, leisure and transportation, professional services, healthcare, pharmaceuticals and biotechnology, and natural resources.

Fraud can also be perpetrated against private individuals but this is often not viewed as seriously as other types of fraud. Fraud victims get very little sympathy, as if being scammed somehow implies being responsible for the victimisation (Cross, 2015). However, fraud against private individuals is still fraud and it is no different from any other type of fraud. Fraud committed against unsuspecting individuals has been going on for centuries and frequently features in children's stories, perhaps serving as a warning about those that may betray our trust (Greenspan, 2009). For example, in the original story of Pinocchio, written in the 1800s by Carlo Collodi, Pinocchio gets defrauded by a pair of swindlers, a cat and a fox, who use the same scamming techniques seen today. He is defrauded several times before he learns his lesson not to trust them (Collodi, 2002). Greenspan (2009) argues that these stories serve as a warning to children, teaching them to avoid being fooled. There are many types of fraud in operation today: holiday scams, health scams, insurance fraud, pension scams, job scams, rental scams, tax frauds, pyramid schemes and other financial frauds, inheritance scams, ticket fraud, charity scams and fake GoFundMe campaigns, psychic scams, fake lotteries and prize draws, advance fee frauds, fake websites, online auction scams, doorstep scams, etc. The list is endless. The diversity of fraud in operation today suggests that fraudsters adapt quickly to current events and are inventive in designing scams that vary in narratives and are highly persuasive. This is why understanding how scams persuade us is important.

Delivery of fraud perpetrated against private individuals has also changed with times. Once upon a time, scams were delivered either face-to-face or by post. This carries considerable cost to the scammer. For example, Nigerian scams, in which a wealthy 'Nigerian official' contacts a potential victim and offers them a hefty fee for help in transferring funds from Nigeria, can be traced to the 1970s, when they were delivered via post and later via fax or phone (Glickman, 2005). However, some researchers argue that this type of fraud has been around for a lot longer, dating back to the sixteenth century (Zuckoff, 2005). But it is the invention of the Internet that allowed Nigerian scams to become omnipresent. They are so well known, obvious and far-fetched, that one theory is that fraudsters use them to identify the most vulnerable and gullible victims, whose details are then sold to other fraudsters as they are perfect candidates for repeat victimisation (Herley, 2012).

The Internet has allowed fraud to be delivered easily, anonymously and relatively cost free to the perpetrator (Button et al., 2015; R. G. Smith, 2010), with email being the most popular delivery of fraud for all age groups (Citizen Advice, 2017). It is, therefore, not difficult to see why fraud is flourishing. It allows perpetrators to defraud people in different countries, which makes it difficult to investigate and prosecute frauds perpetrated online (Button et al., 2012). Therefore, it is not surprising that, since 2009, fraud losses have risen by 56.5 per cent (Gee & Button, 2019). Low prosecution rates and low delivery costs translate to high profits and low risks associated with perpetrating fraud and this is why fraud is growing and evolving so rapidly. Gee and Button (2019) suggested that fraud might be rising due to the erosion of belief in moral and ethical norms, which are part of the society, and the distance between victims and perpetrators, as most of the fraud is perpetrated online. Additionally, the complexity of the processes and systems sometimes allows fraud to go unnoticed.

When is fraud a fraud?

Although deception is a huge part of fraud and necessary for successful execution of a scam, simply deceiving someone without a financial advantage is unlikely to be seen as fraud. What is fraud? I have heard the word 'fraud' used many times to describe different frauds, unethical practices as well as people who lie to their partners. I have heard someone explain that scams are when someone tricks you but fraud is something that happens on a larger scale and is more serious, such as fraud perpetrated against organisations. This is not technically true. Fraud can be perpetrated against private individuals, too, but the legal lines are often blurred there, with many victims told to pursue justice themselves, through civil courts (Button et al., 2013).

There are also unethical practices. Typically, when fraud is concerned there is deliberate deception and/or failure to disclose information, which results in financial gain for the fraudster. Unethical practices are somewhat alike in that, where purchases or services are concerned, information may not be transparent but it will usually be there, just hidden in very tiny terms and conditions. Or the benefit of the product or a service is deliberately overstated in the advertisement, which can be deceiving but is different to fraud, because the customer typically receives a product they purchased (Beals et al., 2015).

In a face-to-face situation, the salesmen may use persuasion techniques to detract from the information they do not want you to notice or to encourage you to comply. For example, I have had, in the past, phone calls following a big purchase with an offer of a warranty for a fee. Often, the representative will say they only have the highlighted terms (usually outlining good things but omitting disclaimers); the only way you can access the full terms and conditions is to sign up. Although they also openly mention a mandatory cancellation period, in which you can cancel the warranty without being charged, many people, once signed up, will not look into the terms and conditions until they need to make a claim, upon which they may find out that they were not told about conditions that make the warranty useless overall. Presenting contract information in this way is highly unethical but not technically fraud because terms and conditions outline terms of the contract. In recent times, certain unethical practices such as these have been exposed and I hope they continue to be frowned upon.

Web design can also contain unethical practices and they are referred to as dark patterns; design patterns based on human desires and behaviour that are used in user experience design. These patterns are typically against users' best interest and are used to persuade. These include making a process too complicated in order to detract from certain actions, redirecting interactions or forcing action in order to access the website or certain functionalities (e.g. adverts disguised as content), misleading questions (e.g. opting out of subscriptions is often worded ambiguously) and delaying or hiding of information relevant to the user (Gray et al., 2018). Dark patterns are frequently used by legitimate companies so they do not always mean the website is fraudulent, but it is certainly not a nice way to treat customers.

While lying and being dishonest are socially undesirable, they are part of everyday life and sometimes even necessary for human relationships (see Chapter 4). Most people would engage in dishonest behaviour given the opportunity, because dishonesty pays and even has a role in the economy (Mazar et al., 2008). Fraud and dishonesty often overlap. For example, I was shopping with a friend a while ago, buying outfits for a function. The sales assistant tried hard to sell my friend an expensive jacket and he was thinking whether he should buy it, given the fact that he would have no occasions to wear it to, after this event. The sales assistant encouraged him to purchase the jacket and advised that he could carefully wear it, without taking the tag off, and return it after the function. This surprised me, not because I am not aware that some people do this, but because I know it is wrong to do this. It is dishonest. And witnessing a sales assistant advising my friend to engage in dishonesty felt, quite frankly, wrong. This is a known practice and a huge problem for retail industry (Speights & Hilinski, 2005). It is considered to be a fraudulent return, yet it seems more acceptable than defrauding a pensioner and more likely to be perpetrated by people who would not otherwise dream of committing fraud. Society likes to think that criminals weigh up the pros and cons of their crimes, taking into consideration the likelihood of getting caught as well as the punishment. But this is not always the case. Good people may engage in dishonesty or cheating because they are able to explain to themselves why this is OK. Being able to categorise the dishonest behaviour as something else means that self-image is preserved. Additionally, dishonesty may depend on whether people are mindful of their moral standards. In fact, research found that dishonesty decreased when participants were reminded of honesty standards (Mazar et al., 2008).

It is often the dishonesty or deception part that causes distress to victims of fraud, even when the victim did not lose any funds, perhaps because they realised they were about to be defrauded (see Dove, 2018). I talk more about the role of deception later in the book.

Who are the fraudsters?

It is not always easy to spot fraudsters and certain stereotypes, especially those painting fraudsters as confident risk takers that are easy to spot, do not help. Wilson (2018) suggests that lack of research is responsible for these stereotypes and that fraudsters are not easily identifiable (also Wilson, 2017). Some of these stereotypes state that fraudsters already have criminal records and are narcissists or psychopaths who enjoy targeting vulnerable victims. However, interviewing fraudsters, Wilson (2018) found that most fraudsters are ordinary individuals who took to crime to protect their families from financial hardship and some reported they felt they had no other alternatives. Some fraudsters stopped when they achieved certain targets, and even expressed regret at causing harm to victims, but others simply adjusted their expectations because a new lifestyle, funded by fraud, becomes enjoyable. Therefore, fraudsters do not fit a single mould. Wilson (2018) also found that many businesses have poor internal control, which creates opportunities for fraud. Some fraudsters specified personal circumstances or unfair conditions at work as reasons for offending, while others highlighted individual characteristics that led them to commit fraud.

There is a distinct lack of research when it comes to fraudsters, especially those that commit fraud against private individuals, as opposed to committing occupational fraud. Occupational fraud, or fraud perpetrated by employees in the organisation tends to be more frequently studied and understood, while not much is known about what motivates fraudsters that target private individuals and businesses they have no links to. Typically, fraudsters that commit fraud within an organisation they work for are in the roles where they are able to override decisions and processes (i.e. a manager) or have worked for the company for a while, which allows them to identify opportunities for fraud. Typically, they commit fraud by billing or tampering with payments (Daigle et al., 2009; Fisher, 2015). These types of fraudsters are typically middle-aged males, who are educated and married, often respected and trusted employees with no previous offences (Kranacher & Riley, 2019). According to CIFAS, a fraud prevention organisation, the majority of the fraudsters are male, especially when it comes to account fraud, lying on employment applications and unlawfully obtaining and disclosing commercial data. However, when it comes to unlawfully obtaining and disclosing personal data (and this may include data that eventually is used to add credibility to a scam), the proportion of women engaging in this type of activity is increasing and the numbers are pretty even now (48 per cent women versus 52 per cent men) (CIFAS, 2019).

So, what makes fraudsters do what they do? Research by Cressey (1953) identified three elements involved in committing fraud: perceived pressure, perceived opportunity and rationalisation. These components became known as the 'Fraud triangle'. Without opportunity, fraud cannot be executed, even if the fraudster is highly motivated to commit fraud. Opportunity relies on two components: an employee's awareness of the fact that their position can help them perpetrate fraud, and technical skill, or the ability to execute fraudulent plans. Another element is the pressure, which can be a financial pressure (e.g. a debt, wanting to live beyond one's means, attain a better lifestyle or status). And finally, the ability to justify the crime so there is no inconsistency between personal values and the crime (Albrecht et al., 1984; Cressey, 1953; Fisher, 2015; Kranacher & Riley, 2019).

However, Wolfe and Hermanson (2004) suggested that fraud could be better explained by adding a fourth element, 'capability', to the triangle, making it a 'fraud diamond'. They argue that without an individual who possesses the right capabilities to commit fraud, fraud may not be possible, even in the presence of the other three components, especially when it comes to complex frauds that result in large losses. This capability may be a mix of personal traits and abilities, such as being able to persuade, lie effectively and consistently, as well as being able to handle stress. This certainly makes a lot of sense, especially where a fraudster must charm or persuade others in order to defraud, or orchestrate a complicated scam that relies on a mix of psychological and technological techniques, which takes time to execute (also Wilson, 2017).

In addition to the components of the fraud triangle, frequent motivations for perpetrating fraud are money, ideology, coercion and ego or entitlement, with money (i.e. greed) and ego (i.e. power) being the most frequent ones. Therefore, a fraudster may be someone driven to succeed, possessing confidence and arrogance, who believes that they would not be caught, someone who may start to feel good about fooling others (Duffield et al., 2001; Krancher & Riley, 2019; Stotland, 1977; Wolfe & Hermanson, 2004). Occasionally, coercion may be the reason for fraud, with individuals (often those in subordinate or less senior positions) unwillingly coerced into the fraudulent schemes by a more persuasive individual, who may even bully those who work under them. Finally, ideology as motivation for perpetrating fraud is less common but it does happen. One example is financing of terrorism or other movements, with perpetrators committing fraud to further their cause (Krancher & Riley, 2019; Wolfe & Hermanson, 2004). Additionally, Wilson (2017) identified factors that influence various stages of fraud. These factors vary from the fraudster's features (e.g. personality, capability, etc.) to context features (e.g. social circle, economy, laws, workplace, etc.). Fraud stages are identified as: tipping points, offending (type and number of offences) and stopping offending (e.g. temporarily or permanently). Research also found that problems that are deemed 'un-sharable' with others, such as financial hardship, can cause someone to commit fraud in order to maintain certain status, when they are too proud to seek help (Cressey, 1953). Reasons for committing fraud can, therefore, be complex and not be able to be identified by one or two things.

It is also important to bear in mind that different types of frauds (e.g. organisational, personal, etc.) are likely to inspire different type of fraudster, therefore their motivations may be totally different and scam specific. For example, gambling addictions have been connected to fraud offending but Albanese (2008) argues that those with gambling addictions that go on to commit fraud may also have other factors contributing to motivation to defraud. These include alcohol or drug addictions or greed. Fraudsters are extremely difficult to recruit as participants, so knowledge in this area will always be limited and only based on fraudsters that have reformed, regretted their decisions and are now helping authorities understand the problem. When caught, fraudsters' motivations for committing fraud are often not explored by police and many are reluctant to divulge their motivations for offending. Even when offenders offer what motivated them to commit fraud, it is hard to know if these are genuine motivations or simply defence strategies. Frequently blamed factors have also been ineffective in explaining why some people commit fraud while others do not. Often, fraudsters rationalise that the fraud they are perpetrating is not serious or that they are led to commit the fraud due to circumstances (Albanese, 2008).

In his book *Catch Me If You Can*, Frank Abagnale, a famous and, dare I say, very successful fraudster, reflected on being tested and studied intently by psychologists in prison, who pronounced him to be low risk when it comes to criminal behaviour. He also reflects on a certain type of fraudster, an extremely smart individual, to whom opportunities for fraud are enticing because they represent a challenge. Where most people would refuse to participate in taking advantage of others for personal gain, because this is socially unacceptable and wrong, to this type of fraudster, it is a game (Abagnale & Redding, 2000). He also talks about how he initially got into fraudulent activities and it seems to be to maintain a certain status, just as Cressey (1953) suggested. However, this was not down to financial hardship, it was simply because he enjoyed socialising with girls who he wanted to impress. Additionally, he also enjoyed a thrill of pulling off his first swindle.

Another, anonymous, fraudster explained in his blog that, despite having a degree from a good university, he was unlikely to earn the amounts of money to enjoy the finer things in life, which could be easily gained through fraud. He also mentioned that laziness, selfishness and lack of strong work ethics may have something to do with choosing that path. Partnering with similar people and sharing tips helped in achieving fraud targets, while pretending that victims were only faceless organisations helped justify the crime. The realisation of how harmful fraud can be to individuals only came when his own parents were defrauded of a large sum of money (Fraudster's Diary, 2019).

Therefore, motivations for fraud offending may not be easy to pin down. Fraudsters can be just like us, but succumb to certain factors, which contribute to fraud offending. Or maybe they start with small things that do not seem that bad and end up committing more serious frauds. Or they are smarter than us, which helps them fool not only victims but also psychologists and do it for the thrill of it, and because it pays. Either way, my advice would be to never ever underestimate them. Not every scammer is bad at spelling and obvious. Some invest time and effort crafting convincing stories, legitimate-looking websites or credentials, have impeccable people skills and know how to play on social norms to get what they want.

Fraud taxonomy

Fraud perpetrated against the government and large organisations tends to be studied more vigorously than frauds perpetrated against private individuals. For a long time, there was also no clear definition or system on how to classify information given to the authorities. Therefore, the Financial

Fraud Research Centre (Beals et al., 2015) developed a system for fraud classification, addressing the problem of information overlap or confusing definitions, which were frequently invented by researchers in the absence of a unified system. This standardised coding scheme improves consistency and allows the results to be compared in a meaningful way. The authors suggest four principles for classification.

- Exhaustiveness – include all manifestations of the phenomenon
- Structure – include hierarchical organisation where similar values are grouped together
- Mutual exclusiveness – each manifestation should be assigned to only one category to avoid overlap
- Description – include detailed description of each incident, to allow for categorisation.

The key concepts outlined by this scheme, which should be captured when fraud is reported, include a target, an outcome, such as a reward offered by the scammer and a type of fraudulent transaction (e.g. what was misrepresented and in what manner). Researchers or practitioners may also apply other tags or codes, such as seriousness of the fraud, which can be categorised by the amount lost and duration of fraud, victim and perpetrator characteristics, method of advertising this fraud (email, letter, etc.), purchase setting (i.e. how the victim responded) and method of money transfer (e.g. cash, card, etc.). Additionally, other categories may be useful, such as different types of fraud (cyber, mail, wire, etc.) and whether the fraud has policy relevance (e.g. fraud perpetrated against vulnerable populations).

The structure of the taxonomy also includes levels.

- Level 1 – the broadest level, consisting of two categories:
  - Fraud against individuals
  - Fraud against organisations
- Level 2 – consists of seven sub-categories for classifying individual financial fraud:
  - Consumer investment fraud (e.g. pyramid schemes and other investments)
  - Consumer products and services fraud (e.g. worthless or non-existent products and services)
  - Employment fraud (e.g. business and work opportunities)
  - Prize and grant fraud (e.g. lotteries, prizes and giveaways)
  - Phantom debt collection fraud (e.g. taxes owed, fines unpaid and court impersonation scams)
  - Charity fraud (e.g. crowdfunding and fake charities)
  - Relationship and trust fraud (e.g. romance scams, friends and relatives imposter scams)

- Level 3 – sub-types of categories mentioned in Level 2, which can be grouped based on attributes such as type of investment, product or a service etc. (e.g. relationship and trust fraud can be categorised as romance fraud, imposter relative, etc.). This category also allows for categorisation of new frauds that may emerge in the future.
- Levels 4 and 5 – not intended to be exhaustive, can be used to account for new emerging frauds or 'other' categories

The taxonomy scheme also suggests appropriate coding, attribute tags and lists examples of different types of fraud and how incidents should be classified. For further information on this, see Beals et al. (2015).

Fraud reporting and sanctions

There is a social stigma attached to fraud victimisation, with fraud victims often typecast as naïve, leading to embarrassment and reluctance to report the crime to the authorities. This is especially true for repeat victims, who often have no confidence in the police. Many victims feel nothing would be done about it, especially if the loss is not significant. Some victims also never tell anyone about it, including their friends and family (Button et al., 2013; Cross, 2013; Dove, 2018; Kerley & Copes, 2002; J. J. Van Dijk, 2001).

However, research by Mason and Benson (1996) found that individuals with strong social ties report fraud more frequently, therefore sharing your experience with friends and family may give them the confidence they need to report what happened to them.

Fraud victimisation is also different from other crimes in other ways too, such as knowing whom to report the victimisation to. Typically, when a violent crime is committed against a victim by a perpetrator (e.g. robbery or great bodily harm), the victim and the perpetrator tend to be in the same location. This makes it easy to identify where the crime should be reported and which governmental agency or body should deal with it (Cross, 2019; Speer, 2000). When it comes to online fraud, it gets complicated, because sometimes perpetrators are located in other countries. This makes it incredibly hard to investigate, arrest and prosecute the crime, unless there is cooperation of other countries, and even with cooperation; there are problems to overcome, such as jurisdiction (Cross, 2019). Who should prosecute the fraudster? The country where the fraudster is located or where the victim lives? Additionally, if the fraud was perpetrated via a fraudulent website, would the country where the domain for this website is registered also be responsible for prosecution?

Prosecution rates for fraud are also shockingly low, which could be down to the jurisdiction problems mentioned above and the manpower needed to investigate and secure fraud convictions. The sanctions applied are also not enough to deter fraudsters. In fact, the relatively low risk of detection and prosecution could lead to the decriminalisation of fraud and tempt honest people to engage in fraud, where they otherwise would not (Button et al., 2012, 2018). The wider fraud justice network system, which goes beyond the police and the courts (e.g. statutory and private organisations who have powers to impose criminal or administrative sanctions) also plays a part in bringing fraudsters to justice (see Button et al., 2018). However, these bodies are unlikely to benefit private individuals who may be defrauded and seeking help from the authorities, and who want the perpetrators to be investigated and punished, irrespective of the amount lost. In fact, frauds that result in small losses are frequently ignored by the authorities. However, many fraudsters know and exploit this to avoid detection by defrauding many people of small amounts. Ignoring victims who have lost small amounts also means that the authorities hold the power over which victims get justice (Button et al., 2009b, 2013, 2015; Doig et al., 2001). Yet fraud often causes devastation even when the amount is low (see Dove, 2018).

Fraud victimisation from the victim's perspective

I want to conclude this chapter with a focus on the victims, which are often failed by society and the relevant agencies for reporting fraud. Fraud victimisation can be extremely harmful to an individual, even though it often seems to be seen as a lesser crime than crimes that cause physical injuries. It can also not be summarised only in terms of financial loss as it causes great psychological distress to victims. Despite this, the effects of fraud are often ignored and fraud victims are rarely extended the same sympathy and support afforded to victims of violent crimes. Victims of fraud are frequently seen as being responsible for what happened to them (Cross, 2015; Titus & Gover, 2001). The victims even blame themselves, often not realising that scammers can be sophisticated and may even use techniques for specifically targeting victims that are easier to persuade (Cross, 2015; Herley, 2012).

Apart from self-blame, many victims suffer loss of self-esteem, have lingering anger or fear, and experience stress and anxiety following fraud victimisation (Button et al., 2013; Dove, 2018). The impact of fraud on its victims can also lead to financial problems or even bankruptcy, leaving victims unable to afford essential items such as food, orr health problems, lack of sleep, breakdown of the relationship and even suicide (Button et al., 2009a, 2010; Cross et al., 2014, 2016).

Support for victims of fraud is lacking, even just in terms of accessing quality prevention advice (Button et al., 2013; Day, 2019). Many victim support services have closed in recent years (e.g. the Office of Fair Trading was an excellent provider of fraud prevention advice but closed in 2014). Even just reporting fraud can be a frustrating experience for victims. The most support is offered to victims who testify in court. Other victims are told to pursue the civil route, but, for many, finding out who defrauded them is difficult without expert investigation. Some also may not have the funds for further legal action, and most victims never recoup funds lost to fraud (Button et al., 2009b, 2012, 2013).

Having multiple agencies also results in victims being told to call other agencies when they try to get help (Button et al., 2013). Many victims expressed great dissatisfaction with how they are treated. For example, Action Fraud, a fraud reporting agency that was meant to make reporting fraud simpler, instead delivered substandard service to victims. Victims were not kept informed and their cases were seldom forwarded to the police. Action Fraud has also recently been exposed in the press, for misleading and mocking victims they were meant to protect (Dove, 2018; Loveday, 2017; Morgan-Bentley & Good, 2019).

The reason this is important is that poor treatment afforded to victims of fraud, when they try to report the victimisation and get help, often causes just as much distress as being defrauded. It erodes the trust in the authorities and the society and can lead to lack of empathy and loss of trust in general. This could result in wider societal consequences, such as less cooperation with the authorities in the future (see Dove, 2018). For example, while I was conducting interviews with victims of fraud, one of the participants, at the end of the interview, told me that part of him is questioning the real reason for the research. Am I really interested in helping victims, or will the research be used to come up with strategies for a more efficient way of ignoring victims of fraud when they try to get justice? This broke my heart. This participant fought for two years to get someone interested in investigating his case, even tracking down the fraudster himself and presenting this information to Action Fraud, lodging several complaints, which were also ignored. He took his complaint to the Health and Parliamentary Ombudsman, which ruled on it without letting him know (this is against protocol). He was contacted by police two years later, due to fighting so hard to have his case investigated, but he was told the trail had gone cold (see Dove, 2018, p. 248).

The system is broken. Fraud is not always easy to investigate and prosecute but treating victims of fraud with respect should be easy. An honest, transparent and sympathetic way of dealing with victims of fraud is sorely needed. Better prevention is needed, especially as the prosecution rates are so low; there seems to be very little risk to wannabe fraudsters when it comes to perpetrating fraud. Sharing stories, raising awareness and destroying stigma attached to fraud victimisation is the key.

Chapter 3

Different types of frauds and scams

A famous magician and showman, P.T. Barnum, wrote a book in the 1800s, called *The Humbugs of the World*. In it, he talks about frauds in existence at that time: fake lotteries, psychic and clairvoyant scams, miracle cures and financial scams (Barnum, 2014). All of these frauds are still in operation today, cleverly adapted to fit current news and events. In this chapter, I will cover some common and enduring scams and perhaps touch on whom they target and how they persuade. Scammers often update their techniques to make scams appear novel and interesting, therefore it is hard to cover all the variants and all the scams in operation. But it will give you an indication of how they work.

Nigerian or advance fee frauds

Nigerian scams are also known as advance fee or 419 scams and they come in many different guises and not all mention Nigeria. Research found that while the majority of these types of emails purport to come from African countries, a large proportion also mention European and American countries (Rich, 2018). Narratives also vary, from legal or bank officials asking the victim to participate in a money transfer, to wealthy widows or lottery winners wanting to gift some of their money. I even saw an example that featured an orphan Syrian girl asking for someone to help her get her money out of the country. These scams often adapt to current events. The size of the reward also varies, but the majority offer at least a million dollars and, in a small number of cases, a billion dollars was offered (Rich, 2018). Hiß (2015) found that scammers perpetrating this type of fraud adopt one of two roles: private or institutional. Private roles include a refugee or a wealthy widow, while institutional roles include some sort of official, such as a bank manager or a lawyer.

Advance fee frauds are designed to appeal to emotions and evoke sympathy or greed (Cukier et al., 2007; Dyrud, 2005). The victim is usually promised a sum of money and before this can be arranged they are asked to pay various fees to arrange this, such as legal fees. Before the Internet, they were perpetrated via phone, mail or fax (Glickman, 2005).

The most ridiculous and highly entertaining example of this scam was a Nigerian astronaut stranded in space asking for funds to come home (Molloy, 2016). Even though they are incredibly common and even quite ridiculous at times, these types of scams are still successful and prolific despite efforts to curb them (Brody et al., 2020). So why are they effective? Rich (2018) analysed a very large number of these types of frauds to look at language used in such emails, specifically terms that evoke trust and how the trust terms correspond to the reward offered to the potential victim. Rich (2018) wanted to see how potential victims would feel about these types of emails and what they may find appealing. In order to do this, different templates of this type of email were created and given to participants to rate. The first version made no references to trust (e.g. using words such as trustworthy, honest, reliable, etc.), while another version made several. For the reward, the first version offered 3 million dollars and the second 30 million dollars. Both of these reward amounts were consistent with emails analysed in this research study. In total, four versions were made, manipulating higher/lower offers and no appeals/appeals to trust, and given to participants who were asked about their perceptions of the letters. The study found that evoking trust and offering large rewards is only marginally effective, possibly due to the fact that these emails are prevalent and many people have been exposed to them in the past. However, the majority of the participants also said the offer was appealing to them and, although only a small amount said they would respond to offers like that, what people do and say are often two different things. In the study, Rich (2018) removed other valuable components to be able to test the effects of trust cues and reward cues, components that are part of the narrative, which could also prove persuasive. Participating in an experiment is also vastly different than real life, especially when it comes to scams, as many phishing scams work by evoking either panic, excitement or greed, which can cloud judgment. Additionally, often, once the victim responds, they are hooked in with additional persuasion and scam techniques. I will explain these factors in the following chapters.

There is also a very dark side to these types of scams too. Some researchers suggested that these scams are now used to identify the most vulnerable victims who are then repeatedly defrauded by different scammers, because their details are sold for profit (Herley, 2012; Nikiforova & Gregory, 2013). Nigerian scams have also been connected to kidnapping for ransom (such as in cases where a victim travelled to meet the scammer) and even murder. There are also cases where victims have been charged with fraud after getting involved (Cukier et al., 2007; Dyrud, 2005; Glickman, 2005; Zuckoff, 2005).

Identity and synthetic fraud

Fraudsters commit identity fraud by stealing and using an individual's personal details to obtain goods or services. They may also redirect victim's mail to a different address or intercept mail, especially if a victim lives somewhere where a mail is delivered to a shared hallway or a letterbox. This means that the victims frequently do not find out this is going on until they get demands to pay off the debt (Experian, 2010). Fraudsters may open new accounts or take over a victim's existing account, and may even clone credit cards once they have a victim's financial information (Saunders & Zucker, 1999).

Identity theft, a more sophisticated version of identity fraud, is where a perpetrator steals a victim's identity. This allows the fraudster to get more important documents, such as a birth certificate or passport, which are frequently used for criminal activities, including funding terrorism (Button et al., 2009a; Regge, 2009).

There is a lot of information publicly available online on governmental websites about businesses and their directors. This information is useful to a fraudster because it adds credibility (Button et al., 2009a). In fact, when I was conducting my own study, talking to victims of fraud, I had a participant say that he was reassured when he checked the company in question and found it to be registered on governmental websites (Companies House and VAT registration). It did not occur to him that a fraudster would go to such lengths and, to be honest, it did not occur to me either until I heard his story. And when he tried to report the fraud to both governmental bodies, he was told the company information is taken at face value (Dove, 2018). It is literally that easy for fraudsters to look like a legitimate company.

But this is not the only way fraudsters utilise publicly available information. They may look up information about the company's CEO, and target the relevant staff, asking for bogus invoices to be paid, pretending to be the CEO (Button et al., 2017). While everyone is vulnerable to identity fraud, there are some groups that are more vulnerable than others. These include company directors or business owners, people with successful careers or those with large income, including wealthy retired people. It also includes young single people living in rented accommodation (Experian, 2010).

Synthetic fraud is perpetrated when a fraudster creates synthetic identities. These are fabricated identities that are constructed using factual and fictitious data. Synthetic identity could be constructed by combining a mailing address from one victim, using a date of birth or other sensitive information from another victim and credit information from a third victim. Often, public records of demographic or credit information is used to create these identities (Experian, 2017). So why synthetic identities when there are real identities to steal? Because the real victim will eventually alert the authorities when they realise they have been a victim of identity theft. An invented victim can never alert anyone, therefore synthetic fraud can be more difficult to spot. Therefore, it is difficult to calculate what the magnitude of synthetic fraud is but Experian (2017) states there was an increase of 35 per cent between 2015 and 2016 and this is likely to continue. There is readily available information out there due to frequent data breaches making it easy to pick and choose information for synthetic fraud.

Romance scams

Romance scams target victims on dating sites and social media, in hopes of developing a romantic relationship, which leads to exploitation. Relationships develop very quickly through frequent and lengthy communication, which is highly intense. Scammers often profess love for the victim early on, appearing as an ideal partner due to shared interests or circumstances (Buchanan & Whitty, 2014; Whitty, 2013). However, the relationship is solely conducted online, because for whatever reason the fraudster is unable to meet. Frequent excuses include working abroad, serving abroad as a soldier, or being part of some charitable cause abroad (e.g. a doctor volunteering in a poor country). This part of the story often leads to why the funds are needed later on. Research found these narratives vary according the victim's gender. Male characters are often army generals or businessmen. They frequently present themselves as recently widowed, with a child to take care of, possibly to invoke emotional response and sympathy. Female characters, on the other hand, are young and vulnerable and needing help (Whitty & Buchanan, 2012b).

Often, people do not understand how persuasive romance scams can be until it happens to them. Online relationships are often more intimate than those developing face-to-face, as intimate details are discussed early on and professions of love are made. Research has found that high self-disclosure led to increased intimacy, especially when the communication is delivered online or through texting (Jiang et al., 2011). Romance fraudsters may also employ specific grooming techniques, to make the victim comply with their requests (Whitty, 2013; Whitty & Buchanan, 2012b).

In some cases, romance scams can lead to other crimes, such as identity fraud (Rege, 2009). During the relationship, victims are persuaded to commit crimes, such as money laundering or even drug smuggling. In order to remain undetected while receiving funds, some fraudsters ask their victim to receive payments and then send them on, usually to another country. Or they might ask them to open bank accounts, receive goods purchased with stolen or cloned credit cards, or help transport drugs. While some victims are unsuspecting and are doing it as a favour, others may be paid for this. Often, victims have also been defrauded themselves, therefore they accept the risk in order to recoup lost funds or they do it because they are afraid to lose the relationship. Threats are also not uncommon. Sadly, some victims have been imprisoned for their part in the crime (Better Business Bureau, 2020a). Strong emotional bonds and feelings make persuasion easier, so it is perhaps easy to see why romance scams can be so harmful and lead to very serious consequences for the victim.

Phishing and other social engineering attacks

Social engineering attacks such as phishing use social interaction as the means to persuade the victim to comply (Mouton et al., 2014). They are highly versatile and can be delivered via emails, through social media or via phone calls and text messages. Typically, they are designed to look like legitimate emails from known organisations, with known logos included to visually prime the victim. However, they also usually have a demand or a request, such as to pay a bill or amend details, and will encourage the victim to click a link (Cross et al., 2014; Orman, 2013; Parrish et al., 2009). Phishing attacks work by taking the victim to a malicious website that mimics a legitimate business, which could be collecting information from users or encouraging installation of malware.

There are different types of phishing attacks. Phishing and pharming collect personal information via fake websites, smishing does so via mobile text message and vishing (voice phishing) via telephone (Orman, 2013). Then there is spear phishing, highly targeted attacks where an email is sent from a trusted sender, such as a work colleague, but in reality the email is spoofed by a scammer. Spoofed emails look highly legitimate, are extremely successful and have led to high-profile breaches (e.g. Google). They may be time-consuming for the scammer, as specific information is needed to execute them, but they also have a greater rate of success (Orman, 2013; Parmar, 2012). In their research study, Jagatic et al. (2007) simulated phishing attacks that lured participants to, what in real life would be, a malicious website collecting personal data. They found the emails coming from a friend more successful than those coming from a stranger. This makes sense because we are socially wired to trust our friends. They also found that emails were more successful if they came from an opposite gender and this effect was stronger for men.

Voice phishing, where fraudsters call the victim to try and get personal information, is also more effective than emails, and is equally anonymous as fraudsters make the calls over the Internet (Maggi, 2010). Fraudsters will already have some personal information when they call their victims, and this info is used to make the call appear legitimate. They then ask the victim for their security information or passwords. Sometimes fraudsters will pretend to be the police, telling the victim their account has been compromised and someone has been arrested for this. The victim is then encouraged to give out their pin number and told someone will come to collect the compromised bank card as evidence. Or they may ask the victim to transfer the funds into a new, safe account.

Typically, phone phishing attacks are difficult to research, because there is no physical evidence such as an email or a text (J. H. Chang & Lee, 2010; Maggi, 2010).

Phishing attacks can also be perpetrated via text messages and work similarly to emails, usually mimicking legitimate organisations and luring victims to click the links. Smartphones are particularly vulnerable because they contain more sensitive information due to banking apps, and allow fraudsters to reach the victim via email, phone, text, Bluetooth or web applications (Foozy et al., 2013; Jeon et al., 2011; Yan et al., 2009).

Frauenstein and Flowerday (2016) suggest that the use of social media made us less cautious when it comes to links, because we are used to sharing and clicking links to access information. Also, fraudsters have figured this out, as phishing attempts are now increasingly common on social media. As humans we also use shortcuts when it comes to information-processing and are often visually primed by the known logos we associate with well-known brands (Blythe et al., 2011).

Psychic or clairvoyant scams and cold readings

These types of scams fall under 'bogus products and services'. Typically, they offer a prediction of the future or some sort of life or personality explanation for a fee (e.g. astrology, clairvoyant or palm reading). Psychics or clairvoyants may mention having qualifications (e.g. parapsychologist, cosmologist, etc.), which add authority to communication (Lea et al., 2009).

Younger people, women and individuals who have been recently bereaved are especially vulnerable to this type of fraud (Button et al., 2009a; Lonsdale et al., 2016; Olivier et al., 2015). Victims often find themselves emotionally dependent on the communication with the psychic due to psychological techniques used by these types of scams. For example, a psychic may evoke fear by making references to danger or threat. They appear to be caring and looking out for the victim and frequently promise monetary gains can be made by removing bad luck (Button et al., 2009a; Lea et al., 2009).

Miracle cures

When people are desperate, they will try anything, and scammers know this. Long-term, embarrassing conditions that are not easily treated and that can cause severe distress to sufferers are usually at the core of these scams. Research found that the most frequent conditions mentioned in fraud correspondence offering miracle cures were weight issues, diabetes, impotence, loss of libido, arthritis, baldness and cancer (Lea et.al., 2009). Some of these have an embarrassment factor (see Chapter 9 for an example), which means that the victim may not seek help elsewhere. Others may include chronic pain, which is probably hard to live with. These factors alone could be enough to influence a potential victim to give them a try. In addition, these types of scams use social proof cues to persuade, such as fake testimonials of people who have, supposedly, found relief for their condition in a short amount of time. Not only ineffective, fake cures can also be extremely dangerous if taken. People defrauded in this way tend to be women. It is also a rarely reported crime (Button et al., 2009a).

Charity scams and crowdfunding campaigns

Many individuals donate funds to charity and GoFundMe appeals, especially after natural disasters, when these types of efforts are common. We do this because it is a decent and human thing to do, which is part of our social norms (i.e. how we were raised). However, this is also exploited by scammers. The likelihood of giving money to charity increases fraud vulnerability, as the potential victim is targeted with other appeals (Herley, 2012; Titus & Gover, 2001).

Recently, GoFundMe campaigns have become increasingly popular as a way of raising funds for various things, and scammers are now also exploiting this. Zenone and Snyder (2018) found that campaigns that aim to raise funds for medical treatments can frequently be fraudulent. Categories of fraud identified in the study included faking or exaggerating one's own illness or that of another, impersonating people who are ill and misapplication of funds. Crowdfunding scams can also be asking for money to fund products (Lake, 2019; Parker, 2015). Fraudulent crowdfunding campaigns often show more pledges, possibly so that a potential victim is influenced by how many other people have already donated (social proof), and have less sophisticated descriptions. This could be a deliberate tactic, to target more vulnerable individuals (Cumming et al., 2020).

Frequently, these crowdfunding campaigns get us in 'the feels'. We like to hear an uplifting and honourable stories such as the one that featured a homeless man giving the last of his money to a woman who was stranded by a highway. She started a GoFundMe campaign to help him get off the street and the story resonated with people, raising a lot of money. In reality, the woman, her boyfriend and the homeless man came up with the fraud. The fraud only came to light when the homeless man sued the couple for not giving him his fair share of funds. This prompted the authorities to investigate and everyone involved is now facing fraud charges (Victor, 2019). This is probably not an isolated case. The problem with such scams, as well as fake charities, is that victims do not always realise they were defrauded, therefore many are never reported.

Lotteries, prize draws, sweepstakes and giveaways

Who does not like to win something? These types of frauds tend to follow a similar pattern. First, the victim is sent a communication that tells them they have won a prize or have a potential to win a prize if they act quickly (e.g. first 100 people get a voucher). However, in order to get their winnings there are often various administration fees involved (Button et al., 2009a; Cross et al., 2014). Both fake sweepstakes and lotteries offer large prizes, to encourage excitement. Some even enclose a mock cheque with the victim's name on it. This may lead to less scrutiny of the information. Such scams also evoke urgency by giving deadlines, and exude authority due to fake watermarks or seals that give a feel of credibility.

Fake lotteries also have a unique characteristic. Typically, they do not ask for funds but instead encourage the potential victim to get in contact with an agent to start claiming their prize. This encourages commitment and makes the victim likely to comply with further requests. In some cases, victims have been passed between different agents and asked for several fees. Sometimes scammers target people who participate in lotteries, which is likely to make the scam more convincing (see Lea et al., 2009; Button et al., 2009a).

Investment or business opportunities and job scams

Known as 'boiler room fraud' because they use high-pressure tactics, investments scams often impersonate legitimate companies to add credibility and victims tend to be people with some degree of financial knowledge, who are confident in their decisions (Button et al., 2009a; Kerr et al., 2013; Lea et al., 2009). Often, rewards are big for very little effort, in order to entice a victim to participate. This is also true of scam job offers, often advertising for remote workers, offering easy work and flexible hours. These job scams serve as mini testimonials too, as scammers describe how the job benefitted them when they were in a similar position. These types of frauds target individuals that may not be able to get conventional jobs, either due to family commitments or disability (Lea et al., 2009). Sometimes fake recruitment agencies advertise fake remote jobs. One of the participants I interviewed for my research told me that she applied for a job through what seemed a legitimate recruiting agency. They offered her a job, provided she bought a training pack and completed some easy training. Needless to say, she never received her training pack. At the time, she was in an unsuitable job with a child to care for and working from home was an attractive option. She reflected on the fact that her situation made her desperate for a better job, which meant she was willing to take the risk, even though she was uncertain about this job offer. She was willing to risk it in case this was a legitimate offer that could help her improve her circumstances. Therefore, sometimes these types of opportunities are not all about excitement and big gains but rather about existential struggles, which makes us more vulnerable at times (Dove, 2018). Some may offer high rewards but others will advertise hourly rates that do not stand out in any way from a legitimate jobs and will mimic legitimate recruitment agencies.

Business opportunities such as pyramid schemes are also common. They work by asking victims to invest in a pyramid, paying a fee, and then recruiting others so that they can get a pay-out themselves. Rewards are often enticing and returns within reach. Pyramid schemes tend to target certain groups of people, such as those working or socialising together, as they rely on social influence. Often, unsuspecting victims recruit other victims (Button et al., 2009a).

Sextortion and extortion scams

Extortion, and especially sextortion, emails have become more and more common in recent years and have also evolved (see Figure 3.1). Extortion and sextortion emails use aggressive threats to extort money from victims, such as exposing the victim's activities in real life (e.g. cheating on a partner) or online (e.g. visiting porn sites or masturbating) to their loved ones or work colleagues. Some even threaten to harm or kill the victim. They frequently ask for payment in bitcoin or other cryptocurrency. The reason for this may be that bitcoin, as virtual money, has no legal regulation, making it a perfect choice for criminal activities (Lim et al., 2014).

Correspondence may include time limits of 24–48 hours and cite the victim's data (phone number, password, etc.) to enhance credibility. Some even give lengthy technological explanations on how the victim was hacked. Almost all examples of sextortion emails I have seen contain direct and implied threats to the victim (see Dove, 2019).

In the past, sextortion victims were usually women, blackmailed by their ex-partners who were in a possession of private or sexual images obtained during the relationship. Additionally, sometimes a perpetrator was someone that met the victim online, and obtained the images from the victim or by some other means (Wolak & Finkelhor, 2016). Additionally, some victims were blackmailed or threatened to supply pornographic content of themselves (Wittes et al., 2016). Now, sextortion (and other types of extortion) emails are prevalent and target individuals that have never had any prior contact with their perpetrator. Instead, they are sent as phishing emails to catch whomever happens to believe what they say.

Just like many other types of phishing emails (e.g. your account is compromised), sextortion emails work by evoking fear. Fear is a visceral influence or a primal drive, under which careful thinking can be compromised (Langenderfer & Shimp, 2001; Loewenstein, 1996). When someone is under visceral influence, they often focus solely on the goals associated with what has been evoked. For example, when hungry, you focus on food and

Theme	Description
Credibility	Credibility of the correspondence was enhanced by quoting victim's details, mentioning affiliation to hacker groups or dark web, by giving technological explanations about capture of compromising evidence and offering reasons for poor grammar and spelling.
Threats	Correspondence included direct and implied threats, where victims were reminded of how their friends and family would feel finding out shameful secrets and some correspondence used secondary threats, such as locking the computer, should the victim decide to disobey.
Scam techniques	Specific scam techniques were used, such as grooming the victims on how to buy bitcoin and to lie if questioned what it is for. Criminals also adopted a role of a friend at times, berating the victim about being caught in this position or advising that the only prudent decision is to comply. Urgency was induced by limiting the amount of time victims had to comply.
Legitimacy	Extortion was justified by alluding to legitimate and reasonable transactions. Many stressed they could have asked for more money but chose not to, and justified the amount asked for by calling it 'confidentiality fee' rather than ransom. Scammers also often pointed out to victims that the attack is not personal, it is just business for them.
Psychological torment	Correspondence was designed to inflict considerable emotional and psychological anguish either by taunting the potential victim or drawing attention to humiliation and shame and social norms to humiliate the victim (e.g. your tastes are weird).
Inducing helplessness	Correspondence alluded to helplessness by outlining that, should a victim choose to go to the authorities, they will run out of time and catching the perpetrator was unlikely. This could make the victim feel it is hopeless to fight and enhance compliance with the request.

Figure 3.1 Components of extortion and sextortion phishing correspondence identified by Dove (2019).

forget anything else. This is why the advice 'Never go shopping for groceries hungry' is wise. The same with fear. When afraid, we concentrate on fight or flight, which is often decided according to the effect fear has on us. Fear evokes certain physiological responses, such as increased heart rate, cortisol levels and so on and an emotional response. This emotional response is very unique to each person. While some people enjoy a bit of fear by watching scary movies or doing things that induce fear, like extreme sports, others are more fear averse and cannot cope as well (Adolphs, 2013). I am not going to go deeper into this because I will explain how visceral influence affects us in scam situations (and what other types there are), later on in the book, but it is good to bear in mind that this is how many scams work and sextortion scams do too, except that level of fear is likely to be higher due to threats they contain.

Sextortion emails can be extremely damaging to self-esteem as they aim to inflict intense shame, therefore potential victims will undoubtedly worry about impact to their reputation. For example, some people consider visiting porn sites to be shameful and would prefer this to be hidden from their friends and family. Others may not think there is anything wrong with it and will therefore feel less fear when threatened with exposure of such behaviour on their part and be able to withstand it. Understanding these underlying emotions and how they govern our behaviour can greatly help with resisting demands for ransom.

Mortgage fraud

Mortgage fraud is on the rise. It happens through deception or omission of information vital to approve a mortgage loan but it can also have several different variants. This type of fraud can be perpetrated for profit (committed by industry insiders) or for housing (committed by a borrower by omitting or misrepresenting information). Fraud for profit often includes involvement of several key players in the industry, such as bank officials, lawyers, mortgage brokers etc. Borrowers, too, can commit fraud by lying about the use of property, saying they live in the property when they are renting it out, because investment properties are often subject to higher interest rates due to increased risks (Carswell & Bachtel, 2007; O'Connell, 2018).

Carswell and Bachtel (2009) found that factors such as unemployment, poverty and vacancy rates, as well as house prices were associated with mortgage fraud. In two out of the three states they looked at (Ohio and Missouri), they found higher unemployment, poverty and vacancy rates (e.g. owner occupies the property). In these areas, property values were lower. However, this was not true for all states. In Georgia, fraudsters were attracted to neighbourhoods that demand higher house prices, and unemployment, poverty and occupancy rates were lower. This suggests that there may be environmental factors that influence mortgage fraud activities.

Additionally, research suggests that mortgage fraud may lead to an increase in foreclosures (i.e. repossessions). For example, foreclosures were higher in areas where mortgage fraud has been identified previously (Baumer et al., 2013; Carswell & Bachtel, 2007).

Additionally, fraudsters also use stolen identities to commit mortgage fraud, or spoof emails and pretend to be the buyer's solicitor, asking the victim to transfer a deposit into fraudulent account. Sometimes mortgage fraud can be down to inadequate regulations or non-stringent qualification requirements. Reducing this type of fraud is also often not seen as a priority by banks, despite the long-lasting effects for the community. Often artificially inflated prices, a direct result of such frauds, have a detrimental effect on the neighbourhood, leading to property devaluation (Carswell & Bachtel, 2007; Nguyen & Pontell, 2010; O'Connell, 2018).

Food fraud

Food fraud is a long-standing issue that is becoming a concern for the food industry (Shears, 2010; Spink et al., 2017). Almost everyone can remember the horsemeat scandal when horsemeat was found in Findus beef lasagne. In some cases, up to 100 per cent of the meat was horsemeat that was also contaminated with drugs given to horses, which can be dangerous for humans (BBC News, 2013). Food fraud can be perpetrated in different ways: by compromising product or process integrity, people employed by the company or by compromising data integrity (Manning, 2016). It can include production in an environment that is unsafe or unapproved and fraudulent health certificates. Additionally, there can be adulteration, dilution, substitution, tampering, mislabelling, misrepresentation, etc. (Robson et al., 2020; Spink et al., 2017).

Some food fraud can also be extremely dangerous and lead to serious injuries or even death (Cohen et al., 2009; Gossner et al., 2009; Yang et al., 2013). For example, a baby milk scandal in China, where baby milk was poisoned by melamine, resulted in six deaths and injuries to 300,000 children. Melamine was added to boost protein content. This led to an investigation, which found similar contamination in other countries (Gossner et al., 2009). Therefore, food fraud can have serious consequences.

This brings me to the end of this chapter. I cannot cover every possible scam there is but I hope I gave a good indication of most frequent and long-lasting frauds in operation. Although there are many additional types of fraud (e.g. credit card fraud, bank application frauds, insurance frauds, etc.), which affect everyone in the long term (higher charges, etc.), the frauds mentioned above are most likely to immediately affect the intended victim.

Fraudsters gather around our activities. Shopping online, selling and buying through classified adverts or even banking, are all activities that are likely to be exploited by scammers. I want to leave you with this message: where there is money to be made, there is fraud and fraudsters will stop at nothing to make money. This is illustrated in the paper on surrogacy fraud by Mohapatra (2012). Without a surrogacy agreement, potential surrogates from poorer countries were promised large sums of money (typically higher than a legitimate surrogacy agreements) if they carry a child for a family they have never met. However, they were later told the family changed their minds, which left the women not only without the promised funds but also responsible for a child, which they were encouraged to give up for adoption. Couples who had paid to arrange a surrogacy would lose their money, too. Since scammers falsified surrogacy agreements and different countries and laws were involved, there were problems with adoption, leaving some of these children stateless (Mohapatra, 2012). It is heartbreaking to read that someone can be so callous as to concoct such cruel fraudulent activities. The best advice I can give you is to be aware of the long-standing scams I have mentioned above and how they can vary in narratives at times and to use social media to follow good fraud prevention accounts which are likely to mention new frauds as they emerge and get reported.

Further reading

Button, M., & Cross, C. (2017). *Cyber Frauds, Scams and their Victims* (1st edition). Routledge.

Abagnale, F. W. (2019). *Scam Me If You Can: Simple Strategies to Outsmart Today's Rip-off Artists*. Portfolio.

Chapter 4

Deception and communication

The purpose of this chapter and Chapter 5 is to explain some of the processes that are important for fraud: communication and deception. This chapter aims to give you an overview of research on deception and explain the communication process, because both feature heavily within the fraud landscape and even touch on one another. Most frauds use communication to deceive, whether written or verbal. Sometimes the body language, mannerisms or gestures the fraudster projects can influence our decisions, because this, too, is communication. As such, it is good to understand how communication happens and what affects it. Deception, too, plays a pivotal role in fraud, as successful deception is likely to lead to compliance. Therefore, knowing the factors that influence how deception is perceived and detected might be beneficial in understanding how fraud happens.

The process of communication

As humans, we can communicate in different ways and, usually, we communicate with intent. What this means is that we want something to happen as a result of the communication. We may want to tell a story, in order to gain sympathy or praise, or persuade and influence someone's behaviour. As such, communication is pivotal in any fraud where a perpetrator needs to communicate with a potential victim, either verbally or through written communication (some frauds happen without communication, such as identity fraud).

We can communicate through art or music, writing, gesturing while we talk, by touch or sound and through action (e.g. doing something). There is usually someone who produces the message and someone who receives it. However, the message can also reach an unintended receiver, posing problems, as it may affect someone in ways we did not anticipate. We also need to be mindful of what the purpose of the communication is. When we share our message, do we simply want others to share our satisfaction or opinion (consummatory purpose) or are we hoping that our message will influence their behaviour (instrumental purpose)? A receiver of the message may also have a consummatory or an instrumental purpose in how they process the message and messages may have more than one purpose. Communications in which there are more than two participants or the ones that are not conducted face-to-face are often less personal and interactive (Berlo, 1960; Buller & Burgoon, 1996).

The message could be informative and used for one's own rewards (e.g. reading about something of interest) or it can be used to inform others or solve problems. Although every communication is different and unique, there are common elements they all share. Berlo (1960) proposed a model of communication that explains how we communicate. The SMRC (source, message, channel and a receiver) model comprises the following components;

- The communication source – a source of the message, who has a purpose and needs to use their communication skills to translate that purpose/intention of the message to the receiver
- The message – way for the communicator to express their purpose
- The channel – medium or carrier of the message (we can receive a message by hearing it, seeing it, by touching it, or by smelling and tasting it)
- The receiver – the target of the message who must decode the received message using the same skills as the source.

In simple terms, communication happens when a source with a purpose sends a message through a certain channel to a receiver. The source might be a person, with a purpose to covey specific message to the person they are communicating with, the receiver. If a source is skilled at communicating, it is likely that the message will be effective, because it was communicated (encoded) in a way that can be understood (decoded) by the receiver. We can receive messages through our senses (e.g. sight, hearing, etc.) and respond to them in different ways. Response is a reaction to the received message, which can be observable (overt) or not observable because it is happening within us (covert). Usually, when we receive a stimulus we have to interpret it. The first response we make to stimuli may be cautious and hesitant, and we do this to test and control the response. If the consequences are rewarding, we retain the response, and if not, we may discard it. We tend to repeat the responses that are rewarded and get in the habit of responding a certain way to certain type of messages (Berlo, 1960).

Communication is successful if the source communicates the purpose of the message in a way that is easily and accurately understood by the receiver. For that to happen the message must be good quality (i.e. not merely garbled words), or as Berlo terms it, high fidelity. Fidelity of the message is affected by certain factors, which may lower or enhance its effectiveness. Some pertain to the source and the receiver, some to the message and others to the channel through which the message has been communicated. There are four factors that affect both, the source and the receiver, but in different ways. These are: communication skills, attitudes, knowledge level and a position within a social and/or cultural system. Communication skills are crucial for communicating. They include writing and speaking (which are important for encoding the message), reading and listening (important for decoding), and thinking and reasoning, which are crucial for both encoding and decoding a message.

Communication skills determine fidelity of the message too because they affect our ability to analyse our own purposes and decode messages. For example, someone with learning disabilities may be less able to decode fraud communication correctly due to the fact that their thinking and reasoning skills are not as good as those of someone who has no such difficulties. This also works in terms of encoding the message. A sender must have an adequate vocabulary to express the purpose of the message (i.e. to encode), know how to spell and arrange the words so they form a meaningful message. In a face-to-face interaction, we need to know how to pronounce the words, label things we talk about and gesture accordingly as we speak. We must know how to interpret feedback we get from the receiver of our message (e.g. a look of surprise or a question) so we can adapt the message as we communicate. Communication skills help us produce a carefully structured purpose, which in turn affects how and what we think. For example, without names or labels we attach to things and objects (i.e. dog, coat, tree), we would have difficulties thinking about them (Berlo, 1960).

Our attitudes (e.g. desires, viewpoints, tendencies, etc.) also affect the way we communicate. For example, if a communicator has a negative view of themselves it could affect the way they structure a message. I remember Frank Abagnale saying in his book *Catch Me If You Can* that one of the ways he got people to like him when he was a fraudster was being friendly and positive (Abagnale & Redding, 2000). I guess people are more drawn to those that make them feel good and it is hard to do that if you have a negative attitude about yourself.

Communication is also affected by our attitudes. If the communicator does not appear to be excited about the message they are conveying, or appear as if they believe in it, it is likely that the receiver will not believe in it either. Finally, if a communicator appears to have a negative attitude towards the receiver (e.g. projecting dislike), communication will suffer, because we are less critical of messages coming from people who project liking. I have a personal story that comes to mind as I write this. Years ago, I was buying an apartment and went to see one in a new building in London. The building was not even finished yet; however, the units were being sold. This would appear strange to any buyer (I hope) and it did so to me. But I was ready to have a look at the show apartment and discuss the options. The person that was showing me the property acted as if she had already made up her mind that I was not a serious buyer. I remember asking a question about the price of fitted wardrobes and she responded that they were very expensive. I had to insist on finding out the price. She did not make me feel good; in fact, I started to feel bad and became defensive. As a result, I became more critical about the building not being finished, the area it was in and the lack of amenities, and I ended up not wanting to pursue this property any further. On another occasion, I remember being treated similarly at a department store. That was the first and the last time I visited that department store. Also, whenever I see it in any other town, I avoid it because somewhere deep down I still remember how I felt in that store. This goes to show how negative first impressions can make a long-lasting impact on us but so can positive first impressions. Fraudsters frequently work hard at appearing positive and likeable, because this makes it easier for them to convince potential victims to comply.

Another factor that affects message quality is the amount of knowledge the source has about the message they are trying to communicate because it is fairly hard to talk about topics you know little about. Even if the communicator has sufficient knowledge, they must be able to communicate it effectively. They must be aware of their own attitudes and how these attitudes impact the quality of the communication, because often our attitudes affect our behaviour. If the person selling me that apartment was aware of her attitudes towards me as a buyer, she might have been able to suppress them and act in a more friendly way. Instead, her behaviour communicated to me that she had something against me, and, as a result of my negative experience, I did not want to communicate further. The way we communicate with others is also affected by our social and cultural norms and systems, as well as our cultural contexts, beliefs and values and our position within the society. For example, people of different social class may communicate using different words or phrasing. This is also true of different cultures (Berlo, 1960).

Receivers of the message are affected by the same factors as senders. Just like senders, they must have good communication skills, such as listening, reading or thinking, without which they may not be able to receive the message. Similarly, their attitudes determine how they decode the message (e.g. do they like the sender, how do they feel about themselves, etc.). Receivers also need to have some degree of knowledge about the message and how the communication process works, otherwise they may unwittingly respond in ways that are against their best interests. Their social and cultural norms, memberships and roles greatly influence how they interpret the message. This is why, as a communicator, you must always think of your audience, structuring and conveying your message in ways that are easily understood by your target audience (Berlo, 1960).

Messages we communicate can take many forms (e.g. speech, pictures, writing, sound, gestures, expressions, etc.). They are affected by code, content and treatment. Each of these factors comprises elements that have a structure. For example, when writing, we use letters, organising them in a specific structure to form a word. In any communication the goal is to structure these elements, so a receiver can easily decode them.

Code can be anything that can be structured into a composition that can be meaningfully received by someone (sound, words, etc.). Codes consists of elements, as well as procedures for structuring those elements in a meaningful way. Language, dance, music, writing etc., are all products of consistently structured elements. Coding a message can be delicate as it requires decisions. Which code are we going to use, what elements and how will we structure these elements so that they appeal to our audience? Our messages also need to have content, which conveys our purpose, judgements or arguments. This content, too, must have elements and structure, otherwise our content will not make sense. The communicator's choice of code, elements, arrangement of those elements and so on, represents a treatment of the message, or their communication style. Treatment of the message helps receivers infer the communicator's purpose, communication skills, attitudes, knowledge and social status. Using the right codes, content and treatment, when communicating, can help us achieve the right response from the receiver (Berlo, 1960).

Finally, the channel – in order to send a message to the receiver, both the sender and the receiver must have a channel that allows them to accomplish this. If I speak to you, you need to be able to hear me or lip read, otherwise I will not be able to send the message effectively. I am writing this and you will be reading it, therefore, we are communicating. Often, the choice of a channel is crucial in how effective the message will be and since the source of the message is the one choosing the channel, they must think about certain factors that could hinder successful delivery. Some of the things that the sender should think about are: what channels are best received by people, what makes the most impact, what channel is the most appropriate for the purpose or the type of content (Berlo, 1960)? To give you a fraud-related example, if a scammer wanted to visually prime a potential victim with a well-known bank logo, they must chose an email or written correspondence to which the logo could be added. Trying to visually prime someone over the phone would be futile, unless the phone has a camera attached, which could convey visual content.

It is clear to see how communication could play a pivotal role in fraud. Careful selection of the right components and factors that form a successful message, delivered by a skilled communicator through an effective channel, can greatly influence how this message will be perceived by the desired receiver.

Deceptive communication

Our everyday social interactions comprise interpersonal communication where we engage in dynamic and interactive exchanges of information with others. Sometimes we are senders and at other times we are receivers of this information. But what happens when a sender or a communicator controls and manipulates the information? Effectively, communication becomes a deceptive act in which the receiver of the deceptive message has to decipher that the sender is not truthful and credible. A communicator's character (e.g. how knowledgeable are they), composure, sociability (e.g. are they warm) and energy (e.g. how outgoing or assertive they are) is evaluated. Communication may be adjusted (e.g. topics changed) according to feedback between the sender and the receiver. It is a strategic interaction (Berlo, 1960; Buller & Burgoon, 1996).

Deception happens in daily life. People deceive others for different reasons; to save face, to guide and influence social interactions and personal relationships, to avoid conflict and to gain power over others (Camden et al., 1984; R. E. Turner et al., 1975). Deceptive messages typically comprise certain components. These include the central deceptive message, which is usually communicated verbally, ancillary message, which can be verbal or non-verbal and which supports the credibility of the central message or its source (e.g. the deceiver), and unintentional behaviours on the part of the deceiver. These behaviours are typically non-verbal and are known as leakage cues. Leakage cues are things that the deceiver does not want to give away, such as their intent. Unintentional behaviours may detract from credibility of the message, therefore more skilled and strategic deceivers will appear more trustworthy. In addition to leakage cues, deception cues may be detected. For example, a deception cue may be a hunch that deception is going on, without knowing what is going on. The person doing the deceiving has to continually monitor the reactions of the person they are communicating with, to see how successful they are in their efforts to deceive. Equally, the person being deceived may want to reveal their suspicions and this is more cognitively demanding than non-deceptive communication (Buller & Burgoon, 1996; Ekman & Friesen, 1969).

Deceptive communication is not always malicious, sometimes it can be beneficial or altruistic. Also it can be viewed more favourably in some relationships, such as when we lie to a friend or a partner as opposed to a stranger (Seiter et al., 2002; R. E. Turner et al., 1975). White lies are often more tactful than the truth. For example, if you did not feel like going to your friend's party, because you disliked their other friends, you would probably invent an excuse rather than tell them the truth. In such cases, deception can actually be beneficial for everyone and is seen as a part of maintaining interpersonal relationships. Most people tell small lies frequently because they are part of communication competence. We use deception for personal gain (e.g. embellishing job accomplishments to make a good impression) and most of us are used to politicians not always being truthful. Deception can also be beneficial when used for self-defence or in situations where one's life is at stake and parents often lie to children as a means of controlling their behaviour (Bok, 1999; Buller & Burgoon, 1996; Camden et al., 1984; Lippard, 1988).

However, some researchers argue that deception can cause harm (Bok, 1999; Teasdale & Kent, 1995). For example, Bok (1999) argues that if deception is excused in certain situations (e.g. when the truth would be considered worse), we are causing harm in the long run. Implications created by excusing deception may go beyond deceptive situations. If we accept deception as a 'normal' part of life, it may increase and encourage more deceptive practices. Also, since deception gives rise to distrust, this may encourage more deception. Equally, if deception is not seen as serious and harmful and this means it is rarely punished, this may encourage more deception.

View of deception through cultural and societal conventions

How we feel about deception, whether benign or malicious, varies across cultures. In some cultures, rather than being perceived as morally unacceptable, being good at deceiving is considered valuable. These cultural norms allow us to decipher and anticipate what people around us are likely to do. Therefore our moral judgments will be greatly influenced by our culture and typical conventions that are seen as 'reasonable' in a certain society (Anderson, 1989; P. J. Taylor et al., 2015). For example, a research study by Sims (2002) looked at cultural differences in attitudes regarding the use of deception in the workplace. Sims looked at deception for personal gain and deception that benefits the organisation and found no differences between Israeli and United States employees in attitudes towards deception that benefits the organisation. However, United States employees were more likely to use deception for personal gain. Cultural differences with regards to how deception is perceived may also have implications for online fraud, since one can commit fraud from anywhere in the world. And if the person perpetrating fraud is perceiving deception they are engaging in as more socially and culturally acceptable than the victim, they may not even be aware of the magnitude of their actions.

Research by Seiter et al. (2002) aimed to explore the perception of deceptions across cultures with regards to motives for deception and the nature of the relationship between the liar and their target. They compared scenarios that involved different motivation for lying, such as whether the lie benefits or harms another and how these differ across different relationships (e.g. spouse, friend, boss, etc.). Motive for lying was the most influential factor in whether deception is found to be acceptable. More altruistic motives for lying (e.g. avoiding conflict or benefitting others) were found to be more acceptable, while malicious or self-serving deception was seen as less acceptable. Lying to a spouse was found to be the most acceptable, while lying to one's boss was found to be the least acceptable. However, while lying to one's spouse to avoid conflict was found to be acceptable, deception to protect privacy was not. With strangers, deception to protect privacy was perfectly acceptable. Lying to one's boss was acceptable in case of self-protection. This shows that not all lies are equal; some lies are seen as more acceptable in different relationships.

Although Seiter et al. (2002) also found that Chinese participants are more accepting of deception than American participants, this could be down to specific motivations and relationships. They argued that the motive for deception defines how acceptable it is, and cultural differences could be responsible for what types of deceptions are acceptable within different motivations. For example, Chinese participants found it less acceptable to deceive a teacher than American participants but found it more acceptable to deceive a spouse, even maliciously or when aware it is causing harm. Perhaps in Chinese culture, teachers are held in higher regard and therefore demand more respect, which would discourage deception, but this does not extend to one's spouse. Therefore, cultural differences with regards to deception, may vary across different situations.

Cultural differences also influence whether we are able to spot deception. People are able to recognise deception better within their own culture than when judging people from other cultures (Bond & Atoum, 2000; Bond & DePaulo, 2006; Lewis, 2009). When someone behaves in a way that is not familiar or expected, we are likely to seek an explanation and if we cannot find it, this may arouse suspicion (P. J. Taylor et al., 2015). Research also suggests that when people evaluate the accuracy of a message, they may be using cultural norms as a guide, and base their evaluations on what they feel others would think about the message (Park & Ahn, 2007).

Language matters too. People are more likely to rate native speakers as telling the truth than people who are not native speakers, therefore we may be biased when it comes to people who speak our language and this could give scammers an advantage. Additionally, there are cultural differences when it comes to how people tell stories and use the language (i.e. verbiage), which may contribute to how truthful or deceptive someone comes across when they lie (Da Silva & Leach, 2013; P. J. Taylor et al., 2015).

Detecting deception

Is deception easy to detect? Extensive global research survey conducted with participants from 75 countries found similarities in what participants thought were stereotypical cues of lying, with the most prevalent cue being averting gaze (Global Deception Research Team, 2006). However, extensive research suggests lying is not associated with averting gaze and people frequently do so when telling the truth (DePaulo et al., 2003). Additionally, a large percentage of worldwide participants believe that shifting posture and excessive touching can give the liar away. They also believed that liars tell longer stories – their speech is flawed with pauses or fillers. However, it is not always easy to tell if someone is lying and authors suggest that stereotypes about lying might have a purpose: to discourage lying. If lying can be detected because the liar feels bad and therefore appears nervous, they will be caught in a lie. Therefore, these stereotypes may be a form of social control and passed down through generations (Global Deception Research Team, 2006).

Detecting deception is not particularly easy, despite its prevalence, and it is even harder to detect deception online because of the lack of audio and visual cues we may have in a face-to-face situation (Lewis, 2009).

Bond and DePaulo (2006) reviewed available research in order to examine the accuracy of deception judgments, shedding light on factors that influence whether a message will be perceived as truthful or deceptive. Overall, people are more likely to classify messages they receive, both deceptive and truthful, as truth. It is harder to judge if someone is lying without audio. Authors found that accuracy is lower in video judgments as opposed to audio-visual or audio examples, as well as transcripts. Messages are also perceived as less truthful when audio is not present. Written messages (e.g. transcripts) are perceived as a bit more truthful than video messages that lack audio but less truthful than video messages with an audio. Lie detection also suffers when parts of a deceiver are obscured (e.g. when face is obscured and participants are asked to only look at the body gestures or vice versa). Bond and DePaulo (2006) suggest that this could be down to typical stereotypes people have when it comes to liars, which are mostly visual (e.g. shifting posture, looking uncomfortable, etc.) and these stereotypes are evoked when no other evidence is present, such as in a video. This also means that people who exhibit these signs may be seen as liars when they are telling the truth.

Other factors that influence correct classification of the message, are the motivation of the person conveying the message and whether the individual is a native speaker or not. Lies are spotted easier when they are conveyed by someone who is motivated. This is problematic because in studies truth tellers report being more or just as motivated as liars (Leal et al., 2018). What this means is that, when we are afraid that we will not be believed, we may come across as a stereotypical liar, because we appear motivated and eager to be believed.

Planning a lie is also important. Unplanned lies were easier to detect than planned messages in some studies (Bond & DePaulo, 2006). I think this finding is particularly important for fraud because of typical stereotypes that accompany fraud victimisation and fraudsters in general. Fraudsters are often seen as opportunists that act on a fly rather than calculated, intelligent and organised criminals who plan their cons meticulously.[1] Therefore, we may think that, because we have spotted clumsy and unplanned lies in the past, we would be good at spotting a good con man too. Just as the poorly spelled and inconsistent phishing email will alert to danger, a badly orchestrated scam, or a fraudster that is not personable and convincing, will do the same. Just as in life, fraudsters differ in the amount of skill and patience they invest in the frauds they perpetrate. The ones that are more skilled and patient will probably tend to do better.

DePaulo et al. (2003) analysed a number of studies looking into differences between truth tellers and liars, and found that, compared to truth tellers, liars provided fewer details and their accounts were less plausible and were less likely to be structured logically and showed discrepancies. Additionally, liars were less engaged, verbally and vocally, when presenting their message and used fewer gestures. They also made more negative statements and projected less pleasant facial expressions, as well as producing more irrelevant details when telling a story (Leal et al., 2018). However, these findings, although interesting, make me wonder if we can compare lab experiments, usually done on young, undergraduate students, to successful liars who are skilled at communication. For example, earlier in this chapter, I outlined factors that affect successful communication (e.g. message structure and treatment, the communicator's attitudes, background knowledge, etc.). It is probably fair to suggest that a skilful communicator, when lying, may not exhibit these deception cues. They may be aware how negativity may come across and work hard at coming up with logical, compelling and well-structured arguments, accompanied with details and appropriate gestures that appear sincere. As such, they may be difficult to discern from people who are telling the truth. In fact, DePaulo et al. (2003) suggested that, while in the lab, differences between liars and truth tellers are observable, in real life the line is often blurred. One reason for this is that, in an experiment, participants' motivation to lie convincingly may be lacking. They were instructed to either tell the truth or lie rather than choosing to do so. In real fraud situations, a fraudster would be highly motivated to lie convincingly, appear credible, motivated, friendly and articulate, in order to get the potential victim to comply with requests, especially if defrauding victims was lucrative.

Deception is probably fairly difficult to research, given the fact that most successful and skilled liars would probably not be volunteering to participate in research, and be open about their lies, just as fraudsters rarely are. They also may differ from people who occasionally tell white lies in order to maintain interpersonal relationships or for self-promotion.

How fraudsters deceive

Some frauds are better than others when it comes to deception, with fraudsters using persuasive techniques to make their deceptive practices look more appealing. Not all frauds are equal in the amount of deception they contain. I will concentrate on those with more elaborate and intricate deception, such as where the victim is groomed over time and several actors may be present. Rather than being a 'one off' lie, sometimes victims can be deceived in several stages and by several actors who are all part of the same fraud (remember romance frauds). Many people still believe that fraudsters are opportunists, looking for gullible victims. Some are; however, when there are large sums of money to be made, you can be certain that you are getting extremely talented fraudsters. They can be organised and work on systematically building social relationships with victims, in order to abuse them and often there are specific stages in how victims are handled and guided through the experience (Goffman, 1952). This is frequently the case in some romance frauds, which are orchestrated in a way that encourages the victim to help the perpetrator (e.g. a love interest has been in a car crash and a doctor calls the victim asking for funds for treatment). Additionally, some advance fee frauds can also have this level of complexity and have been found to involve different actors, pretending to be lawyers and officials to enhance credibility (Glickman, 2005). Fraudsters may also use the power of certain groups to execute deception. Targeting a group of people who are friends or colleagues is a way of spreading deception in a more natural way. Instead of deceiving each person in the group, a fraudster may concentrate on one person who will unwittingly become an advocate of whatever fraudulent practice is being offered (e.g. pyramid schemes often work this way), and convince others to join (Abagnale, 2019; Abagnale & Redding, 2000).

According to Mitchell (1996), successful deception relies on rational beliefs people have about the world, and the way they respond to it. A deceiver needs to know what the victim perceives as 'regular', in order to act accordingly, and this requires extensive knowledge that incorporates psychology, cultural conventions and regular life patterns of the victim. The more the potential fraudster knows about the intended victim, the more successful the deception will be. Let me illustrate with an example. In one of my studies, I spoke to a participant who invested in shares after being promised a quick return. He then received another call from the broker, telling him the merger was about to happen (proximity of the prize being used as a lure here), and that he should invest more to maximise the return, so he invested more, after taking a loan. When nothing happened in the promised time window, he started to complain, and this is where he was put in touch with a new contact. This person would call him daily and was extremely friendly and approachable. He was enquiring about the victim's personal life and thoughts and shared details about his. Over a few weeks of daily conversations, they became friendly. After a while, the victim found it uncomfortable complaining about his investment and there is a reason for this. Research indicates that people may find it uncomfortable suggesting that individuals familiar to them are deceptive (Bond & DePaulo, 2006).

This is a common tactic in financial frauds. When a victim starts to complain, they are likely to go to the police and this may mean that the fraudster will have to shut down the venture. This is where an 'operator' will engage with the victim to 'cool' them off (Goffman, 1952). What does that mean? Effectively, it means that the victim is unconsciously encouraged, using deceptive, psychological techniques, to accept their fate without commotion. This illustrates that some fraudsters are extremely skilled, using elaborate deceptive practices, usually when large sums of money are at stake, that go far beyond simple lies.

Deception and its role in fraud victimisation

It would be fair to mention the role of deception in fraud because it is complex. In a nutshell, deception is an act of making a person believe something that is not true and, as I explained previously, deception used for personal gain is fraud. Deception in fraud is not just about how fraudsters lie to get what they want, it is about how this deception affects victims beyond the loss of funds. There are wider implications of deception when used for fraudulent activities, such as loss of trust, which can lead to lack of empathy towards others (Dove, 2018). So why is deception used in fraudulent activities so harmful? Generally, being truthful is virtuous and we praise those that are truthful. Even though sometimes truth can hurt and there is benefit in lying, we generally value those that are truthful (Bond & DePaulo, 2006). Telling the truth is morally the right thing to do while telling lies is not. Titus and Gover (2001) suggest that deception used in fraud causes considerable harm to fraud victims because it goes against social norms and degrades the 'moral fibre' of the society, undermining trust (also Bok, 1999). Lies that are seen as the worst kind of lies are the ones that are planned, repeated and cause the most harm (Bok, 1999). As most frauds use planned and repeated deception to convince the victim to comply, it is clear to see why they would also inflict the most harm. Some frauds can use quite deliberate and prolonged deception, usually where a victim has continued contact with the perpetrator. This includes romance frauds, clairvoyant frauds and even some financial frauds, where a victim may be encouraged to invest more over time. Continuous deception, in these cases, ensures repeated victimisation but can also be extremely harmful to victims once the fraud is revealed (Buchanan & Whitty, 2014; Whitty & Buchanan, 2016).

When used in fraud, deception will almost always cause harm to the victim, unless the victim is not aware they have been defrauded (e.g. they gave money to a fake charity and never found out it was fake). Fraud victims experience anguish not only through losing funds but also through being deceived. The majority of people are brought up to be upstanding citizens who would not dream of defrauding or deceiving others. Therefore, when fraud victimisation happens to us and we are successfully deceived, it makes us see the world in a different light. We may have previously helped others indiscriminately or given people the benefit of the doubt, but now, we do not trust anyone and end up questioning people's motives. This is something many fraud victims I spoke to told me. The experience changed them as a person and how they see the world around them. The realisation that you have allowed yourself to be deceived can have a detrimental effect and many fraud victims I spoke to referenced being deceived as a bigger insult than the funds they lost. Even frauds resulting in relatively insignificant loss left some participants upset, because a realisation that some people can callously lie to others for personal gain can be quite a sobering and disappointing one (Dove, 2018). One of the fraud victims I spoke to did not lose any funds because he realised in time it was a scam and walked away. However, prior to purchasing a tour, the scammer pretended to book him and his friend a hotel, which they had difficulties booking at the next destination. He remembered being so grateful that he shook the scammer's hand at the time but later, when he realised that the scammer only pretended to be on the phone, as no reservation was made, he felt deeply upset that he was deceived.

Fraud victimisation also frequently leads to secrecy. People dislike the feeling of being deceived or tricked, because this realisation may have an impact on their self-esteem. Many participants that I personally interviewed about their fraud experience told me they would feel embarrassed to go to the police because they allowed themselves to be deceived and they felt culpable (Dove, 2018). Fraud victimisation is still seen as something 'you deserved because you allowed yourself to be deceived'. This is often not the case with other crimes, even when a victim may have done something to make the crime easier for the perpetrator, such as leaving their house unlocked. Even in experimental contexts, people have difficulties admitting they have been deceived. In the study by Jagatic et al. (2007), the majority of participants succumbed to the simulated phishing attack, but no one wanted to admit to falling victim to the attack, focusing instead on the unethical aspects of the study. Fraud victimisation, therefore, even in experimental contexts, may evoke secrecy.

The reason I think deception might be responsible for secrecy is that while almost all identity frauds are reported, this is not the case of other types of fraud. Identity frauds mostly do not require cooperation from the victim, so there is no deception to speak of, apart from pretending to be the victim. Identity fraud victims may not feel as ashamed and culpable. Therefore, deception could also have a detrimental effect on whether we report fraud or not, which can in turn lead to more fraudulent practices, as reporting is vital for good fraud prevention.

Note

1 For detail description of the lengths meticulous and successful fraudsters may go to, see Abagnale and Reading (2000).

Further reading

Abagnale, F. W. (2019). *Scam Me If You Can: Simple Strategies to Outsmart Today's Rip-off Artists*. Portfolio.

Berlo, D. K. (1960). *The Process of Communication: An Introduction to Theory and Practice*. Holt, Rinehart and Winston, Inc.

Bok, S. (1999). *Lying: Moral Choice in Public and Private Life*. Vintage Books.

Chapter 5

How we think and make decisions and why this matters in fraud situations

There are many types of scams. Some work by evoking certain emotions while others work by evoking stereotypes, heuristic and cognitive biases or taking advantage of the processes we rely on to make decisions, which can sometimes be flawed. Fraudsters think about how they design the communication, relying on theories of rationality, cognition and judgmental heuristics (see J. J. S. Chang & Chong, 2010). Therefore, this chapter aims to explain some of these processes in order to highlight how, in fraud situations, thinking can be influenced by a skilful scammer. This chapter is not meant to be an exhaustive guide on how we think, it is rather a quick background on some of the thought processes, heuristics and decision-making styles that may be important in how we process fraud communication.

System 1 and System 2

In his book *Thinking Fast and Slow*, Daniel Kahneman tells us that, as humans, we have intuitions about information being processed; however, this intuition can often lead to imperfect decisions. Kahneman (2011) suggested that we rely on two processing systems, System 1 and System 2. Many alternative terms for System 1 and System 2 processing have been proposed in the past and they have also been called Type 1 and Type 2 processing (Stanovich et al., 2014; Stanovich & West, 2000). In this book, I will refer to them as System 1 and System 2.

System 1 is automatic; it operates fast and without much effort and cognitive capacity. It is often unconscious and involuntary, relying on previous experience or associations. It has lower correlation with intelligence. Since careful thinking is hard and requires cognitive effort, System 1 relies on vividness and emotion for making decisions, rather than on retrieving facts needed to make optimal decisions (Kahneman, 2011; Stanovich et al., 2014). While most of the time this type of processing is fine, it often falls short when it comes to bigger decisions (e.g. complex financial decisions, which are often part of fraud).

System 2, on the other hand, is slow and controlled. It allocates attention and concentration to the task, and engages in effortful cognitive processing. It is often conscious and has higher correlation with intelligence. It is also associated with agency and choice (Kahneman, 2011; Stanovich et al., 2014). System 2 is able to interrupt System 1 processing by offering better responses, engaging in hypothetical reasoning and simulation of the events and actions, which helps us form representations of the real world. However, one important facet of hypothetical reasoning is the ability to separate the representations of the real world from those of the imaginary situations (Stanovich et al., 2014). This is likely to be very important in a fraud situation, because fraudsters often work very hard to present fraud offers in a way that may encourage individuals to picture the benefits of such offers (e.g. a large investment, a good deal or an exciting romantic prospect.). It can be hard to override such thoughts and the emotional impact they may have on potential victims.

Some of the automatic activities of the System 1 include trying to figure out the source of an unexpected sound, detecting distance between objects, recognising hostility in a voice, understanding simple sentences, driving under typical conditions, etc. We need very little effort to perform such activities, which become automated with practice. We share the innate abilities (also part of System 1), such as the ability to perceive the world around us, with other animals (Kahneman, 2011). Activities of System 2, on the other hand, require attention and can be disrupted when this attention is diverted by something. According to Kahneman (2011), such activities may include doing a tax return, focusing on someone's voice in a crowded and noisy room, parking in a challenging parking space, comparing the value of two different products, assessing the validity of a complex argument, etc. Such situations require careful attention, a focus, and the inability to direct and maintain attention where it is needed may affect performance. This requires effort.

System 1 runs automatically and is responsible for most of the decision making, while System, 2 is in the background, in a low effort mode, overseeing the operations and only engaging when required. System 1 and System 2 work together. For example, suggestions and inspirations generated by System 1 (e.g. feelings, intuitions, impulses) are processed by System 2, and if they pass the inspection, they are adopted and become beliefs and voluntary actions. Because System 1 processing can lead to systematic errors, it may request System 2 to lend support for more detailed processing, such as when the answers are not immediately apparent or when there is complexity. System 2 is also responsible for regulation of our behaviour in certain situations and under certain conditions, when behaving the right way is hard, such as being polite and calm when angry. In short, System 2 steps in when it detects errors are likely. This division of labour leads to greater efficiency, since, most of the time, decisions we make, using mental models based on familiar situations, are appropriate (Kahneman, 2011; Shleifer, 2012).

Another downside of System 1, apart from the limitations mentioned above, is that it cannot be switched off, creating a conflict between an automatic reaction and control. For example, even when we do not want to stare at someone, perhaps because they are inappropriately dressed or are behaving in a way that is out of the ordinary, we cannot help it. For this we need self-control. Therefore, another task of System 2 is to overcome the impulsiveness of System 1 and exert self-control. Self-control is also very important in resisting fraud offers.

Elaboration Likelihood Model (ELM) of persuasion

Petty and Cacioppo's (1986) model of elaboration aims to explain how individuals process messages. The model consists of two routes of processing, central and peripheral. Central route concentrates on the facts and the argument quality, while the peripheral route may be influenced by superficial cues, such as attractiveness of the offer, or how charming a scammer appears, taking attention away from the facts. However, there are other factors that come into play. In order to choose a central route of processing when a persuasive communication is received, an individual has to be motivated to process information, which may be influenced by how much they enjoy effortful thinking in general. They also need to have an ability to process the message (e.g. message comprehensibility, lack of distractions, etc.). The message may evoke favourable thoughts and, if so, it will lead to a positive attitude change, while negative thoughts will lead to a negative attitude change. In both cases, this central attitude change will be relatively enduring and resistant to change and in line with one's behaviour.

If an individual is not motivated or not able to process the message, they are likely to focus on any peripheral cues that may be present. For example, how they feel about the communicator or the source of information (e.g. attractive and well-presented scammer, professional-looking website, etc.), number of arguments or the feelings evoked by the offer. Based on these cues and how persuasive they are, there will be a peripheral attitude change, which is relatively temporary and susceptible to further persuasion, and generally not predictive of one's behaviour. However, it is often enough for a quick decision, which scammers rely on and encourage. Peripheral attitude change may also happen in cases where an individual is motivated and able to process information, but is not sufficiently influenced by the facts in the positive or negative direction. They may, at this point, look for peripheral cues to make up their mind (Petty & Cacioppo, 1986).

It is worth pointing out that scammers bargain on leading you 'up the peripheral path' (pun intended) and away from facts, which could raise suspicions, therefore the superficial cues may be very persuasive. A polite, friendly, well-dressed and eloquent scammer will be highly persuasive and appear credible; however, this also extends to websites or processes orchestrated by scammers (see Dove, 2018). Scammers may also use scam techniques, to speed up the process, such as imposing time limits or offering testimonials.

Decision-making styles

People make decisions relying on habitual patterns and this can be very individual. For example, it may be defined by the amount of information that is sourced and considered while making a decision, or the number of alternatives considered or even how we make sense of the information we gather to support decisions we are trying to make (Driver et al., 1998; Hunt et al., 1989; McKenney & Keen, 1974). In the information gathering stage, we may rely on 'perceptives' or a categorisation system that has been established previously and that is used to filter data. Or we may focus on the 'receptives' or the stimulus (i.e. a message we are considering) and its details. During information processing, we may focus on methods that are likely solutions to our problem or 'systematics' or rely on trial and error or 'intuitives' (McKenney & Keen, 1974). We may also have more than one decision style. For example, Driver et al. (1998) suggest that individuals have a primary style (i.e. the one used most often) and backup styles, used when the primary style is not used. According to their book, there are five decision styles:

- Decisive – great for getting things done and deciding today
- Flexible – adaptable, being able to see things from different perspectives
- Hierarchic – conclusions are reached by using all of the available information
- Integrative – seeks maximum amount of information and generates multiple possible solutions
- Systemic – the most complex, this style combines qualities of hierarchic and integrative styles and focuses on detailed strategies for addressing problems/

Being rewarded for one's decision style when the decisions work out (e.g. being decisive is likely to be seen as a good quality in a job where decisions must be made quickly), reinforces the reliance on that decision style. However, while a certain decision style can work out in some situations, in others it can prove to be disadvantageous. For example, while advantages of the decisive decision style are speed, consistency, order, etc., disadvantages are short-sightedness, avoidance of data, inflexibility, etc. (see Driver et al., 1998). In a scam situation, decisiveness and rushed decisions could certainly work against you. For example, people with a preference to consider facts and not rush their decisions were more likely to spot phishing emails (Dove, 2018).

Other researchers also proposed that we differ in our decision making. Harren (1979) proposed three different decision-making styles when it comes to choosing careers. This included dependent (depend on others for decisions), rational (use logical and deliberate approach to make a decision) and intuitive (quick decisions based on a hunch). Although these decision-making styles are specific to choosing one's career, they illustrate that there may be differences in how we make decisions and this could add to our vulnerability. Decision-making style can also be influenced by the situation we find ourselves in. In certain situations, we may prefer to choose a different decision style (Scott & Bruce, 1995).

Finally, Scott and Bruce (1995) developed a decision style measure and tested it on different samples (e.g. military personnel, part time and full-time students and engineers). The authors identified five decision styles: rational, intuitive, dependent, avoidant and spontaneous and noted that, as suggested by Driver et al. (1998), decision styles are not mutually exclusive. Instead, people tend to use a combination of different decision-making styles. The study also found additional information on different decision styles. Individuals with a rational decision style tend to approach problems, rather than avoid them; however, they were also less likely to be innovative than individuals with an intuitive decision style. Individuals with a dependent style were more likely to avoid decision making (also Harren, 1979). When it comes to scams, decision-making styles may facilitate or moderate vulnerability. For example, someone who avoids making decisions may look to others to decide for them and could, therefore, be more influenced by the scammer or more susceptible to take notice of bogus testimonials.

Cognitive biases

In a nutshell, cognitive biases are errors in judgments. For example, we value things we created ourselves more than we would value an identical thing or product that was created by someone else. We might also even expect for others to feel the same about our creation. We are biased. This is known as an Ikea effect (Norton et al., 2012). The Ikea effect is just one of the cognitive biases; there are many more. I will mention a few, which I think might be important to watch out for regarding fraud, but this list is not exhaustive, it is a start to get you to think about how our decision-making processing can be exploited by fraudsters.

Framing effects

Every successful salesman knows that a carefully worded statement can make a difference to a potential customer. For example, if you are purchasing a product that is 80 per cent effective you would probably feel better about it than you would about purchasing a product that fails 20 per cent of the time. These choices are the same, but what is different is how they are framed. Framing the same choice differently, for example, by using different words, could heavily influence our decisions (Twersky & Kahneman, 1981). A financial product or a service (including a fraudulent one) will be perceived as more attractive if it is framed in a way that accentuates gains rather than losses, as most people try to avoid losses (Twersky & Kahneman, 1979). In their study, Twersky and Kahneman (1981) gave participants a choice to save 200 lives by adopting a program A, or 1/3 chance of saving 600 lives, but with a 2/3 probability that no one will be saved if program B is adopted. The majority chose to save lives, because saving lives is more attractive than entertaining the idea of not saving any lives. However, they framed the question differently. Participants were asked to choose program C, which would lead to 400 people dying, or program D, which gives a 1/3 probability that no one will die and 2/3 probability that 600 people will die. Needless to say, the majority chose to not let 400 people die. However, these two choices are identical, just framed in different ways, in terms of gains (lives saved) and losses (deaths). We see choices that involve gains as risk averse and those that involve losses as risk taking.

Framing effects can be extremely influential in decision making in all walks of life. For example, studies have found that framing effects can be influential when people are evaluating mortality rates (manipulating words such as people will die/be saved) or economic policies. For example, focusing on employment rates rather than unemployment rates tends to result in more support (Druckman, 2001a, 2001b). It was even found to work in home purchase price negotiations. Sellers who used sales prices as a reference point were more likely to make concessions than those who used equity as a reference point (Witte et. al, 2008). Framing effects also seems to work differently for groups; sometimes they are reduced and sometimes they are increased, depending on manipulations (Cheng & Chiou, 2008; Milch et al., 2009; Paese et al., 1993). There are many studies on framing effects that found varying results, depending on what is being framed, as well as on population groups. For example, testing framing effects on students and targeted populations, such as professionals, in a particular field will likely yield different results. It will also differ according to conditions, such as when people are asked to reflect on decisions or when they are under pressure (Kühberger, 1998; Levin et al., 1998).

Levin et al. (1998) suggest that there are three different types of framing effects: those affecting risky choices, attributes and goals. In case of risky choices, a set of options with different risk levels are presented, affecting risk preferences, such as in the examples by Twersky and Kahneman (1981). For attributes, characteristics of an object or an event are presented, affecting item evaluation, for example, when consumers are judging a quality of a certain product and they are being told it is 90 per cent effective vs that it fails in 10 per cent of cases. For goals, consequences or implied goals of a behaviour in question are framed in order to persuade. For example, a problem might be framed in a way that focuses the attention on the benefits of a certain product, such as a large investment return or a benefit of a useless miracle cure (e.g. it cures cancer), as well as its potential to prevent negative consequences (e.g. losing out on a large investment or dying of cancer).

Goal framing effects are particularly important when it comes to persuasive communications, with positive manipulation focusing attention on positive or negative consequences (Levin et al., 1998). Lots of scams work by accentuating large rewards or miracle properties of products (positive manipulation) and by limiting 'good offers', which are lost tomorrow (negative consequence). Even phishing scams, which tell you your account is compromised, frame the message in terms of consequences (i.e. your account will be deleted, locked or suspended) if you do not update your account. The effectiveness of goal framing effects will likely vary according to situation. For example, if you do not care much about your iTunes account being suspended, it is likely that the effect will not have a strong influence, but it also may depend on the cognitive effort needed to assess the problem (e.g. in cases of complex investments).

The Barnum effect

In 1949, psychologist Bertram Forer gave his students psychometric tests to complete and promised to give each of them their own personality feedback. Instead, each student received the same feedback, compiled out of daily horoscopes. Students were then asked to rate this fake feedback for how accurate it was as a description of their personality. The feedback received high scores. Everyone thought it was a reasonably accurate description of their personality (Forer, 1949). This is known as the Forer effect or, as it was later named after a famous magician, the Barnum effect. So how can this be done? Certain statements are so vague and universally valid (i.e. they apply to most people) that they will seem very accurate when given as a description. In this vagueness, everyone can recognise themselves. In fact, O'Dell (1972) found that when participants were given both, the vague, fake feedback and their own personality feedback, the vague feedback was seen as more accurate.

The Barnum effect comes in handy for any type of cold reading (e.g. clairvoyant or psychic reading, astrology, palm readings, etc.). The Barnum effect can be very influential as people are not able to see that it applies to most people. For example, when asked how true this feedback is of them and people in general, participants often rate it as less accurate of other people, even when they did not complete any psychometric tests beforehand (Johnson et al., 1985; Snyder & Larson, 1972). People also tend to accept more positive statements as true of them and reject more negative statements, but when they are asked to rate people in general, this pattern is reversed (Dana & Fouke, 1979; Furnham & Varian, 1988; Layne, 1978; Macdonald & Standing, 2002). Therefore, if the clairvoyant starts the reading with vague feedback that appears highly accurate, the victim is more likely to think they are legitimate and trust them. Once the trust is established, it can open doors to exploitation.

In one of my studies, I gave participants different measures to complete, after which they received feedback consisting of neutral 'Barnum' type sentences as well as positive and negative sentences. Participants were told this was their personalised feedback; however, everyone received the same sentences. These sentences were sometimes extreme (e.g. 'You are extremely popular' or 'You can be extremely critical of others', etc.). For each sentence, participants were asked to rate how well the sentence described them and to rate how well the sentence describes other people. The idea was to see, first and foremost, if participants are able to tell that the neutral or vague statements apply to others just as much as them. Also, to see if positive and negative statements, which were quite specific and therefore not as applicable to everyone as the neutral statements, will evoke the Barnum effect. Typically, participants accept positive and reject negative sentences when rating for how well the sentences describe them, but the reverse is true when they are rating how well the same sentences describe people in general. They were also asked whether they have been scammed in the past.

Participants who reported being scammed in the past were more likely to rate positive items as true descriptions of their personality but not as true descriptions of other people (i.e. people in general), than people who have never been defrauded (see Dove, 2018). This may indicate that fraud victims may be more prone to flattery, which is something that scammers often exploit, and which I explain in the following chapters.

Anchoring effect

Anchoring effect is a reliance on some information we have received, when we make subsequent decisions (Furnham & Boo, 2011; Kahneman, 2011). I guess the most common example would be seeing something reduced in a shop. If you saw a product that cost 300 pounds, without some information on the price of such products, you would not be able to tell if this product was expensive or not; you may price it in your head at 250 or even lower. But if you saw that the product has been reduced from 600, suddenly you might think this is a good deal because, in your head, you now assess a value of the product at 500, therefore 300 sound like a good deal. Scammers frequently use these techniques, as do legitimate companies. But anchoring can work in different ways too. For example, an example that Kahneman (2011) mentions in his book is of driving on a motorway, where a speed limit is much higher than on an ordinary road. The motorway speed acts as an anchor, and when you get off the motorway, you are more likely to speed. In a review on anchoring effects, Furnham and Boo (2011) reflect on many studies in this domain, some of which found that higher cognitive ability and knowledge decrease the anchoring effects. Mood, too, can play a part, with sad individuals more susceptible to anchoring effects. I found similar results regarding emotional state in one of my studies. Some fraud victims told me that they think their emotional state made them more vulnerable and open to considering fraudulent offers they engaged in (Dove, 2018). Even without anchoring effects, emotional state can make one vulnerable to fraud but even more so, perhaps, if other factors are present also.

This type of cognitive bias is probably the most effective in frauds that rely on emphasising great deals or rewards. However, Iuga et al.(2016) found that people sometimes exhibit the anchoring effect when assessing phishing emails. By giving participants web pages to assess for authenticity, they watched to see if the first pages would influence what participants look for in consequent pages. They found this to be the case and suggested that individuals' recent history influences the ability to assess phishing correspondence.

Illusion of control and just world hypothesis

Sometimes, things that happen to us are random and out of our control; however, we often believe that we can influence or control them. This is known as illusion of control (Langer, 1975; S. E. Taylor & Brown, 1988). People were found to believe that an accident would be less likely to happen to them if they are the ones driving the car, instead of being the passenger (McKenna, 1993). Or that a lottery win is more likely if they choose the number instead of having them randomly assigned, which is literally what happens during lottery draws (Cowley et al., 2006).

Many people believe that fraud could never happen to them because they are fully functioning and intelligent adults who could tell if someone is about to scam them. Or that they would be protected because the authorities would take care of people who commit fraud (Dove 2018; Lea et al., 2009). However, this is not always so easy. Scammers can be sophisticated, scams may be realistic and not so obvious, therefore thinking that this would never happen to someone like you may lead to less caution.

Also, the likelihood of falling for a scam increases the more scam communications someone receives. The more scams you are exposed to, the more likely it is that one will resonate with you and work. Also, one cannot control how many scam offers they receive. This vastly depends on many factors, such as if a potential victim's details have been traded between scammers or if they have been a victim of fraud before (scammers like to go after people that have proven to be lucrative in the past). It is also worth noting that some scams are not offers at all, such as compromised

Figure 5.1 Illusion of control can make us think we have control over random events.

accounts or fake crowdfunding campaigns, and the common adage that 'fraud victims are greedy' often does not apply. Sometimes fraud victims are just unlucky to be hit with the right scam, at the right time, which looks convincing. It can, effectively, happen to anyone.

It is worth mentioning that often, people exhibit Just world hypothesis bias when they think of fraud victims. Just world hypothesis or belief in a just world, as it is also known, is an erroneous belief that bad things eventually happen to bad people (i.e. karma) and good things happen to good people (Dove, 2018; Lerner & Miller, 1978). This is not always the case. However, fraud victims are often seen as deserving of what happened to them. Because they were silly or greedy, they learned their lesson. Both illusion of control and belief in the just world are, in the fraud domain, related to control we think we have when it comes to being defrauded. By blaming fraud victims for what happened to them, we feel it would never happen to us because we would be able to spot and avoid fraud. I explain belief in the just world further in later chapters and how it relates to fraud vulnerability.

Sunk-cost fallacy

The sunk-cost fallacy is connected to decision making. It is a tendency to keep investing in something we have already invested in rather than invest in something we have never invested in, be that time, money or effort. Some examples would be staying in a long-term relationship despite knowing it is not working, investing in an investment that has already failed, eating a meal that you dislike because you paid for it, sticking with a dreadful movie because it is paid for, where you would not if it was free (Kahneman, 2011; Strough et al., 2008; Van Putten et al., 2010).

Some researchers suggest that the sunk-cost effect happens because people want to avoid losses (Frisch, 1993; Soman, 2004). For example, admitting that your ten-year relationship is over would mean you lost those ten years for nothing. Quitting a boring movie would mean that you lost money you paid for it. These sunk costs are used as justification for sticking with something that is not working out. This is relevant to several types of frauds. First, financial investments but also advance fee and lottery frauds, where potential victims are asked to send small admin fees in order to collect a reward. These scams ask for fees one after another, usually pretending it is a legitimate administration fee or a lawyer's fee so that the payment can be arranged legally. To a potential victim, this may feel like something they have already invested in, which would be silly to abandon because it is about to pay out, even when they start having legitimate concerns. Sometimes, even when the victim realises they have been defrauded, scammers may contact them pretending to be legal representatives who are able to help the victim recover the funds lost. The victim is then asked for further funds (Button & Cross, 2017). They may pay thinking they would be able to recover the funds and avoid losses they incurred.

Van Putten et al. (2010) found that people who have a tendency to dwell on past events were more prone to sunk-cost effects than people who are quick to get over past events. However, strength of association between the current investment and the sunk costs is also an important factor, which depends on the mindset as well as situational factors. For example E. Van Dijk and Zeelenberg (2003) found that participants who were given the exact amount for the incurred sunk costs (500K or 1.5 million), were more likely to continue a hypothetical project that supposedly incurred those costs, than those who were told sunk costs are ambiguous (i.e. they fall between 500K and 1.5 million). Ambiguity may therefore act as protection from sunk-cost fallacy.

This chapter has, hopefully, made you aware how our thinking and decision-making processes can enhance vulnerability to fraudulent messages. I tried to keep the information brief and not go too deep into the literature; however, there are many good sources on this that can offer deeper understanding of what are, effectively, complex processes.

Further reading

Driver, M. J., Brousseau, K. R., & Hunsaker, P. L. (1998). *The Dynamic Decision Maker: Five Decision Styles for Executive and Business Success*. iUniverse.

Kahneman, D. (2011). *Thinking, Fast and Slow*. Farar, Straus and Giroux.
Petty, R. E., & Cacioppo, J. T. (1986). *Communication and Persuasion: Central and Peripheral Routes to Attitude Change*. Springer.
Sherman, J. W., Gawronski, B., & Trope, Y. (Eds.). (2014). Dual-process theories of the social mind. Guilford Publications.

Chapter 6

Persuasion and scamming techniques

Fraudsters frequently use deceptive and coercive techniques in order to encourage compliance. Many of these are known persuasion techniques, which bypass careful thinking. In this chapter, I will explore these techniques and how they influence our judgements.

Evoking visceral influence

Visceral influences or primal drives, such as hunger, fear, greed, sexual desire, etc. can be very powerful. When people are under the visceral influence, all they can think about is how to address the needs of that state. For example, when hungry we think about how to get food, when afraid, we prepare to fight or flight (Loewenstein, 1996). This can lower our perception of risk and make us act more impulsively and this is why scams are frequently designed to evoke visceral influence (Langenderfer & Shimp, 2001; Slovic & Peters, 2006).

For example, many people will have a strong urge to act quickly when they receive a phishing email informing them their account has been compromised (provided they believe it is legitimate, of course). To increase the likelihood of quick action, scammers also often add time limits to the correspondence. They do this because visceral influence is temporary and they need the potential victim to act while they are still under the visceral influence and unable to fully concentrate on facts (Langenderfer & Shimp, 2001).

Phishing emails often use this technique, either evoking fear (e.g. compromised account) or evoking excitement and greed (e.g. free prizes, vouchers or winnings). However, romance scams, too, can be designed to do this, by evoking sexual desire. Figure 6.1 explains what rational advice may look like when we are in a state of fear.

Figure 6.1 Rational advice is often useless when one is in a visceral state.

Liking and similarity

Fraudsters will often appear very friendly and likeable and pretend to like their victims, by giving compliments or having frequent contact with a victim (Lea et al., 2009). When we communicate with someone who appears to like us, we will be less likely to scrutinise the facts in the message being communicated (Berlo, 1960). Additionally, when we like the person communicating, we are more likely to assign the positive characteristics we attributed to that person to other things connected to that person (e.g. their work). This is known as the halo effect. It also works in reverse. When we dislike someone, we may attach negative attributes to their work, irrespective of quality (Nisbett & Wilson, 1977; Thorndike, 1920). Here is a fraud example: if one is communicating with a sharply dressed, good looking, pleasant and friendly fraudster, one might decide, based on that information, that they look credible. The idea of credibility is then assigned to the information being presented to us, and is based on our impressions of the fraudster, rather than on careful evaluation of facts. The same information may appear less credible if the fraudster looks scruffy or they appear to not like us, because we may pay closer attention to it in the absence of positive attributes, or we may assign negative attributes to the information, simply based on what we think of the fraudster.

Fraudsters also try to strike similarity with a victim, such as having things in common or being similar in some way, such as having the same background. Similarity increases the feeling of closeness and reduces perceived threat (Cialdini, 2014; Silvia, 2005; Whitty, 2013). For example, famous fraudster Frank Abagnale used to join what he termed 'affinity groups' in order to defraud people. An affinity group is any group of people that shares a common interest (Abagnale & Redding, 2000). Having this common ground means that people may let down their guard and those we see as similar to us will appear as more trustworthy. In one of my studies, a participant told me that what made him trust his scammer was the fact that the scammer mentioned local landmarks, making him think he was a neighbour (Dove, 2018). We do not think of neighbours as fraudsters, so this will affect whether we see someone as a threat.

In written communication, similarity can be evoked by using specific phrasing. Lea et al. (2009) analysed scam communication and found that fraudsters use phrases such as 'I was just like you' or 'I was in your situation'. This technique works in many types of frauds. It works well in fake testimonials for miracle cures, where a fraudster might allude to the fact that they were like other people, desperately looking for a solution, before they were cured. In romance scams, a love interest may pretend to have similar circumstances to their victim, such as being recently divorced, having children, etc. (Whitty, 2013). Striking that similarity with the intended victim often makes the scam appear credible and can aid compliance.

Credibility and legitimacy

Scams would not be convincing if they were always obvious. Scammers go to great lengths to design credible and legitimate-looking correspondence, which mimics genuine organisations and services. Perhaps not a typical scam technique, but when interviewing victims of fraud, the concept of legitimacy and credibility came up a lot. Many participants mentioned the correspondence or a website looked legitimate and professional and nothing stood out. In face-to-face situations, scammers appeared immaculately presented and professional, which generated positive impressions. Some even checked company details, only to find them legally registered on a governmental website (Dove, 2018). Other research also found this to be true (see Lea et al., 2009). Often, scams look the same as legitimate marketing offers, frequently adding official-looking seals or warranties as this gives the impression that the source can be trusted (Grazioli & Jarvenpaa, 2000; Langenderfer & Shimp, 2001).

Phishing emails are also more effective when they pretend to be coming from a person known to a victim, as this adds to credibility. Despite this being more labour intensive for the scammer, some invest time and effort in crafting such attacks because they are highly effective (Parmar, 2012). For example, Jagatic et al. (2007) simulated a phishing attack in order to see the difference between a phishing email coming from a friend and a stranger. Unsurprisingly, emails from a friend were more successful. Sextortion emails also work on credibility by giving a detailed technological explanation as to how the information about the victim was collected. Even though they are often not technically correct (I checked with friends who are cybersecurity professionals), to many recipients the explanation may appear credible (Dove, 2019).

Evoking social norms

There are certain socially prized characteristics that make us human. Being kind, helpful, charitable, law abiding or simply returning favours. These are all social norms that scammers frequently exploit by pretending to be in need (Lea et al., 2009; Whitty, 2013). Often, when there is a natural disaster, which is publicised in the news, fake charity appeals crop up, because we are likely to be inspired to help. Or fraudsters may hijack someone's social media account or email, and target their friends, asking for financial help to get out of an unexpected situations (e.g. being robbed abroad and having money and credentials stolen). These requests are powerful because they play on what we were brought up to value and understand. Helping friends and family or simply being charitable when people are in need of help.

Reciprocating favours is also something fraudsters rely on. This is a frequent technique in romance frauds, where a fraudster may send small gifts in the beginning of the relationship. This not only makes the scammer appear genuine but also facilitates compliance later on, because the victim is likely to feel they have to somehow return the favour (Whitty, 2013).

Another way reciprocation can be exploited is by making a request that is extreme and that is likely to be rejected immediately. This is followed up by a smaller request, which, in comparison, seems reasonable and that is often accepted (Benton et al., 1972; Cialdini, 2014).

I remember my friend explaining how they justify spending money on clothes to their partner. By telling them the jeans they bought cost £600, they evoke a strong reaction (and possibly some chosen swear words), which is followed by a feelings of relief when the partner finds out the jeans were really £300. Although still expensive, this feels more acceptable when it is compared to £600 than it would be on its own. Although technically no reciprocation took place in this case, the example illustrates how our minds can be manipulated by framing things in a certain way.

Authority

We are brought up to trust and obey authority figures as this is seen as correct social conduct. Some professions are also seen as more trustworthy such as doctors, lawyers, etc. Therefore, requests coming from police officers, doctors, lawyers, bank officials or even clergy will inspire less scrutiny than requests from random people (Cialdini, 2014; Lea et al., 2009; Whitty & Buchanan, 2012a). Authority is used in different frauds, from phone calls in which a scammer pretends to be a bank official or a police officer and encourages the victim to cooperate, to romance scams in which authority is used to make the scam more believable. Researching romance frauds, Whitty and Buchanan (2012b) found that in later stages of the scam, when a scammer is ready to ask for money, the victim is told that the partner is in some kind of trouble. This is where a third person is introduced, often a lawyer or a doctor, which effectively confirms the story and thus makes it more believable.

In written correspondence, authority is evoked by offers purporting to come from someone who is authorised to facilitate the offer. For example, lottery scam offers can be signed by a 'director of promotion' or 'president' while advance fee frauds often pretend to come from bank officials. In addition, sometimes authority can be evoked by having fake signs of authority, such as fake seals of approvals or guarantees (Fischer et al., 2013).

Authority cues can be highly influential. Skagerberg and Wright (2009) found that people, when trying to remember an event, are more likely to be influenced by statements about the same event, that are made by people in a position of authority (e.g. police). Obedience to authority can also lead to social engineering attacks, such as phishing (Workman, 2008). Imagine a slightly strange request coming from a peer versus coming from a director or an influential manager in the company you work for. Which one are you less likely to question? A research study by Modic and Lea (2013), looking into susceptibility to persuasion and its impact on likelihood of scam compliance, found that being influenced by authority figures predicted responding to scam offers. Additionally, responding to a fraud offer increases the likelihood of compliance due to another persuasion technique known as commitment and consistency. Therefore, authority can be a very persuasive factor when it comes fraud.

Commitment and consistency

Have you ever met a person that says one thing and does another? It is pretty annoying when people are inconsistent. Personal consistency is a personality trait that is highly valued. It refers to our personal beliefs being in accordance with our behaviour. We appreciate when people are consistent and a person that is inconsistent may be seen as two-faced (Cialdini, 2014). Many frauds, such as lottery or advance fee frauds, ask potential victims to simply reply, in order for the forms to be processed. This fosters commitment, which makes it easier to comply with any future requests (Cialdini & Goldstein, 2004; Lea et al., 2009). A need to honour previous commitments was also found to predict responding to scam offers (Modic & Lea, 2013).

Scarcity and urgency

When something is not easily available, people value and desire it more. Scarcity also skews perception of quality. This is frequently manipulated by limiting the quantities or limiting offer duration (Cialdini, 2014). By emphasising that the offer is unique (e.g. a one-time offer), scammers encourage potential victims to make instant decisions to avoid missing out on a great opportunity (Stajano & Wilson, 2011). However, research found that some people are able to recognise this as a scam technique and actually become more suspicious and cautious, when they see scarcity cues in a correspondence (Fischer et al., 2013).

Urgency is frequently used in phishing scams, those that evoke fear as well as excitement. Most phishing emails that evoke panic or fear, such as 'your account has been compromised', tell the victim that they have a limited amount of time to sort out the problem, usually 24 hours. This limit can lead to more fear. In scams that evoke excitement, such as those offering free vouchers or free first-class flights for a year, urgency may be evoked by stressing that the offer is only available to the first 500 recipients or that the offer expires soon.

Urgency can also be evoked more subliminally, especially where a scammer can talk to the victim (e.g. on the phone or face-to-face). They may create circumstances that imply urgency. One fraud victim told me he was involved in a face-to-face scam where a scammer compromised his car while he was shopping for groceries. The scammer then alerted him as he approached his car that his engine was in danger (the engine was smoking) and that he could help as he was a car mechanic (Dove, 2018). This would obviously create urgency without the scammer having to specifically mention any deadlines or limitations. Often, a good storytelling can do most of the scamming if the scammer is skilled.

I have recently come across a video from a cybersecurity conference, where a cybersecurity expert showed how easy it is to compromise company protocol and policy on data security by spoofing a number and inducing urgency (Oracle Mind, 2016). Pretending to be the wife of a man whose account she was trying to compromise, the cyber security specialist started the call by playing crying baby sounds in the background. I have seen many examples of urgency being induced in written correspondence or even verbally. I have never seen it being induced completely via auditory means and, quite frankly, it blew me away. A crying baby in the background and a mother apologising on the call because the baby is crying will send a strong message that the customer service representative must sort the request out as soon as possible. Here is another interesting thing about crying in general. Crying is a survival tool. Without it, an infant cannot communicate its needs and humans are hardwired to respond to crying. Research found that mute mice infants were quickly abandoned by their mother, despite the mother being able to see and smell them (Hernandez-Miranda et al., 2017). In their study, Parsons et al. (2013) found that exposure to an audio of a crying baby activated a region in the brain called the periaqueductal grey area, which is responsible for survival-related behaviours, much faster than other audio sounds. They suggested that this rapid response encourages protective caregiving. Therefore, it is clear how hearing a crying baby in the background can evoke urgency.

Social proof and social influence

We shape our world by looking to others, seeing how they behave, what they believe in and what they do. This is why fake reviews, testimonials and recommendations can be so lucrative for fraudsters. Seeing other people benefit from an opportunity lowers our risk perception and makes us more likely to try it out (Cialdini, 2014; Lea et al., 2009; Stajano & Wilson, 2011). Bogus feedback will inspire confidence in a product and make us more likely to buy it.

Fraudsters exploit social influence in other ways too. Creating fake social media accounts or buying lots of fake followers can give a fraudster an appearance of a legitimate company online. Creating aliases and posting on social platforms or forums where they can influence others can also go a long way. One victim told me he took his time to research the company online, before buying an expensive training from them. He found several postings on various forums where people discussed this type of training, which appeared to be from a genuine person telling others about their experience, almost like a word of mouth recommendation. But it was left there by a scammer.

Social influence can also be used in other ways. For example, targeting people that work or socialise together with pyramid schemes has been found to be extremely useful to fraudsters, as they only need to persuade one person and encourage them to talk to their friends, exploiting social influence friends and co-workers have over each other. This includes people worshipping in the same church or belonging to groups that share common interest (e.g. hiking, singing etc.). A scammer would affiliate themselves with a group and use this similarity to gain the trust of the group, which makes compliance easier and the potential pool of victims larger (Abagnale, 2019; Abagnale & Reading, 2000). This way a scammer can target a large number of people, while individuals feel more comfortable going along with it because their friends are also part of the deal or have good things to say about it (also Dove, 2018). Being easily influenced by peers or one's social circle has also been found to predict responding to scam offers in general (Modic & Lea, 2013).

Dishonesty and distraction

Some scams work by telling the victim they are getting involved in something illegal and this is why the victim is getting a good deal. Often, scammers will also focus the victim's attention the on size of the reward they are getting, such as in advance fee frauds where a victim is promised very large sums of money for some money laundering. So, when a victim is defrauded, they may feel afraid to report it, because they feel they would also get in trouble (Stajano & Wilson, 2011).

Fraudsters can also distract the victim by alluding to the proximity of the prize and making the prize more vivid or approachable. Proximity and vividness increase visceral influence, which has already been evoked (Langenderfer & Shimp, 2001). For example, in financial frauds, the rewards are often quick, because no one would get excited about investments that mature many years from now. But a quick investment, maturing in a couple of weeks from now, seems more enticing. Fraudsters may also tell the potential victim of other people, just like them (similarity) who have benefitted from the same opportunity, thus making the offer more vivid in one's mind. As we shape our world by looking to others (social norms), we are better able to decide if something is possible if we hear stories of people similar to us succeeding at something we want to attain.

Priming

I also want to mention priming effects. Priming is frequently used by scammers in fraudulent correspondence. I encountered this a great deal when I analysed sextortion emails and I think we will probably see more of this as scams evolve and become more sophisticated.

In cognitive psychology, priming is a technique used to evoke a response by exposing an individual to a specific stimulus (Hong et al., 1997; Molden, 2014). In its simplest form it works something like this. If we wanted to prime someone to take us on a holiday without asking, we could talk to them about things that are associated with holidays, such as having a rest, recharging, experiencing something new, being somewhere sunny, etc. They may then associate these things with a holiday and come to an idea that it would be good to go on a holiday.

Priming can influence our memory in a positive or negative way. For example, words such as shame, stupidity or embarrassment will have a totally different effect on us than the words cake, birthday or picnic. One will conjure mostly positive memories (if your birthdays were mostly nice events) while the other could make us feel uncomfortable and experience negative images and memories. Sometimes we may even experience physical reactions to certain words. They arouse feelings and reactions we would feel if this was a real event. Primed ideas could have an impact, through association, on other ideas we have, as well as on our behaviour. However, although priming can be powerful, it doesn't affect everyone equally (Kahneman, 2011).

We can be primed in different ways. For example, in terms of fraudulent communication, having testimonials with before and after pictures will

Let's get straight to the point. I do know [redacted] is your password. More importantly, I know about your secret and I have evidence of it. You do not know me and no one hired me to investigate you.

It's just your misfortune that I stumbled across your misdemeanor. Actually, I actually setup a malware on the adult videos (sex sites) and you visited this web site to experience fun (you know what I mean). While you were busy watching videos, your browser initiated functioning as a Rdp (Remote desktop) with a keylogger which provided me with access to your display as well as cam. Right after that, my software gathered your entire contacts from fb, and email.

Next, I gave in more hours than I should've exploring into your life and created a two screen video. First part shows the video you had been watching and second part shows the capture of your web cam (its you doing nasty things).

Frankly, I am ready to forget exactly about you and allow you to continue with your life. And I am going to offer you two options that will accomplish that. Those two choices either to ignore this letter, or simply pay me $2900. Let's explore above two options in more details.

Option 1 is to ignore this email. Let's see what is going to happen if you pick this path. I will definitely send your video recording to your entire contacts including close relatives, coworkers, and so on. It does not shield you from the humiliation your self will feel when relatives and buddies learn your dirty videos from me.

Second Option is to make the payment of $2900. We will name it my "confidentiality tip". Now let me tell you what happens if you choose this path. Your secret remains your secret. I will destroy the video immediately. You continue on with your daily life like nothing like this ever occurred.

At this point you must be thinking, "Let me call cops". Let me tell you, I have taken steps in order that this e-mail can't be linked returning to me plus it will not stop the evidence from destroying your daily life. I am not seeking to steal all your savings. I am just looking to be compensated for my efforts I place into investigating you. Let's assume you decide to make all this disappear completely and pay me my confidentiality fee. You will make the payment through Bitcoin (if you don't know this, type "how to buy bitcoins" on google)

Required Amount: $2900
Bitcoin Address to Send to: [redacted]
(It is case sensitive, so copy and paste it)

Tell no person what will you use the Bitcoins for or they will often not give it to you. The task to have bitcoin may take a couple of days so do not wait. I have a special pixel in this e-mail, and now I know that you have read this e mail. You now have 2 days in order to make the payment. If I don't receive the BitCoins, I will definitely send out your video recording to all of your contacts including members of your family, co-workers, and so forth. You better come up with an excuse for friends and family before they find out. Nonetheless, if I do get paid, I will destroy the video immediately. It is a non negotiable offer, thus please don't waste my time & yours. Your time is running out.

Figure 6.2 An example of a sextortion scam.

visually prime us to think the product on offer is effective. Or, a phishing email bearing familiar bank logos will prime us to think it is legitimate because we came to associate these logos with legitimate organisations. In a study by Blythe et al. (2011), participants were sent phishing emails imitating legitimate companies and bearing logos associated with those companies. The authors included blind participants, thinking that they would show greater vulnerability to phishing emails due to not being able to visually process the correspondence. Instead, they found that blind participants were better at spotting phishing emails. Unable to be visually primed by familiar logos, blind participants concentrated on the message, which was read by their computer. Where we would typically miss odd grammar or slight spelling mistakes when reading the message, computer software alerted to even the tiniest mistakes.

I just want to say, since bad spelling is so frequently associated with scams, that good scammers will craft perfectly spelled correspondence. Therefore, concentrating on spelling gives people the impression that a well-constructed email, luring them to click a link, is legitimate. A better way would be paying attention if an email is asking you to perform an instant action.

In sextortion emails, priming is done by using specific words that are likely to evoke negative emotions and encourage avoidance. So, a potential victim wanting to avoid these highly negative feelings and images is more likely to comply with the demands to pay the ransom.

Figure 6.2 shows an example of a sextortion type correspondence. I highlighted words that repeat, which are likely to evoke feelings of shame and embarrassment, as well as fear.

Look at the chosen words: secret, misdemeanour, nasty things, humiliation, dirty. These words are likely to influence the potential victim to think that what they were caught doing is shameful, disgusting and would cost them their friends and family. The key is to persuade the victim to think that visiting porn sites would be seen as socially unacceptable by others and should be kept a secret, so that the victim sees no other way out but to pay the ransom.

Altercasting

Although altercasting has not specifically been identified as a scam technique, I think it could be classed as one. It is a compliance-gaining technique and scammers frequently rely on it (Lea et al., 2009), therefore I think it is important to be aware of it. Altercasting involves projecting an identity, which is then assumed by the other. This projected identity serves a purpose, such as to get the other to comply with something or behave in a certain way (M. M. Turner et al., 2010; Weinstein & Deutschberger, 1963). For example, scammers may pretend to be dependants and put a victim in a position of a protector. I have seen a Nigerian type scam that purported to be from an orphan Syrian girl looking for a guardian to help her sort a visa and transfer money. The recipient is put in a role of a confidante and a protector, while other scam techniques were also used to encourage compliance (see Chapter 9 for an example).

Scammers may also put a victim in a position of a friend. Additionally, scams using authority also work via altercasting, by persuading the victim to act in a way that is consistent with social roles, such as trusting and respecting authority figures (Lea et al., 2009). Altercasting can be positive or negative (e.g. messages can be framed in positive or negative terms). Positive altercasting messages tend to be more successful than negative, which may be perceived as inappropriate (M. M. Turner et al., 2010). For example, study by Kendall et al. (2018) found that positive altercasting can be used as a persuasive tool to gain compliance and encourage desired behaviour, so it is no surprise that scammers sometimes rely on it, too.

Grooming

Some frauds work by employing specific grooming techniques, especially romance frauds. The grooming of the victim can go on for several months before the victim is asked for funds. And when they refuse, the fraudster may threaten to leave the relationship to influence compliance. This is effective because, at this point, the victim is emotionally invested and afraid of losing a partner (Whitty, 2013; Whitty & Buchanan, 2012b).

Whitty and Buchanan (2012b) identified a pattern of grooming that takes place in romance scams. First, the victim will be encouraged to talk about their deepest thoughts, feelings, desires and fears and this creates intense bonds. The fraudster will only ask for funds when the victim is emotionally invested in the relationship. Even then, they may ask for a small favour to test the water. After this there tends to be a crisis, where a fraudster pretends something terrible happened to them (e.g. car accident) and this is when they request more money. Frequently, at this crisis stage, a third party may be involved to make the stories sound more believable, such as a doctor telling the victim their partner needs funds for hospital bills. The victim ends up sending money because they believe they are helping their loved one. Elaborate romance frauds are incredibly harmful to victims, because as well as losing the money, the victim also ends up losing their relationship. Some victims even find it hard to believe the relationship is fake, even when there is ample evidence to suggest it is, and this leaves them open to being victimised again (Buchanan & Whitty, 2014; Whitty & Buchanan, 2016).

There are other frauds that also employ grooming techniques. In order to remain undetected, some fraudsters will attempt to manage the victim, when they realise the victim is about to report fraud. Many organised scams use professional-looking websites or other operations and it is in their interest to remain undetected. When a victim starts to complain, one of the fraudsters will attempt to 'cool' them and guide them to accept the loss (Goffman, 1952). One fraud victim I spoke to told me how, when he became suspicious about an investment he participated in, he was put in touch with a new liaison. That individual called him daily and they spoke about the investment but also about private life. The liaison person was likeable and pleasant and eventually it became increasingly difficult for the victim to complain about his investment (see Dove, 2018). The reason for this is that, for most people, the suggestion that people familiar to them are deceptive is uncomfortable (Bond & DePaulo, 2006).

I hope this chapter helps in understanding how complex frauds can be. This list is probably not even exhaustive as fraud is evolving all the time and we are likely to see new ways in which scammers hope to persuade us.

Further reading

Button, M., & Cross, C. (2017). *Cyber Frauds, Scams and their Victims* (1st edition). Routledge.

Chapter 7

Human factors in fraud

When an individual receives a fraudulent offer, it does not mean they will automatically be interested in it, because people have different needs and interests that govern how they respond to offers in general. Even when the fraud offer appears interesting and enticing and is being evaluated, it is likely that different individuals with the same interest in the offer will act in different ways. Ultimately, it is not always easy to pinpoint individual vulnerability to fraud, mostly because it is complex and can comprise many different factors. Titus and Gover (2001) suggest that the likelihood of engaging with fraud offers is often a combination of personality characteristics, demographics and life events.

According to Alseadoon et al. (2013), when a fraud offer is received, such as a phishing email, there are phases an individual might go through before they respond. This includes a susceptibility stage, detection, confirmation and action. If an individual has a high susceptibility level, they will likely miss the detection and confirmation phase and respond. Lower susceptibility may either lead to detection or doubt. If the fraud is detected, a phishing email is rejected and if there is doubt, this may lead to a check and, if the doubts are confirmed, to a rejection. If a doubt is denied, it may lead to a response.

So, what exactly is fraud susceptibility? Often, fraud susceptibility is defined in terms of someone being foolish or stupid to fall for it, but research indicates that it is not as simple as that. In reality, fraud can happen to anyone. Some fraud victims are fully functioning and well educated and do not appear to be vulnerable (Cacciottolo & Rees, 2017; Lea et al., 2009; Zuckoff, 2005). However, sometimes their personality can contribute to how they are targeted by fraudsters and how they respond to the offers. All of us comprise many individual characteristics that make us who we are, such as our personality, circumstances, education, interests, behaviour, beliefs etc. In this chapter I will discuss the factors, which can make people more vulnerable to fraud.

Impulsivity and self-control

Some fraud victims engage with fraud offers because they cannot control their emotional responses (Holtfreter et al., 2008; Langenderfer & Shimp, 2001; Lea et al., 2009). Van de Weiyer and Leukfeldt (2017) found that people who were more emotionally stable were less likely to be victims of cybercrime. Since many scams typically work to evoke strong emotions (e.g. you won a lottery etc.), having the ability to regulate emotional response and exerting self-control could help in avoiding such scams. However, self-control is hard, especially when we really want something. Therefore, it comes as no surprise that people who lack self-control could be more vulnerable to fraud. Self- control and impulsivity have been found to increase vulnerability to fraud. Inability to control impulses compromises decision making (Bayard et al., 2011) and this can greatly influence evaluation of the fraud offer (e.g. not concentrating on the facts). Lack of self-control increases the risk of criminal victimisation, especially when victimisation takes place without a contact, such as online (Pratt et al., 2014; Schreck, 1999; Schreck et al., 2006). Therefore, it comes as no surprise that it is also implicated in fraud victimisation (Langenderfer & Shimp, 2001; Lea et al., 2009). Individuals with lower levels of self-control are more likely to engage in behaviours that could lead to fraud victimisation (Holtfreter et al., 2010). In research studies, when given hypothetical fraud scenarios to evaluate, participants that had lower self-control and that were unable to foresee consequences of their actions (premeditation), were more likely to respond to fraud offers (Holtfreter et al., 2010; Modic & Lea, 2012).

Impulsivity is somewhat similar to lack of self-control in that it affects decision-making and makes one more likely to act without deliberation. It is also connected to risk taking and patience. For example, individuals who were less impulsive took less risk when completing the gambling task and were less likely to pay more to get the desired items delivered quickly, showing greater patience (Frederick, 2005). Sometimes patience and delaying gratification can be useful in spotting warning signs and lowering the intensity of the emotional response towards the offer (i.e. letting visceral influence subside). Fraud offers are often designed to evoke strong, quick reactions, which impact rational thinking and impulsivity exacerbates this. During the course of my research in this area, I found that individuals who are more impulsive also has less self-control. Additionally, impulsive individuals were more likely to report they have responded to fraud offers in the past, were more likely to be fraud victims and were less able to spot a phishing attempt (Dove, 2018). Other studies, too, found a link between impulsivity and vulnerability to fraud. Impulsivity was found to be higher in fraud victims (Knutson & Samanez-Larkin, 2014). It was also connected to risky cyber security behaviours and cybercrime (Hadlington, 2017; Hadlington & Chivers, 2018). Additionally, Whitty (2017) found that romance fraud victims were more impulsive, also scoring high on urgency, which means they are likely to comply with scammers requests early on. Therefore, impulsivity can drastically increase fraud vulnerability. It is not all bad news. Being aware of your own vulnerabilities can be a protective factor. In fact, I have had fraud victims tell me how the experience made them become less impulsive, by drawing attention to their own vulnerabilities.

It is also important to mention age and how it may relate to lower self-control and impulsivity. Holtfreter et al. (2015) found that individuals over the age of 60 with lower levels of self-control tend to make more purchases after receiving unsolicited emails from unknown vendors, which can leave them open to identity theft and more unsolicited offers. However, this could also be down to the fact that people over the age of 65 show increased levels of dysfunctional impulsivity (i.e. act with less forethought or make quick decisions) compared to adults and adolescents (Morales-Vives & Vigil-Colet, 2012).

Compliance and obedience to authority

People who are more compliant may be particularly vulnerable to fraud. Compliance does not necessarily mean that a person is not aware of the danger, it rather means that they consciously decide to go along with something (Gudjonsson et al., 2002). In my own research, I defined compliance as a likelihood of going along with others, which is down to persuasive techniques (e.g. activation of social norms, liking and similarity, time pressure).

I found that compliance was connected to greater impulsivity, social influence and lack of vigilance (Dove, 2018). This would suggest that compliant individuals may be vulnerable to different types of fraud. For example, impulsivity may be important when it comes to clicking links, buying things on an impulse or making quick, uninformed decisions, whereas social influence would be most influential in scams that offer testimonials or in groups that invest together. More compliant individuals were also less able to recognise that hypothetical fraud scenarios could in fact be real situations, and were less able to recognise a phishing attempt (see Dove, 2018).

Compliance was also connected to external locus of control (Dove, 2018). Locus of control refers to a belief that people hold when it comes to control over their lives. For example, people that believe they have no control over things that happen to them have more external locus of control, while people with internal locus of control believe they control their life (Rotter, 1966). This means that compliant individuals may be more likely to accept things that happened to them because they feel they cannot control them anyway. Additionally, compliant individuals were also more likely to believe in powerful others (see Sapp & Harrod, 1993), and thus may be particularly vulnerable to fraud offers that use authority cues, such as those pretending to be from the police (Dove, 2018).

Perhaps the most worrying thing about compliance is that it has been linked to low self-esteem and inferiority, as well as a negative view of self (Dove, 2018; Gudjonson, et al., 2002; Fischer et al., 2013). This could leave more compliant individuals particularly vulnerable to all sorts of fraudulent attempts, but particularly those that use threatening or negative communication to force the victim to comply with requests.

Obedience to authority can also lead to greater vulnerability to fraud, as scammers frequently use authority cues to encourage compliance (Fischer et al., 2013; Modic & Lea, 2013; Workman, 2008). Fischer et al. (2013) found that scam victims were more influenced by fake signs of authority in fraud correspondence than non-victims. Similarly, Modic and Lea (2013) found that being influenced by authority predicted whether someone is likely to respond to scams. Trust in authority was also found to be related to lack of vigilance, which could mean that trusting authority figures has a potential to lower one's vigilance (Dove, 2018).

Risk assessment and sensation seeking

Sometimes people recognise that an offer they are evaluating may be a scam and that there is a risk involved, but decide to go for it anyway. They may decide to look at it as a gamble. For example, if the reward is large, paying a small amount of money for a chance of getting a large pay-out may seem worth it (Lea et al., 2009). Even in romance fraud, this rationalisation is present, as some victims view their fraud experience as a 'near win' and hope that next love interest will work out. Additionally, romance fraud had higher scores on sensation seeking measure than non-victims (Whitty, 2013, 2017).

However, sometimes our circumstances can influence risk assessment. When we feel like we have no other options, taking a risk on something that does not look quite right is about survival. One participant told me they were so desperate to find a new job due to their circumstances at home and work that they dismissed initial doubts when asked to pay a fee for a training pack, after being offered a job without an interview. Without better options on the table, there was nothing else to do but hope that this could be a genuine offer (Dove, 2018). If the offer is enticing, small amounts of money asked by scammers are seen as 'worth the risk' (Lea et al., 2009; Olivier et al., 2015). There are many scams that exploit this by asking for various fees, for example fake lotteries or prizes.

Large prizes (e.g. lottery win or a big investment return), which are often part of fraudulent offers, can stir up emotions and positive feelings, lowering risk perceptions, affecting rational thinking and making us more likely to engage in actions that are not optimal (Greenspan, 2009; Lea et al.,

2009). For example, Fischer et al. (2013) found that, when recalling the scam experience, victims often recall positive emotions, as well as the size of the prize, therefore, when it comes to scams, positive emotions affect the assessment of risk.

Additionally, risk assessment also depends on how we evaluate the risk. If we concentrate on the gains, instead of the losses, we are more likely to only choose information that supports positive aspects of the offer. This is likely to lead to confirmation bias, or a tendency to selectively seek information that supports our beliefs and enhance confidence in our decisions (Fischer et al., 2008; Nickerson, 1998). Risks associated with our online behaviour also play a part in how suspicious we may be when encountering fraudulent correspondence. Higher perceived risks will result in more cognitive effort invested in processing the message (Vishwanath et al., 2018).

Flattery and intimidation

Susceptibility to flattery and being easily intimidated have also been found to fraud vulnerability (Abagnale & Redding, 2000; Buchanan & Whitty, 2014; Langenderfer & Shimp, 2001; Whitty, 2013). Flattery can be influential and is used in many types of frauds, especially in face-to-face situations or where lengthy communication takes place (e.g. romance). We like people who like us, and will therefore respond well to flattery, and it may even positively influence our opinion of the message being communicated to us, just because the fraudster is pretending to like us. We tend to be less critical of messages communicated by those who appear to like us (Berlo, 1960).

However, some scammers go the other way and use intimidation tactics, to bully and intimidate people into complying with fraudulent schemes, and older people are more likely to be victims of online intimidation (Van de Weijer & Leukfeldt, 2017). However, this does not mean that every elderly person who happens to be a victim of intimidation will comply with requests, as people differ in how susceptible to intimidation they are. But it is worth mentioning that threatening correspondence will be more effective if an individual is susceptible to intimidation. For example, extortion and sextortion type emails use direct and implied threats to scare the potential victim, hoping that the fear will make them pay the ransom (Dove, 2019). Someone who is easily intimidated or fear averse may have harder time dealing with fear and shame evoked by such correspondence.

Information processing and need for cognition

How we process information and the attention we pay to communication we receive can have a great impact on decisions we eventually make. I will explain how this may work in a scam situation, using the Petty and Cacioppo's (1986) Elaboration Likelihood Model of persuasion.

For example, when a persuasive message is received, we may take one of two routes of processing: peripheral or central. If we are motivated to process information and are able to do so (e.g. people with learning disabilities may not be able to process it, even when motivated), we are likely going to choose central route of processing. We will concentrate on the quality of the message and its arguments and this will lead to attitude changes based on the quality of the arguments we just assessed. However, if we are not motivated to process the information carefully, we may concentrate on the superficial cues, such as how charming the scammer is or, if online, how good the website or email looks. Or simply how attractive the offer is, rather than look for evidence that could confirm or dispute the credibility of the offer, something that is needed to make an optimal decision. This is a peripheral route of processing. Our attitude change will be temporary but that is all the scammer needs to get us to part with our money. Additionally, we may, if we like the scammer, carry the positive attributes we assigned to them, and apply them to the message. So even when we think the arguments make no sense and are weak, we will still feel the offer is credible because we see the person presenting the offer as credible (see Petty & Cacioppo, 1986).

How we process information also comes down to 'need for cognition'. Need for cognition is a tendency to enjoy effortful thinking. Cacioppo and Petty (1982) suggest that people who have high need for cognition tend to process information using the central route of processing. In fraud terms, this would mean that they would also be less likely to focus on superficial cues and instead, concentrate on the quality of the message. In contrast, people low in need for cognition may be more vulnerable. In a research study by Cacioppo et al. (1986), participants low in need for cognition reported using less effort in evaluating the arguments in the task. They also did not discriminate between high-quality and low-quality arguments as much as participants with a high need for cognition. Additionally, they were not able to recall as many arguments when asked after the task. Other studies found that individuals with a high need for cognition were less likely to be persuaded by an affect-based information about a product. Instead they preferred fact-based information (Haddock et al., 2008). Kaufman et al. (1999) found that people high in need for cognition are not as influenced by source credibility, but instead pay attention to quality of the argument. This is important as fraudsters frequently pretend to be legitimate sources. Therefore, people who naturally enjoy thinking may be better at concentrating on factual information when it comes to fraud correspondence, which could alert to danger.

Trust and gullibility

Rousseau et al. (1998) defined trust as "psychological state comprising the intention to accept vulnerability based upon positive expectations of the intentions or behaviour of another" (p. 395). They also suggest that trust is a psychological condition, which can cause a behaviour or be the result of a certain behaviour (e.g. cooperation) or a certain choice (e.g. taking a risk). Trust is a component in all cooperative relationships, without which many of our activities would be limited. We often have to take a risk and trust others (Luhmann, 2000). Every time we shop online, we trust that the goods we purchased will be sent to us and we take certain amount of risk while waiting for our purchase. In other words, we trust that the other party will cooperate. As such, trust equals accepting the uncertainty, when it comes to intentions and motives of others (Kramer, 1999; Luhmann, 2000; Misztal, 2013). Scammers can manipulate our trust by employing techniques, which impact risk perceptions, such as adding seals of approval, fake warranties, product information, fake testimonials or third-party endorsements and security protection. These things can influence trust and lead to a purchase (Grazioli & Jarvenpaa, 2000; D. J. Kim et al., 2008). Additionally, people differ in the propensity to trust others, which can also vary according to our perceptions of online risks (Corritore et al., 2003; Cramer et al., 2009; Mayer et al., 1995). Personality traits and situational factors such as reciprocity (a known scam technique), may also influence trust and therefore lead to fraud compliance (A. M. Evans & Revelle, 2008).

Is there connection between trust and gullibility? Often, this seems to be a popular belief, as they are frequently interconnected. For example, Greenspan (2009) suggests that gullibility means trusting someone or something. Gullibility is more prevalent in certain people (e.g. children, people with learning disabilities or cognitive impairment), however, Greenspan (2009) argues that anyone can engage in gullible action (i.e. acts against our best interests) in certain contexts. Often, gullible action can be down to several factors: cognitive or personality factors, situation or the emotional state (see Chapter 8). In fraud terms, this may mean that an impulsive purchase from an unknown vendor could be down to our personality factors, such as impulsivity and lack of self-control, an emotional reaction towards the offer and how well we are able and willing to process information. Therefore, even smart people can sometimes engage in gullible action, especially when we trust the source and as I said above, trust can be manipulated by scammers.

Langenderfer and Shimp (2001) suggest that the difference between victims of frauds and non-victims is down to gullibility and trusting nature, because often, rather than evaluate the offer, the potential victim may concentrate on how trustworthy the scammer appears to be. Other research studies also found a link between a trusting nature and fraud victimisation (Fischer et al., 2013; Whitty & Buchanan, 2012a; Workman, 2008). One reason for this could be that people who are inherently honest expect others to be the same (A. D. Evans & Lee, 2014), but this, sadly, is not always the case. However, being trusting may not necessarily imply that the person is also always gullible (Judges et al., 2017; Markoczy, 2003; Yamagishi et al., 1999). Sometimes this is down to other factors. For example, in the research study by Markoczy (2003), participants had to predict the behaviour of others (Yamagishi & Kakiuchi, 2000). The study found that those who were trusting but vigilant were better at predicting others' behaviour than those who were less vigilant or even less trusting but lacking vigilance. Rotter (1980) argues that trusting someone when there are warning signs that the person is not trustworthy is connected to gullibility, whereas just trusting someone in the absence of the warning signs is not. And as stated above, we need to trust to be able to cooperate and function in our daily life. However, trusting nature, coupled with a lack of vigilance, may result in actions that are not always optimal and leave us open to fraud.

Vigilance, delayed decisions, scam awareness and background knowledge

Just as there are factors that increase vulnerability to fraud offers, there are some that offer us protection. The ones that I am going to discuss are vigilance, preference to delay decisions, healthy scepticism and scam awareness.

In situations where a fraud offer is being evaluated and the visceral influence is relatively low (i.e. no extreme emotional reactions towards the offer), we may still erroneously decide the fraud offer is legitimate and go for it. In such cases, there are certain, protective, factors that can help us avoid victimisation. Scepticism and scam knowledge (e.g. general knowledge how scams operate and target people), could help by making us more aware that offers we receive could be fraudulent (Langenderfer & Shimp, 2001; Norris et al., 2019). Since scams go hand in hand with current events, people who take little interest in what is going on in the world may also be more vulnerable to frauds as they will have no awareness of the latest frauds (Titus & Gover, 2001). For example, in their study Alseadoon et al. (2013) found that some victims do not even consider the idea of a phishing email when they respond to correspondence, which leads them to believe the email is legitimate. For such people, knowledge about scams in operation would help. Additionally, the study found that there are other types of victims, those that do have initial doubts but do nothing to confirm or deny those doubts. For example, participants in the study said they verified with peers (who got the same phishing email) or relied on the source of the email to make a decision. However, good scammers can fake where the email is coming from. Being vigilant and cross-checking information might have protected such individuals, rather than relying on social proof or source credibility. In this case, security and computer knowledge may have helped avoid a phishing attempt, as previous studies have found this to be the case (Alseadoon et al., 2013; Wright & Marett, 2010). For example, being aware that scammers can make emails appear credible and legitimate may lower trust levels when an email, which seems to be coming from a legitimate source but which seems out of character, is received.

Having background knowledge also helps. For example, if someone presented an exciting investment opportunity to you, knowing how financial investments work and what is a reasonable return on such investments could help raise red flags. Having said that, background knowledge can also lead to overconfidence in our decisions and this can mean less caution (Langenderfer & Shimp, 2001; Lea et al., 2009). Therefore, it is good to bear in mind that having the knowledge is generally good, but it is also good to be cautious.

Another factor that offers protection from fraud is vigilance. When our vigilance is relaxed, fraud victimisation is easier (Grabosky & Duffield, 2001). For example, in the study by Markoczy (2003) trusting individuals that were also vigilant were more likely to accurately predict how others would behave than those who were less vigilant. This may be important for fraud because, often, a potential victim needs to evaluate fraudster's behaviour. In insurance fraud, vigilance has been connected to better detection of fraudulent claims, such as spotting irregularities in claimants' stories (Morley et al., 2006).

In my own research, vigilance was related to awareness of others' motives, as well as willingness to check the provided information. If you are more willing to check facts rather than believe what you are told, it could help you avoid situations and things that may not be in your best interest. Vigilant individuals had more self-control, were less likely to be influenced by others, were less impulsive and less compliant. What this may mean in fraud terms is that they are less likely to act without carefully considering what they are getting into and are also less likely to go along with what others want them to do. Additionally, vigilant individuals were better at recognising potentially fraudulent situations and better at spotting a phishing email than non-vigilant individuals (Dove, 2018).

Delaying decisions is also a good way to avoid scams. Most frauds rely on quick thinking (e.g. today only, one-time offer, etc.) and visceral influence will intensify this. Therefore, having a preference to take your time to consider things properly and consider the information is likely to be protective (Greenspan, 2009). Many fraud victims that I interviewed during the course of my research told me they regret rushing their decision and this is why I looked at this in subsequent studies. People who prefer delaying decisions were less impulsive and compliant, had more self-control and were less influenced by others. Similarly, to vigilant individuals, they would be less likely to rush into things they did not consider carefully and would not be as vulnerable to frauds that utilise social influence or social proof. They were also more vigilant, so these two things may be related. Additionally, they and were less likely to respond to fraud offers and were better at recognising a phishing email (Dove, 2018).

Demographics and circumstances

Sometimes, our vulnerability is down to circumstances we find ourselves in, which we cannot control, but which, none the less, make us vulnerable to fraud. For example, major medical treatment, marriage, birth or death in the family may mean that we are likely to be targeted by certain offers, as these details can be easily obtained by legitimate and illegitimate people (Titus et al., 1995; Titus & Gover, 2001). These major events can make people vulnerable to fraud because they present a new target opportunity that the scammer did not have previously. If you have just had or are going through medical treatment, miracle cures may look particularly enticing where they would not be otherwise. Bereavement or divorce, as well as illness in the family, can increase vulnerability, because they leave us emotionally vulnerable and this vulnerability can lead to engagement with scams. Negative emotional states, such as sadness due to a bereavement for example, anxiety or depression, are also likely to add to vulnerability to fraud. Such states can make us focus on alleviating the distress instead of focusing on the facts (Isen & Patrick, 1983; Williams et al., 2017). Communication with a sympathetic scammer may, in such cases, offer escape from grief and alleviate loneliness (Olivier et al., 2015). Being out of a job can make one more willing to take a risk in order to find work, and thus more vulnerable to job scams (Dove, 2018).

Some scams are even specifically designed to target people's circumstances, such as financial problems, illness, addiction and even breakdown of a relationship. In times when people are going through difficult circumstances, the scam can appear more attractive than it would be at other times (see an example in Chapter 9). Circumstances can change and vulnerability to fraud connected to circumstances may, therefore, not last for ever (e.g. vulnerability to romance fraud diminishes when people enter genuine relationship).

Perhaps the most important life circumstance that makes us very vulnerable to frauds is ageing. With increasing age our cognitive abilities diminish (Andrews-Hanna et al., 2007; Callahan et al., 2002; Griffiths & Harmon, 2011; Langenderfer & Shimp, 2001; Salthouse, 2009), which means that it will be even harder to discern if the offers we are receiving are genuine. Elderly people are also aggressively targeted by scammers (Harries et al., 2014; Muscat et al., 2002; Reisig & Holtfreter, 2013), perhaps due to the cognitive complications that arise with age, and this increases the likelihood of becoming a victim. Other factors could also add to vulnerability. For example, financial stability and home ownership may increase vulnerability, as elderly individuals that were less financially stable were less likely to be defrauded, possibly due to lack of available funds (Kerley & Copes, 2002).

Old age also increases likelihood of dementia, which not only leads to greater manipulation by scammers, but has also been connected to exploitation by legal guardians appointed to manage financial affairs (R. G. Smith, 2000). It also increases dysfunctional impulsivity, which can lead to fraud (Morales-Vives & Vigil-Colet, 2012). This does not mean every elderly person is vulnerable, it just means that there is a greater likelihood of being vulnerable due to certain factors that are part of the ageing process. In fact, a study by James et al. (2014) found that in elderly participants without dementia, those with lower levels of cognitive functions, suffering poor health and having lower psychological wellbeing were the most vulnerable, as were those with lower financial literacy. In fact, knowledge of financial concepts often helped prevent fraud irrespective of cognitive abilities.

Research also suggests that social isolation, which is more prevalent in old age, increases fraud vulnerability (Langenderfer & Shimp, 2001; Lea et al., 2009; Martin, 2009; Olivier et al., 2015), but some researchers suggest otherwise (see James et al., 2014). However, loneliness can, at any age, make someone more open to talking to unknown people and therefore, more vulnerable to fraud, but again, this may not be true of all scams and all people (Buchanan & Whitty, 2014; Dove, 2018). One of the participants in my study told me that, at the time an investment scammer was persuading him to invest his money in the venture, he was living alone, away from his family, having just separated with his wife. The daily conversations with a scammer were friendly and pleasant. He specifically connected living alone and being stressed over his family with being less able to spot that the venture was a scam (Dove, 2018). Often, when we have a support network around us, we are able to discuss situations and decisions over with friends and family and get perspectives that are not available when we live alone.

Some studies have also found gender differences for certain scams. Van de Weijer and Leukfeldt (2017) found that men were more likely to be a victim of a cybercrime than women and elderly people, while miracle cure type scams tend to affect women more than men (Button et al., 2009a). Men were also more likely to be victims of romance fraud; however, when targeted, women tend to lose more money to romance fraud than men. Romance fraud scenarios also vary according to gender, which I talked about in Chapter 3 (Whitty & Buchanan, 2012b).

There may also be cultural differences that could potentially influence vulnerability to fraud. For example, propensity for trust differs across cultures (Weber & Hsee, 1998; Yamagishi & Yamagishi, 1994). Research found that American participants were more likely to trust strangers that belong in the same category group as them than Japanese participants, which could make them particularly vulnerable to frauds affecting affinity groups (Yuki et al., 2005). Additionally, some individual characteristics can be more pronounced across certain cultures, such as conforming to social norms, something that is frequently exploited by scammers (H. Kim & Markus, 1999).

Behaviours and beliefs

The way we behave and what we believe can also influence vulnerability to fraud. Often our beliefs shape our behaviour and this is known as consistency (Cialdini, 2014). Therefore, what we believe in can have an impact on how we behave. Often, we seek information to support our belief and ignore information that contradicts it (see Nickerson, 1998) and this can also lead to greater fraud vulnerability, especially as scammers often tell their victims what they want to hear.

Often, people believe that people who are scammed somehow deserved it and that this would never happen to them (Cross, 2013, 2015). Many fraud victims told me that they never thought it would happen to them because they considered themselves to be intelligent (Dove, 2018). But intelligence is not enough when it comes to fraud as some scams can be well executed. Additionally, intelligent people may be lacking practical or social intelligence, which is more influential when it comes to recognising deceptive cues (Greenspan, 2009). Erroneous belief that fraud only happens to some people can enhance vulnerability as it may lead to less caution (Dove, 2018).

Many fraud victims report that they believed that if they were defrauded, their perpetrator would be caught and punished, and many are disappointed when this does not happen. I named this belief 'Belief in Justice' or a belief that justice prevails and people get what they deserve. Belief in Justice was found to be connected to greater trust in authority, greater impulsivity and inability to correctly identify a phishing email, all of which can enhance vulnerability to fraudulent messages (Dove, 2018). Similar findings were reported by Cox et al. (2020), who found differences in how individuals assess the risk when it comes to them, as opposed to others, believing they would be less likely to fall for a phishing attempt than other people. This erroneous belief could be down to a cognitive bias known as a just world hypothesis. People want to believe that the world is a fair place where everyone gets what they deserve. Just think about how much people love when karma catches up with someone bad, even though karma is nothing more than a random sequence of events, otherwise we would always be able to rely on it. However, the illusion that we can control our environment has an important adaptive function (Lerner, 1965; Lerner & Miller, 1978). When something bad happens, we want to find a reason for it, because if we believed that bad things can happen to us randomly, this may have a negative impact on our wellbeing. For example, belief in a just world was found to contribute to life satisfaction and maintaining self-esteem (Dalbert, 1998, 1999).

When it comes to romance fraud, having strong romantic beliefs can add to vulnerability. Fraudsters exploit these beliefs by giving victims exactly what they need, by professing love early in the relationship and discussing future plans, fuelling romantic beliefs. This heightened emotional state, in combination with romantic thoughts of the future, is likely to influence potential victim when the perpetrator asks for funds (Whitty, 2013; Whitty & Buchanan, 2012b).

Some behaviours also increase our vulnerability to fraud. The obvious ones are ignoring security or fraud warnings (Furnell & Thomson, 2009; Modic & Anderson, 2014) and only actively seeking information of how to avoid fraud after being defrauded (Citizen Advice, 2017). Some studies indicate that joining online groups, using social media, entering contests and prizes, online and phone purchases, and giving to charity increase the likelihood of being targeted by scammers and, therefore, becoming a victim (Parish et al., 2009; Titus & Gover, 2001). What we share on social media can be of particular concern, as birthdays, friends lists and photographs can be used by scammers in order to orchestrate scams. Consequently, using social media can often result in security and fraud attempts, while the information we share on social media via links (and those oh so cute cat videos) is making us less aware of dangers that links can represent (Frauenstein & Flowerday, 2016; Kunwar & Sharma, 2016). Using smartphones to engage in these online behaviours carries even more risk, because smartphones tend to contain a lot of sensitive data (think banking apps) and because fraudsters can deliver different types of attacks through the smartphones (Foozy et al., 2013; Jeon et al., 2011).

Human factors and information security

Many organisations believe that as long as they have good security protocols in place, this is enough to ward off cyberattacks. Many do nothing to address human factors that can greatly compromise the security of the whole organisation. Security protocols are often ineffective when it comes to protection from cyberattacks, mostly due to the fact that people either ignore the advice or put themselves at a greater risk by engaging in behaviours that lead to cybercrime (Hadlington, 2017; Hadlington & Parsons, 2017; Herath & Rao, 2009). For example, Herath & Rao (2009) found that employees are guided by intrinsic and extrinsic motivations when it comes to security behaviour. They are more likely to comply with security if they believe their behaviour has a positive impact on the organisation. However, they also found that social influence can influence security behaviour. Employees are more likely to comply with security policies if they see their peers and supervisors doing the same (social influence). Additionally, the study also found that severe penalties can be counterproductive when it comes to security intentions. Similar findings were noted by Pahnila et al. (2007), who noted that sanctions for non-compliance with security have little impact on intentions to comply. This is also consistent with other research on rewards and punishments (Bénabou & Tirole, 2003; Oliver, 1980).

So why pay attention to human factors in organisations and why should you concentrate on educating your employees on their vulnerabilities? First and foremost, because they exist and no protocol will be a foolproof way of accounting for these vulnerabilities. For example, studies conducted by Workman (2008), looked at individual characteristics associated with security breaches in the workplace. The study orchestrated various social engineering attacks (e.g. phishing email, phone calls). Employees have previously filled in the measures on obedience to authority, commitment and trust. The study found that phishing and phone phishing was connected to obedience to authority, high normative commitment (e.g. reciprocity), and trust. This means that some employees would be more susceptible to phishing attacks targeted at businesses. Other research found a connection between impulsivity and risky cybersecurity behaviours in the workplace (Hadlington, 2017). Therefore, individual characteristics may affect security attitudes and behaviours in the workplace.

It is impractical to control your employees and what they do all the time, but once there is a breach or customer data is compromised, the publicity in the media can be extremely damaging for the organisation and lower the public's confidence in the brand. Many employees will not be aware of a social engineering attack when it is taking place, because scammers can be incredibly skilled at orchestrating attacks that are likely to be lucrative, such as those aimed at businesses. When people are under visceral influence or in the presence of other highly successful persuasion techniques, they are likely to forget any protocol they have been asked to follow (see Oracle Mind, 2016 video to see how an organisation's protocol can be compromised by a social engineering attack in less than 5 minutes). Therefore, making them aware how these attacks target individual vulnerabilities may raise awareness and lead to more employee engagement when it comes to security. This is needed because studies have found that the abundance and complexity of security advice is causing security fatigue, leading to avoidance, and security outcomes could be improved by designing prevention around individual differences (Dove, 2018; Egelman & Peer, 2015; Furnell & Thomson, 2009; Stanton et al., 2016).

OK, we are done. I am sure this chapter was a lot to take in. We are all composed of so many different characteristics that it is impossible to pinpoint one or two. Fraud vulnerability is likely to be different from person to person, as personality characteristics, circumstances, behaviours and contexts collide. But having an awareness is a start. Finally, I want to conclude this chapter by highlighting research that found that some victims are simply attracted to scam offers even though they make good decisions in every other aspect of their lives, while others are not tempted by small or large amounts (Fischer et al., 2013; Lea et al., 2009). Additionally, romance scam victims were found to be highly educated, middle-aged people with no obvious vulnerabilities, such as those that affect elderly people (Whitty, 2017), therefore fraud vulnerability may be less obvious and more individual.

However, being aware of some of these vulnerabilities and why scammers target them, as well as actively slowing down reactions to any kind of offer received can help in avoiding them.

Further reading

Button, M., & Cross, C. (2017). *Cyber Frauds, Scams and their Victims* (1 edition). Routledge.
Cialdini, R. B. (2006). *Influence: The Psychology of Persuasion, Revised Edition*. William Morrow.
Greenspan, S. (2009). *Annals of Gullibility: Why We Get Duped and How to Avoid It*. Praeger Publishers.
Misztal, B. (2013). *Trust in Modern Societies: The Search for the Bases of Social Order*. John Wiley & Sons.

Chapter 8

Theories and models that could explain why we fall victim to fraud and scams

There are different theories, psychological models and errors in judgments that can assist in understanding why we fall for scams, how we process information and make decisions when it comes to fraudulent offers. In this chapter, I will outline some of these theories and models, in hope that they may piece all the information so far together and offer a deeper understanding.

Errors in judgment

Lea et al.'s (2009) research into scams and scam compliance identified different factors that affect how we process fraudulent offers. Although they also belong with processes explained in Chapter 5, I thought it would be more useful to explain them here, with other theories and models of fraud vulnerability.

These factors fall into two groups, motivational and cognitive, and they can influence judgments. Motivational factors, such as visceral influences, liking and similarity, reciprocation, commitment and consistency and lack of self-control, are frequently exploited by fraudsters, as explained previously. Additionally, when evaluating offers, our motivation to process information could be reduced, either as a result of persuasion (e.g. scarcity of the offer) or evoked visceral influence, such as greed or fear, and this can lead to compliance. However, there could be a more sinister reason behind reduced motivation to process information, such as cognitive impairment.

Sensation seeking, which is associated with risk taking and refers to emotional effects such as excitement, arousal and mood regulation (e.g. alleviating negative moods by shopping) can also lead to errors in judgments. Finally, is a potential victim just seeking information that confirms their preferences or are they looking at the offer in more detail? This preference for confirmation, too, can lead us to make wrong decisions when evaluating offers.

Among cognitive factors, the most obvious is reduced cognitive abilities, which are crucial for making optimal decisions, norm activation, tendency to obey authority, social proof, positive illusions and background knowledge. Too little knowledge on a specific issue can lead to fraud; however, extensive background knowledge can, too, because it may lead to overconfidence. People see themselves in a positive light, due to which they may sometimes overestimate their abilities (positive illusions) and this can lead to vulnerability, especially if the scammer is flattering and offers compliments.

False consensus, or thinking the offer is valid because others are backing it and altercasting, which was explained in the previous chapter, are also cognitive factors that contribute to errors in judgments.

You may notice some similarity with these errors in judgment and scamming techniques that were mentioned earlier. This is because scammers try to evoke these errors in judgment when they present fraud offers or communication, because they do not wants us to think carefully and rationally, they want us to make emotional or rushed decisions.

Lea et al. (2009) also looked at how these errors of judgment affect people that have been defrauded in the past and those that have not. A questionnaire, with statements referring to different errors of judgment related to scam vulnerability, was given to participants. Participants were also asked to indicate their feelings about scam offers they received in the past. Non-victims showed either no agreement or very little agreement with the statements while victims and near victims reported medium agreement with the statements. Lea at al. (2009) suggest this means that victims have a general vulnerability to persuasion and are not merely affected by the right scam at the right time. Instead, they may be susceptible to committing errors of judgements when presented with offers, and are more likely to engage and comply. Additional study, where participants were sent a fake scam correspondence, which was designed to evoke errors in judgements (e.g. high prize, scarce offer etc.) also found differences between previous scam victims and non-victims. People who were defrauded in the past showed less dislike towards the scam communication and were more likely to respond, therefore may be particularly vulnerable to repeat victimisation (Lea et al., 2009).

The Model of Scamming Vulnerability

After evaluating a large corpus of research conducted by the American Association of Retired People, as well as surveying fraud prevention specialists, Langenderfer and Shimp (2001) proposed a model that could explain scam vulnerability. They suggested that attention people pay to fraud communication is down to the Elaboration Likelihood Model of persuasion (Petty & Cacioppo, 1986). When we deliberate on something, such as a fraudulent offer, we may take one of two routes of information processing, central or peripheral. The peripheral route is somewhat superficial, which means we may not concentrate on the message quality and facts, the pros and cons of the offer, but instead we may concentrate on persuasive cues. This includes focusing on how attractive the reward is and what we may do with it, or how friendly and approachable the scammer appears. Taking the central route, we are more likely to concentrate on the argument we have been given and seek information to see if the offer is legitimate. Langenderfer and Shimp's (2001) Model of Scamming Vulnerability considered these two routes of information processing and how we may process fraud communication under the visceral influence (i.e. strong emotions, fear, excitement, etc.) and without it.

Langenderfer and Shimp (2001) suggest that when the elaboration is high (i.e. we are able to and willing to process information), but the visceral influence is low, we take the central route of processing and concentrate on the quality of the argument. This can help us detect deception by spotting warnings signs. However, if the visceral influence is high, we may concentrate on the attractiveness of the offer instead, despite the high elaboration, and this can influence compliance. So even if our preference is for high elaboration, we may still be susceptible to the effects of the visceral influence, especially if the scammer is skilled at making us imagine the benefits of the offer (vividness), which are just around the corner (proximity). However, these influences can be moderated by self-control. For example, imagine being very tempted by a great offer, but you also know that acting on impulse is not good for you, so you frequently take time to decide whether to purchase something. Walking away means that when you make a decision, you are likely to not be under the visceral influence, because the effects of the visceral influence are temporary, and are likely to make an informed decisions based on rational arguments.

Sometimes, the attention may be on the attractiveness of the offer, rather than on the argument quality (peripheral route of processing) but visceral influence is low. In such cases, different factors such as social isolation, cognitive impairment, gullibility and consumer susceptibility to interpersonal influence, can exacerbate scam vulnerability. This vulnerability is lessened in people with scam knowledge (e.g. knowledge of how scams operate) and who are more sceptical (Langenderfer & Shimp, 2001).

Models of Gullible and Foolish Action

People often do something that is later deemed foolish, even by them. It would be hard to find someone who has never done anything foolish. Greenspan (2008) proposed a model of how foolish acts happen. The Model of Foolish Action comprises socially and practically foolish actions. Practically foolish actions tend to result in physical danger, such as petting a wild alligator, while socially foolish actions have interpersonal consequences. Socially foolish actions can be induced by manipulative scammers giving the potential victim false information, which is not in their best interest, and this can lead to gullibility. In his book on gullibility, Stephen Greenspan asserts that gullibility is something all of us can relate to at certain times. He suggests that gullible action tends to comprise four components: situation, cognition, personality and state. Any combination of these components (or even one strong one) can lead to gullible action (see Greenspan, 2009).

How can this model help explain fraud vulnerability? For example, situation may mean a social situation potential victim finds themselves in. Are other people recommending this deal, is the scammer persuasive or likeable, etc.? Cognitive processes may refer to not knowing much about scams or the background of the offer or not being able to determine if the scammer or the offer is genuine and this can sometimes be down to cognitive impairment. However, according to Greenspan (2009), gullibility is not an intelligence problem as it does not signify inability to think, but it may be a sign of lazy thinking. Perhaps the person is not motivated to process the information, leading to errors in judgement (also Lea et al., 2009).

Personality may refer to certain characteristics that the potential victim possesses, such as being impulsive or compliant and therefore more likely to go along with fraud offers or more trusting and less vigilant. State or affect refers to how we feel, our emotions. In this context, it may be that the potential victim is under the visceral influence evoked by the scam communication (e.g. excitement or fear), or that they are in love with the scammer, as in the case of romance fraud. Making decisions under the influence of strong emotions is not optimal. Rational thinking is more likely when we are not under the influence of strong emotions, than when we are under the influence of strong emotions. Cold cognition vs hot cognition. Therefore, it may be good to postpone decisions when under the influence of the strong emotion, as it is likely to lead to hot cognition (Greenspan, 2009).

Phishing susceptibility framework

Frauds sometimes target certain human traits, which makes people with those traits more susceptible to fraudulent offers. Parrish et al. (2009) proposed a phishing susceptibility framework, which can help explain why people fall for phishing. Personality traits they considered were the Big-Five: openness, conscientiousness, extraversion, agreeableness and neuroticism. They argue that, besides personality traits, personal (e.g. gender, age, culture) and experiential factors (past events that shape who we are) can also be implicated in fraud vulnerability. Not only that, each factor can also affect other factors. For example, personal factor, such as age, can influence an individual's experience in some way, while personal and experiential factors could play a role in who we are (e.g. personality). Culture and age can have effects on gender, while personality can shape our experience. Experiences can also be positive or negative. Let me try to give you some examples. Elderly people tend to be targeted by scammers more than other age groups (Harries et al., 2014; Muscat et al., 2002). This alters their experience, compared to other age groups, because it increases the likelihood of fraud victimisation and repeat victimisation. Most fraud victims that I interviewed for my research reported that being defrauded (experiential factor) has changed them as a person in some way. Either they became more aware of people's motives or they altered their behaviour to avoid fraud in the future (see Dove, 2018). One victim told me that she used to be quite impulsive in the past but after being defrauded due to a relatively impulsive decision, she became less impulsive and now weighs out pros and cons when it comes to investments or large purchases, and tends to delay decisions. Initially, some aspects of her personality (e.g. being impulsive) led to a bad investment and this experience made her alter this part of her personality to avoid bad investments in the future.

According to Parrish et al. (2009), agreeableness and extraversion could be associated with phishing vulnerability. Agreeableness contains a trust dimension, which could mean that agreeable people could be more trusting, while extraversion might be connected to how much information is shared online (e.g. more extraverted people would likely share more). Openness to experience, they argued, may also be implicated in susceptibility to phishing, but conscientiousness may in some cases, prevent compliance. For example, if a person is aware of fraud security advice, they will be more likely to follow this advice. Neuroticism, too, could prevent phishing attacks, because those high in neuroticism may be more private with sharing their details online.

It is important to consider that the Phishing Susceptibility Framework, proposed by Parrish et al. (2009) is theoretical, which means it has not been experimentally tested on phishing correspondence. It is not always easy to study scam compliance because in order to do so, one has to mimic a scam, which is not always easy or ethical, and has proven to be problematic (Jagatic et al., 2007). However, Modic and Lea (2013) attempted to assess the Big-Five personality traits in relation to scam compliance, using hypothetical scam scenarios and asking participants about previous behaviour in similar situations. I will quickly go over their findings to see how they compare to the Phishing Susceptibility Framework.

After completing the Big-Five personality traits measure, participants in Modic and Lea's (2012) study also received life scenarios describing potential scam situations (e.g. advance fee fraud, fake listing online, etc.), and were asked if they experienced, responded and lost money to such a scenario. Contrary to Parrish et al.'s (2009) prediction that extraverts could be more vulnerable, Modic and Lea (2012) found that individuals who were more introverted were more likely to respond to scams. They put it down to introverts preferring impersonal contact (e.g. online communication), which makes it harder to tell if someone is trustworthy. Agreeableness, on the other hand, was found to be a predictor or responding to scams. Agreeableness is connected to being considerate and friendly, which could make people who are more agreeable think that other people are similar to them, leading to greater vulnerability to frauds.

There are other factors that could be implicated in vulnerability to phishing, such as additional experiential factors. These include technological experience (e.g. how internet savvy you are and what knowledge you have on how technology works) and professional experience, which includes career or academic experience (Parrish et al., 2009). When I was analysing sextortion emails, I noticed that many offered technological explanation for how data on the victim was captured, which to me seemed believable. However, when I checked a few with some of my friends, who are security experts, I was told the explanations made no sense. This is how technological and professional experience can come in handy when it comes to frauds.

Additionally, there are attack factors, which include lure and the hook, or things that fraudsters engineer to make us comply. The lure refers to the type of phishing email, what it is purporting to offer or communicate (e.g. security upgrades, financial incentives, etc.). The hook is what the email is asking us to do (e.g. reply to an email or click the link). Phishing susceptibility is much greater if the attack factors appear convincing (Parrish et al., 2009).

Suspicion, Cognition and Automacity Model of phishing susceptibility

Vishwanath et al. (2018) proposed and tested a model of phishing susceptibility that takes into a consideration several factors that could potentially contribute to fraud vulnerability.

The first component, suspicion, refers to a process of detecting deception, which can depend on certain conditions (McCornack & Levine, 1990). The way we perceive reality often depends on cognitive evaluation of information available within a certain context. Expectations of what this reality should be is also a reflection of our beliefs of what is acceptable in a given situation. In a potential phishing situation these beliefs may refer to how we perceive risks that are typically associated with our behaviours online. If we perceive our behaviour to be risky, we may invest more cognitive effort in information processing, processing the message systematically (e.g. paying careful attention to information at hand) rather than heuristically (e.g. more reflexively). Therefore, according to Vishwanath et al. (2018), these cyber risk beliefs could greatly influence the level of suspicion in a phishing situation.

The authors argue that many behaviours we do online, such as sending and receiving emails, are habitual and, for the most part, they are benign. Therefore, not a lot of cognitive effort is applied to some of the behaviours we engage in online. This may be why we sometimes ignore the cues that should arouse suspicion. This could be more pronounced in individuals who may have less self-control over their email habits (e.g. checking emails while driving, despite danger).

Vishwanath et al. (2018) tested their model in two separate experimental studies, one using an email with a link and one using an email with an attachment, while testing participants on a series of measures (e.g. suspicion, heuristic and systematic processing, cyber risk beliefs, email habits and deficiencies in self-regulation). The study found that individuals who were more suspicious were less likely to be phished, either via links or attachments. Additionally, participants' level of suspicion and their information processing was connected to their cyber risk beliefs (e.g. when perceived risk was high, messages were processed systematically). The study also found a link between habitual email actions and phishing susceptibility. This supports suggestions by Frauenstein and Flowerday (2016), who argued that our habitual behaviours on social media, such as sharing and clicking links, are making us more vulnerable to phishing attacks.

The Model of Fraud Susceptibility

This model was developed by me, through several research studies, looking into individual characteristics that make people vulnerable to fraud offers (Dove, 2018). Some of the findings were also mentioned previously in this book, however, the Model of Fraud Susceptibility (see Figure 8.1) can be used to provide more holistic view of compliance with fraud offers.

When a potential victim receives a fraudulent offer, whether out of the blue or by searching for solutions to their needs, they are more likely to engage or comply with the offer if certain factors are present, for example their circumstances. Do they have the time to carefully examine all the details? Are they experiencing financial struggles, which could be alleviated by the fraudulent offer (e.g. needing a job)? Are they evaluating the offer as a part of a group and likely to be influenced by their friends or colleagues, which think the offer is good? Circumstances can greatly influence how we feel about fraud offers. For example, a job offer, however dodgy it looks, will always seem more enticing to someone who is desperate to make ends meet, because they are trying to alleviate their problems, and the offer provides a solution.

Fraud offers that mimic the look and feel of genuine offers will also appear more trustworthy and may not arouse any suspicions (e.g. professional-looking websites or a presentable scammer). Additionally, persuasive techniques could also influence how a potential victim perceives the offer, and this too can add to the likelihood of engaging with the offer.

Once an offer is deemed appropriate, immediate compliance is likely to happen if a potential victim is more impulsive, has less self-control or if they are more compliant in general, preferring to go along with things. However, if a potential victim is vigilant, and they decide to check some facts, despite

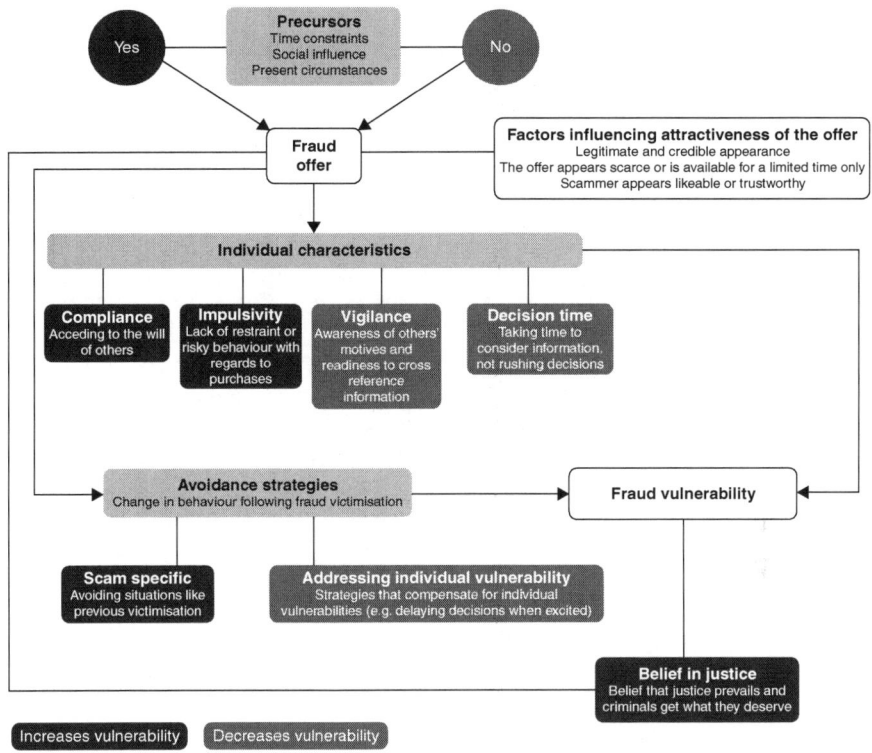

Figure 8.1 The Model of Fraud Susceptibility by Dove (2018).

thinking that the offer looks legitimate, they are more likely to find something that would arouse suspicion that the offer is fraudulent, which could help guide their decision. Even just delaying decisions can be beneficial because it allows visceral influence to subside, leading to more rational decisions. Additionally, awareness of one's general vulnerability can also help in avoiding fraud victimisation. For example, despite the attractiveness of the offer, the potential victim may be aware that in the past, impulsivity led them to make bad decisions, so now they make a point of taking time to decide what to do. Some people are naturally more cautious and take time to consider things carefully, while others became more cautious due to previous life experiences. Other examples of awareness of personal vulnerability may also include being aware that you comply more readily in certain situations, so you try to prepare or avoid such situations or avoiding people who have influence over you, which you find uncomfortable.

Sometimes, our beliefs can also add to fraud vulnerability. For example, believing that scams only happen to some people and that, since you are an intelligent and competent person, it would not happen to you, can lower risk perception and prompt confidence in the decision. In reality, fraud can happen to anyone and some frauds are complex events, influenced by different components that contribute to eventual compliance.

These models and theories certainly come in handy when trying to explain how fraud happens to us and what makes us vulnerable; however, there are certain caveats. Only some of these models were based on experimental studies. Errors in judgements were tested in series of studies by Lea et al. (2009). Additionally, Vishwanath et al.'s (2018) Model of Susceptibility to Phishing was also tested on phishing type correspondence. My Model of Fraud Susceptibility, was a result of series of research studies specifically addressing individual characteristics implicated in susceptibility to fraud, including phishing correspondence (Dove, 2018). The rest of the models or frameworks, while based on solid research, have not been experimentally tested, to my knowledge. What this means is that you cannot be completely sure how they would perform in the real world. And even when new research offers something exciting, sometimes it warrants further testing. However, all of these theories and models offer a solid start in understanding how and why we fall for scams.

Chapter 9

Learning to spot scams, fraud and persuasive communication

Vulnerability to fraud is often down to several factors. Some of those are individual, such as personal circumstances, behaviours or individual characteristics (e.g. level of vigilance or self-control). Some are down to persuasion or scam techniques that fraudsters may use. An individual may be more vulnerable to particular frauds at certain times in their life, depending on their circumstances. For example, if you have recently divorced your partner or are single but looking for a relationship, you will be more likely to engage with someone contacting and befriending you out of the blue on social media or more likely to use dating websites where you may encounter romance fraudsters. On the other hand, if you are desperately looking for work or ways to earn money, certain financial opportunities, schemes or job offers will be more attractive to you than to someone else who already has a good job and is not suffering financial hardship. Even just being lonely can make one more likely to engage with unsolicited calls or correspondence.

Vulnerability to fraudulent offers can also be increased by carefully chosen persuasion or scam techniques. Fraudsters frequently use persuasion techniques to influence compliance and many frauds use more than one at the time. Carefully chosen scam techniques that complement each other can be very influential. For example, a phishing email that evokes strong visceral influence, such as excitement or fear, will be more effective if the fraudster then also limits response time in some way because visceral influence is short lived. Therefore, fraudsters need to ensure that the potential victim will act quickly while still under the influence of the initial emotions that the correspondence may have evoked.

Scam situations and factors that contribute to compliance

So how does everything in the previous chapters translate to real life? Here are some case studies of different frauds and how they relate to personal circumstances, errors in judgment and scam techniques. Although individual characteristics can greatly influence compliance with fraud offers, they are difficult to pinpoint from case studies alone without some sort of psychometric measure. However, many people are aware they may have certain characteristics that do not always serve them well, such as not being able to say no or rushing decisions. The following examples of fraudulent situations have been told to me by victims of fraud, either as a part of my research (see Dove, 2018) or in other conversations. They are real examples; however, they are not the only examples. However, they may, hopefully, illustrate factors that come into play when it comes to scam situations.

> **Case study 1**
>
> Peter was shopping locally for groceries. Upon reaching his parked car, he noticed smoke coming from the car engine. At that point, a man approached him, told him he was a car mechanic and told him not to turn the car on as the engine could seize. The man who appeared friendly and approachable told Peter that he lived locally, even mentioning local landmarks. He also told him he has recently become a granddad and he offered to fix Peter's car for a fee. Peter, who is disabled and has difficulty standing and walking for longer periods, and is often in pain due to his disability, remembered he was a member of a car recovery scheme and quickly contemplated calling them but felt it would take some time for them to arrive and solve the problem. Because he did not want to wait and stand around, he accepted the offer and paid the man to look at his engine and fix it. A few days later, Peter read in the local paper about a fraudster purporting to be a mechanic, sabotaging people's car engines with liquid to make them appear to be smoking and then offering to fix it, and he realised he was a victim of this fraud.
>
> Individual factors
>
> *Circumstances*
>
> Peter was disabled, which often meant being in pain, therefore, for him, waiting for recovery service meant possible discomfort, whereas for someone else this would not be an issue.
>
> *Background knowledge*
>
> Not knowing much about car engines meant that Peter could not tell whether the man was telling the truth or not.

> **Scam techniques used**
>
> *Liking and similarity*
>
> The fraudster stressed similarity between him and the intended victim by mentioning he lives locally and backing this up by giving the victim specific street names. Research found that similarity reduces perceived threat.

Had Peter been someone else, perhaps someone who is not in pain and has no issues standing or walking, he may have felt that it was worth waiting for a recovery service. Had the fraudster been less charming or had he not given Peter local landmarks as a reference, Peter might have been more alarmed that a complete stranger was offering to fix his car. We typically do not trust strangers but we trust friends and neighbours, so pretending to be a neighbour allowed the fraudster to connect with Peter on an interpersonal level, lowering the level of vigilance one may have when dealing with a complete stranger.

> **Case study 2**
>
> Fred needed to buy a vehicle for an upcoming road trip and found a perfect one on eBay for a very good price. Fred wanted to talk to the seller about some details prior to purchase, so he emailed the seller requesting to connect over the phone. However, the seller emailed him to say he was abroad and was not able to talk on the phone until he came back home. Fred realised that if he waited for the seller to come back so that he could find out more information, he would miss the auction, as the auction was ending, so he decided to go ahead. Upon winning the auction, Fred was received a legitimate-looking email bearing relevant PayPal logos, asking for a bank transfer, which he sent. At the time, he did not realise that this was a phishing email and he was not paying through PayPal at all and that PayPal does not cover vehicle purchases.
>
> Individual factors
>
> *Circumstances*
>
> Needing a vehicle for an upcoming trip possibly meant that time might be an issue in finding the right type of vehicle for the trip, leading to rushed decisions as there may not be *another opportunity like this*.

Vigilance

Although Fred appeared vigilant after getting a bit worried that he could not talk to the seller to source more information, he decided to take the risk based on the plausible story the fraudster told him, which created urgency and the fact that he needed a vehicle soon.

Background knowledge

Fred was not aware that PayPal does not include or cover payments via bank transfer and also does not offer cover for car purchases.

Scam techniques used

Urgency

Auctions typically limit the time an item is available for and this will create urgency.

On top of that, the fraudster engineered a plausible situation to escape talking to the potential victim within the time of the auction, a conversation that may have raised some red flags and resulted in the victim pulling out of the sale.

Legitimacy

To most people, legitimate and official-looking correspondence will appear trustworthy.

A professional and legitimate-looking email, designed by the fraudster, reassured Fred that the transaction was legitimate and offered Fred a sense of security. However, Fred's lack of knowledge on PayPal's terms and conditions led to a false sense of security in the transaction that initially seemed a bit risky.

Had Fred had more time to purchase the vehicle for the upcoming trip, he may have decided to wait and purchase another vehicle when the initial doubts set in. The fact that the vehicle was being sold on an auction site and the auction was ending, added to the overall urgency, influencing quick decisions. Correspondence that impersonates genuine organisations, bearing the appropriate logos, is seen as highly credible. For example, research has found that people are primed by visual cues in emails, such as known logos, and this sometimes takes away from careful information processing (Blythe et al., 2011). To Fred, the correspondence looked credible as it arrived after the auction had ended, just as an invoice would, and he did not question it.

Case study 3

Jackie had her Facebook account compromised by a fraudster who then contacted her friends on Facebook, pretending to be Jackie. The fraudster then told Jackie's friends that she (Jackie) was in trouble and needed money and asked each of Jackie's friends for a relatively small sum of money, possibly to avoid suspicion and remain undetected.

Individual factors

This fraud was perpetrated against Jackie's friends, without any cooperation from Jackie, while her friends thought they were receiving a genuine message from her, therefore individual factors may not have been that influential as the scam techniques used in this type of fraud.

Scam techniques used

Evoking social norms

Most humans need social interaction and are brought up to trust and help their friends and family. Whereas one would be wary of a stranger's request for money, when it comes to people we know and like, we tend to be generous and helpful. Therefore, most of us, when we receive a message from a friend and that message looks credible, would help a friend in need. Fraudsters exploit this socially desired behaviour by pretending they need help.

Sometimes, such as in the Case study 3, a well-designed scam is enough to influence compliance. This type of fraud is interesting as it combines aspects of cybersecurity (e.g. someone who is able to compromise or successfully steal Facebook log-in details) and psychology. Frauds that are able to combine these two aspects can be highly effective as they appear very credible (i.e. coming from a friend in this case) and are difficult to discern from genuine situations. Social norms, such as being kind, helpful or charitable are frequently exploited by scammers, whether through fake crowdfunding campaigns or fake charities that frequently pop up after major natural disasters (e.g. earthquakes or hurricanes). It is not always easy to find out which ones are fake and which ones are real and many people defrauded in such a way never find out that they have, in fact, given money to fraudsters instead of charity.

Case study 4

Tim's work colleague told everyone at work about an exciting investment opportunity that he was investing in. Tim was initially hesitant as there was not much information about the investment and this was not something he knew much about. Also, he was told he had 48 hours to make up his mind, which worried him slightly, but the return on the investment was excellent, which appealed to him. Since his work colleagues were also investing, Tim decided to go for it. He felt he would regret if he did not and he wanted to feel he was part of the group. Soon after investing their money, Tim and his colleagues could no longer get in touch with the investment banker who arranged the investment and, after reporting it to the police, they found out that they had been defrauded.

Individual factors

Social proof

Some people are more likely to follow the crowd or look to others as guidance when making decisions. This is not necessarily bad, but in some cases it may mean that one is going against their better judgment to fit in with others who may be making the wrong decision.

Background knowledge

Not knowing much about investments or financial frauds made Tim more vulnerable to this type of fraud as he would not have known what to look for.

Vigilance

Initially, Tim was vigilant and had reservations about investing in the venture due to the lack of solid information available, but the desire to fit in with his friends and the fact that so many of his colleagues thought this was a good idea gave him more confidence in his decision.

Scam techniques used

Social influence

Investment or pyramid schemes often tend to target people that work or socialise together as the fraudster needs to persuade one person to invest and encourage them to tell their friends and/or family about it. People tend to take more risks when they see others taking risks and may feel more confident in their choice when they see it has the backing of other people.

Visceral influence

Offering big returns on investment often evokes strong feelings such as excitement or greed, which may compromise careful thinking.

Time limit

Imposing a time limit ensures that the initial visceral influence is still present when a potential victim makes a decision.

Financial scams often target people in groups, such as people who work together as word of mouth can be a powerful thing among friends or colleagues (Abagnale, 2019). It allows the fraudsters to target more people at once this way and trigger social influence. Often, the investments promise very good returns in a relatively short space of time, which makes it attractive and exciting and evokes visceral influence. By offering a quick return on an investment, fraudsters keep the prize proximate. Proximity is important, because a long-term investment may not be as exciting to potential victims (Langenderfer & Shimp, 2001).

Case study 5

Liz was recently bereaved after many years of happy marriage and was living alone, when she received a letter through the post, advertising psychic services. She engaged with the psychic on several occasions and the psychic appeared understanding and nurturing, which gave Liz comfort. At other times, the psychic called her, and they discussed their daily lives, as one would do with a friend. Soon, it became difficult for Liz to stop engaging with the phone calls.

Individual factors

Circumstances

Recently bereaved people are particularly vulnerable to this type, and other types, of fraud that are based on building a relationship with the victim (e.g. romance fraud and even some financial frauds).

Compliance

Despite not wanting to communicate with the psychic anymore, Liz could not say no. For more compliant individuals, saying no might be more difficult, which makes them more vulnerable to fraud.

Scam techniques used

Altercasting

Fraudsters sometimes orchestrate frauds that put the intended victim in a specific role, such as a role of a friend. When Liz called the psychic for a reading, she was a customer but the psychic changed that relationship by calling her and talking to her as a friend would. This assumed role of a friend made it difficult to sever the ties with the psychic. Fraudsters use this technique in order to keep defrauding the same victim over and over.

Liz found herself living alone and, having lost a partner of many years, was feeling lonely. Engaging with a psychic provided company and comfort. However, when the psychic started calling her and building a friendship, it made it difficult for Liz to sever all ties or go to the police as this is not what one would do to a 'friend'. Many fraudsters use this technique as it allows them to have control over the potential victim. For example, it often stops the victim from going to the police because they feel they are betraying the person they have been communicating with. Some financial frauds also use this technique.

Case study 6

Anna is an office manager for a medium-size company and part of her job is to pay invoices submitted to the company. Anna received an email from a company director himself, asking Anna to pay an invoice attached, by bank transfer. Anna noted that this was out of the ordinary since invoices typically came directly from contractors and service providers the company used. However, the company director mentioned other members of staff who work under him in the same email and provided an explanation as to why he was asking Anna for this request. Anna paid the invoice but the company later realised they were victims of a spear phishing attack.

Individual factors

Background knowledge

Anna was not aware of spear phishing attacks and how sophisticated they can be; therefore, despite the request, which was out of the ordinary, she had no reason to doubt that the email came from the company director.

Obedience to authority

It is possible that an email from someone else in the company would have aroused greater suspicion and, therefore, triggered additional checks. Despite initial concerns, Anna did not want to question the request from the person in a position of seniority.

Scam techniques used

Authority

Scammers use authority to enhance compliance because we are taught to trust and obey authoritative figures. Requests coming from people in authority (e.g. police, solicitors, etc.) are less likely to be questioned. To Anna, a company director is an authoritative figure, therefore she was unlikely to question or undermine their requests.

Credibility

The email looked legitimate and appeared to be coming from a credible source. The scammer enhanced credibility by mentioning other staff in the company, leading to a false sense of security, even if the email initially arose suspicion.

Scammers enhance credibility in many ways, from inserting legitimate logos in the correspondence to impersonating credible and trustworthy people or professions.

Not questioning people who have authority over us or those that we associated with having our best interests at heart, whether at work (e.g. managers, directors) or in our daily lives (e.g. police, legal professionals, doctors) is common. But this is also how scammers encourage compliance, even in the presence of warning signs.

Case study 7

Zara is a busy professional woman in her sixties, who was recently widowed. She tried online dating and soon started exchanging emails with someone who seemed to be perfect and with whom she felt instant connection. He was also recently widowed and was working on a large project abroad. Soon, Zara was talking to him on the phone and they started discussing future plans for when he came back home after his contract ended. After several months of daily conversations and plans, Zara's new man confided in her that he needed to find a large sum of money to secure the contract, which was about to fall through. She offered him the money because, by this time, she believed they were destined to be together. However, after several requests for money, Zara became suspicious and confided in a friend, who encouraged her to report it to the police. By this time, Zara was defrauded of a very large sum of money.

Individual factors

Bereavement

Bereaved individuals are often more vulnerable to being defrauded due to the emotional vulnerabilities that come with bereavement. Sometimes, bereavement can leave a void, which scammers are only too happy to fill.

Background knowledge

Having been in a long-term relationship before becoming widowed, Zara was not fully aware of dangers of online dating and potential for romance fraud, which made her more vulnerable.

Romantic beliefs

Zara desperately wanted to find someone to share her life with again and when she met someone that seemed perfect, she was only happy to help them when they needed it.

Scam techniques used

Liking and similarity

Romance scammers often pretend to be similar to the victim (e.g. having the same circumstances, such as being divorced or having children) and this encourages trust and intimacy.

> *Grooming*
>
> Romance scammers often groom their victims for months before asking for money. After many months of intense emotional conversations, the scammer orchestrated a crisis, hoping that Zara will offer the money without being asked.

Certain life circumstances, such as bereavement, can make people vulnerable to fraud. When it comes to romance fraud, a strong desire for a romantic relationship can override warning signs that may appear during the course of a relationship.

> **Case study 8**
>
> Ivan received a letter in the post, which told him that the sender had been watching him for a while and knew his secret. If he did not pay a ransom in bitcoin within 24 hours, his secret would be revealed to his friends and family. Since Ivan had recently had an extramarital affair, he feared that the sender knew about this and would reveal this to his family, which this would result in the breakdown of his family. The letter also reminded him how much shame he would feel if his co-workers and his family found out about his 'secret' and how pointless it would be to go to the police, as the ransom should be paid within 24 hours. Ivan was under a lot of stress to make a quick decision and he was afraid to lose his family so he paid the ransom.
>
> Individual factors
>
> *Circumstances*
>
> Ivan had an extramarital affair in the past, which his family did not know about. This made him doubt if the sender knew about this.
>
> *Background knowledge*
>
> Ivan has not heard much about sextortion scams, he thought that they only happen online, therefore receiving a letter through the post made the threat more credible. Ivan also thought, since the correspondence was eloquently written and did not have typical scam signs (e.g. bad spelling and grammar), that it must be genuine.

Scam techniques used

Visceral influence

Extortion correspondence (including sextortion) is designed to evoke fear, which will compromise careful thinking and may encourage a fight or flight response. Ivan felt he had no other choice but to pay to avoid the situation.

Urgency

Giving a victim a limited time to comply ensures that that the evoked fear is still fresh and the victim has no time to consult with friends, family and the authorities.

Evoking social norms

Extortion correspondence also works by evoking shame by reminding the victim about correct social conventions, such as that cheating on a partner is something that is shameful, not condoned by society and that would have serious consequences.

Helplessness

The scammer purposely mentioned that they cannot be easily found, especially in the time frame given to the victim to pay the ransom (24 hours). This was done to dissuade the victim from going to the police, as they may be told about this scam, and to feel powerless and helpless and accept the terms of the deal.

Not all fraud attempts result in the victimisation. I think it is helpful to also see how fraud can be avoided, so I will give you some examples of this, too.

Case study 9

Ismail has a small business and was about to purchase a large order of goods from a company he found online. The company appeared to be registered in another country but offered shipping across Europe and had products that he needed, which were sold out elsewhere. The prices seemed appropriate and Ismail initially did not have any doubts so he placed a large order. However, when the company sent him an invoice and a shipping confirmation email came in, with a tracking number, Ismael noticed a small discrepancy in the email he received from the shipping company and started investigating further. He found out that the company address was a residential house, rather than a warehouse, as stated, and that the shipping company did not exist and the tracking number was fake. Additionally, he became suspicious about being asked to transfer money internationally as no credit card payment was provided. Social media links that the company had on the website did not go anywhere. He ended up not paying the invoice.

Individual factors

Background knowledge

Ismael did not have background knowledge on the company he was dealing with but he was aware of frauds that target businesses and therefore he entertained the possibility that the transaction could be fraudulent.

Risk assessment and vigilance

Since he was dealing with an unknown vendor, Ismael realised that there may be some risk attached to the transaction, which made him pay more attention to the facts and he processed documentations received by the vendor more systematically by checking facts, spotting further discrepancies.

Scam techniques used

Scarcity

The products Ismael wanted to source were sold out. The company website alluded to scarcity by listing limited number of desired products they had in stock and marking other stock as sold out. Scarcity can influence the desirability of products.

Credibility and legitimacy

The website looked professional and the invoice had all the usual information, from company registration number (which was a genuine number for a legitimate company, which the scammer pretended to be, but giving a different address) to invoice number.

Ismael was vigilant because he has never dealt with this company before and therefore trust had not been established previously. Being aware of the risks that come with this, he was motivated to do few extra checks, which uncovered discrepancies that made him question if this could be a fraudulent transaction.

Case study 10

Greg was travelling abroad with a friend. They wanted to purchase a tour and were impressed by a well-spoken, nicely dressed person selling tours, who invited them into his shop. While there, a man came in, thanking the shop owner for a fantastic tour. While choosing tours, Greg and friend mentioned not being able to find affordable hotel rooms in the city they were going to visit next, and the shop owner made a phone call and booked them a hotel at a reasonable price, which helped Greg a great deal. The shop owner also said that he would give them a good deal if they booked straight away. Greg and his friend were happy and were about to book a tour; however, they had a rule to always go away so they could check facts on the internet, before booking or purchasing things, to avoid bad deals. They informed the shop owner they needed to get some money and left. Upon checking the tour's reviews online, they found out that this shop owner works with another man who pretends to be a happy customer to persuade the customers in the shop to purchase the tours, which underdeliver. Greg and his friend never went back and they later found out that the shop owner only pretended to make a reservation for a hotel as the hotel did not have any reservations for them. Greg also stated that he frequently lies about going to get some money for a purchase, in order to get out of uncomfortable situations, because he finds it hard to say no but also does not want to be coerced into purchasing something he does not want to buy.

Individual factors

Vigilance

Having a rule to check all available information before any financial decision saved Greg from getting defrauded in this situation, as he was able to find out about the scam.

Compliance

Greg is aware that he feels uncomfortable saying no when he does not want to agree to something, which could make him vulnerable to fraud, so he came up with a lie that he tells in situations where he feels he is being pressured to comply.

Scam techniques used

Credibility and legitimacy

The shop owner's demeanour was professional, making him look trustworthy, and the satisfied customer praising the tour added to credibility.

Evoking social norms

By pretending to book them a hotel, the scammer was hoping to evoke reciprocation and encourage Greg and his friend to book his tour. When someone does something for us, we naturally want to reciprocate in some way and scammers exploit this. This technique was likely orchestrated to encourage compliance.

Time pressure or limited availability

Offering a good deal for an on-the-spot purchase is a typical scam technique. It encourages quick, impulsive decisions, which are often not optimal.

I like this case, specifically because it highlights how sometimes we can be aware of our weaknesses, which in some situations make us vulnerable to exploitation by others. Years ago, I did a talk about frauds for the elderly residents in my area and many told me how they feel uncomfortable saying no, when someone comes to their door selling something, because it feels rude. So many people have been brought up to think that saying no is not graceful or polite, and this can cause cognitive dissonance in situations where they want to say no but also feel this is not a polite thing to do, so it is uncomfortable to do. Inspired by Greg's story, which was part of my research (see Dove, 2018), I advised that group of residents to lie if they have to, in order to protect themselves. My advice was to tell the sales person to come back when a relative, a police detective, is here so they can also see the product or an offer. An honest sales person might be back but a scammer will probably blacklist the address for good.

Spotting scam techniques in phishing correspondence

People get phishing correspondence almost every day. If you are lucky, it will go to your spam folder or it may get filtered by your email provider. But many phishing emails get through and some are better than others. Here are some examples that I have broken into persuasive components, so that you can see what to look for when you receive emails such as these. Figures 9.1 and 9.2 are some examples of a Nigerian or advance fee type scams. Figure 9.1 is an example of a classic Nigerian scam. These scams can be adapted for many situations and I have seen examples with lottery winners looking for people to help them distribute the funds to charity, lonely, dying widows wanting someone to distribute their estate to charitable causes, etc. There are also examples of bank officials or lawyers trying to find someone who would help them transfer or launder the funds. Often, they adapt to current events in order to be more believable.

Figure 9.2 is a more current version of the same type of scam, adapted to reflect current events. Adapting scams to current events is more successful because people are less likely to have heard about the new narrative and are therefore more likely to believe them. They are also more believable, as they reflect what is currently happening. Different narratives may use different persuasion techniques.

Figure 9.3 is also an example of a classic Nigerian scam, using a bank official narrative, which is more widely known.

The reason why I supplied three examples of this type of fraud is because despite being well known, they are still very successful, possibly because they can be adapted to many different situations, making it hard to warn people about them. The key is to look for scam techniques they use rather than to focus on the story they present, as this often changes with current events.

Many phishing scams mimic banks or legitimate companies, telling the victims their account has been compromised. Figure 9.4 is one such example. They work by evoking fear and often mimic legitimate company logos. If they mention you by name in the body of the email, this is likely going to appear more credible, because we have come to associate scams with vague greetings. However, so much of our data is available to fraudsters nowadays that personal information in an email may not automatically mean the correspondence is genuine.

Figure 9.5 is another example of a compromised account. However, note how this is implied rather than stated in the email. The email looks like a receipt rather than a warning. This is a smarter scam correspondence, in my opinion. We are all used to seeing compromised or locked account warning emails, so will be somewhat immune to it. However, receiving a receipt for something we did not purchase is likely going to be alarming and evoke panic. It also uses a familiar logo and evokes urgency but this, too, is done in a more sophisticated manner by telling the potential victim they will be charged further amount unless details are updated.

Figure 9.6 is an example of a miracle cure scam. These scams typically use social proof in order to persuade. In this example, proximity and vividness are also used to entice the potential victim to purchase the product.

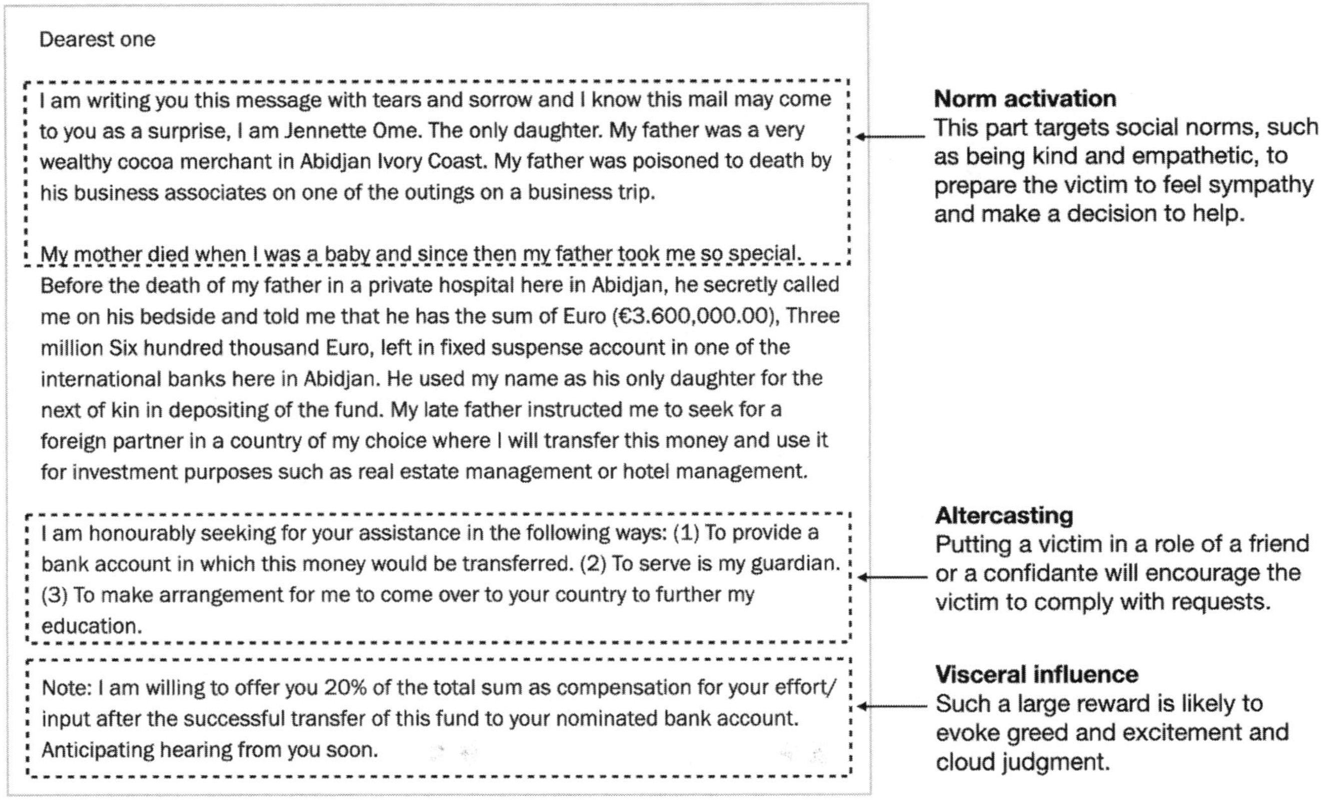

Learning to spot scams and fraud 107

Norm activation
This part targets social norms, such as being kind and empathetic, to prepare the victim to feel sympathy and make a decision to help.

Altercasting
Putting a victim in a role of a friend or a confidante will encourage the victim to comply with requests.

Visceral influence
Such a large reward is likely to evoke greed and excitement and cloud judgment.

Dearest one

I am writing you this message with tears and sorrow and I know this mail may come to you as a surprise, I am Jennette Ome. The only daughter. My father was a very wealthy cocoa merchant in Abidjan Ivory Coast. My father was poisoned to death by his business associates on one of the outings on a business trip.

My mother died when I was a baby and since then my father took me so special. Before the death of my father in a private hospital here in Abidjan, he secretly called me on his bedside and told me that he has the sum of Euro (€3,600,000.00), Three million Six hundred thousand Euro, left in fixed suspense account in one of the international banks here in Abidjan. He used my name as his only daughter for the next of kin in depositing of the fund. My late father instructed me to seek for a foreign partner in a country of my choice where I will transfer this money and use it for investment purposes such as real estate management or hotel management.

I am honourably seeking for your assistance in the following ways: (1) To provide a bank account in which this money would be transferred. (2) To serve is my guardian. (3) To make arrangement for me to come over to your country to further my education.

Note: I am willing to offer you 20% of the total sum as compensation for your effort/input after the successful transfer of this fund to your nominated bank account. Anticipating hearing from you soon.

Figure 9.1 An example of a Nigerian/advance fee scam exploiting social norms.

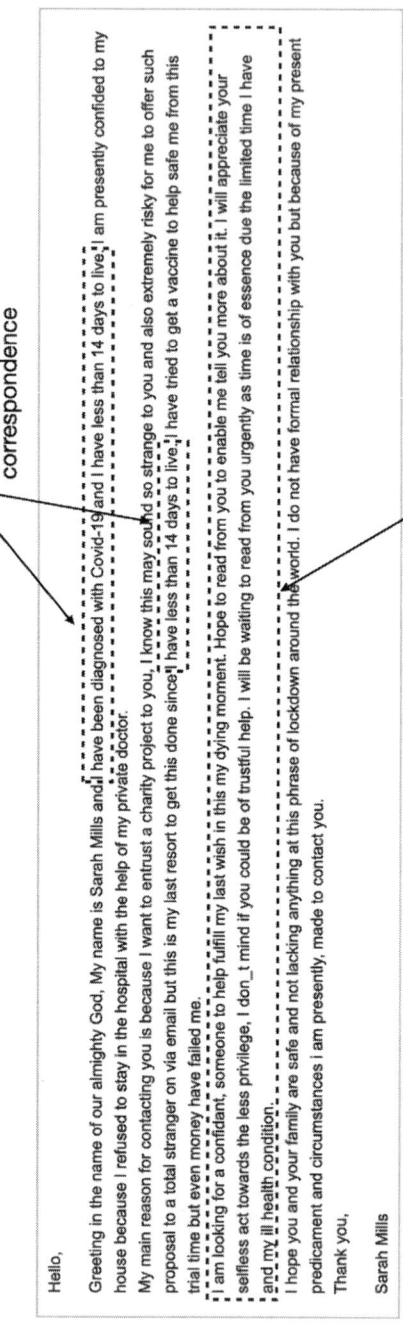

Figure 9.2 An example of a Nigerian/advance fee scam, adapted to reflect COVID-19 pandemic.

Learning to spot scams and fraud   109

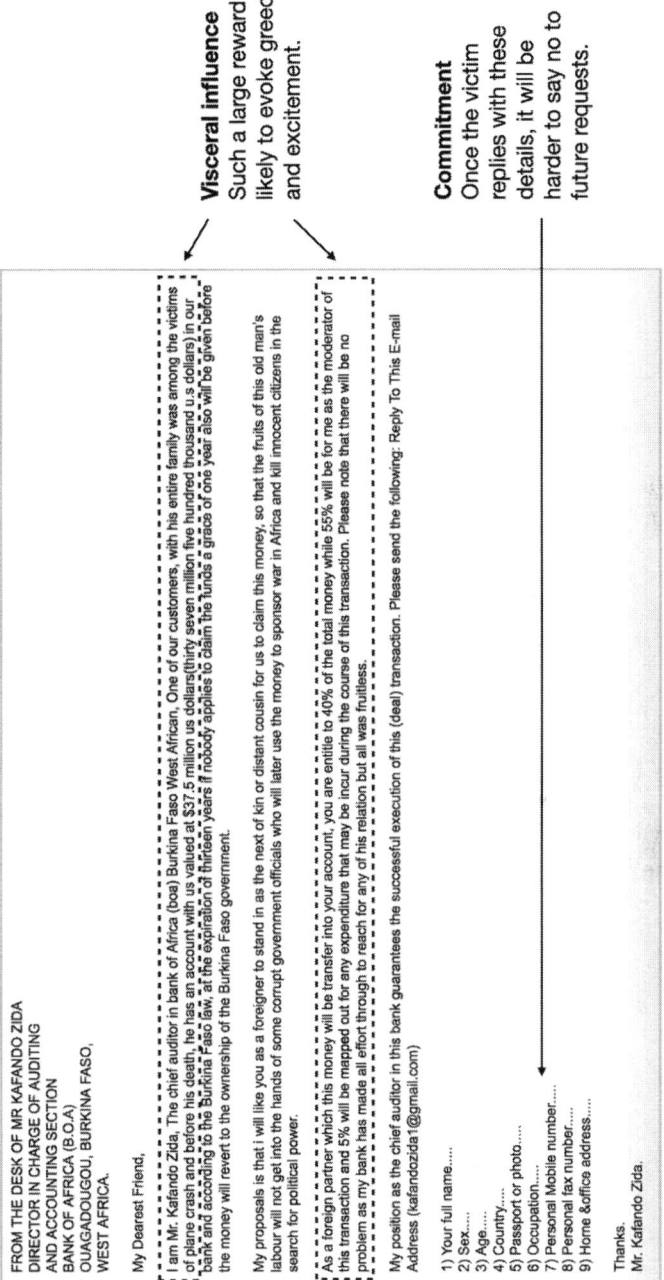

Figure 9.3 An example of a classic Nigerian/advance fee scam.

110 Learning to spot scams and fraud

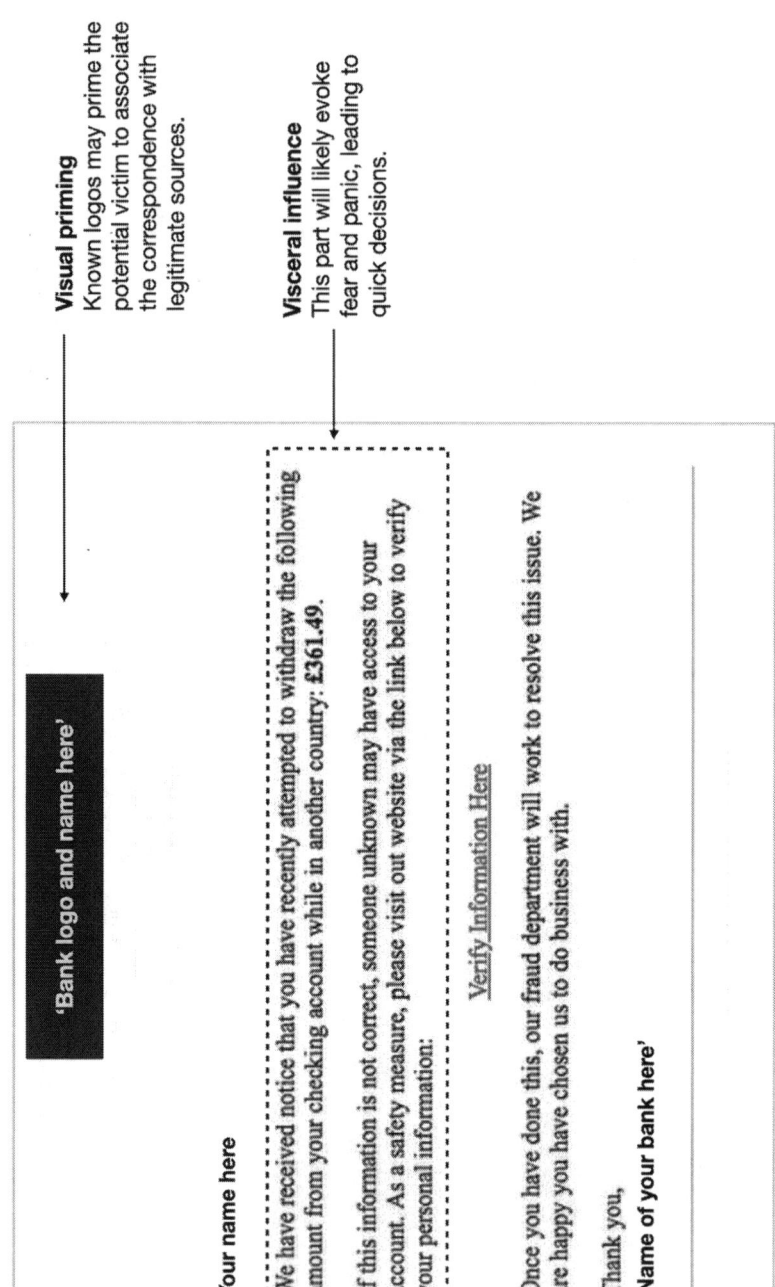

Figure 9.4 An example of a 'compromised account' scam.

Learning to spot scams and fraud 111

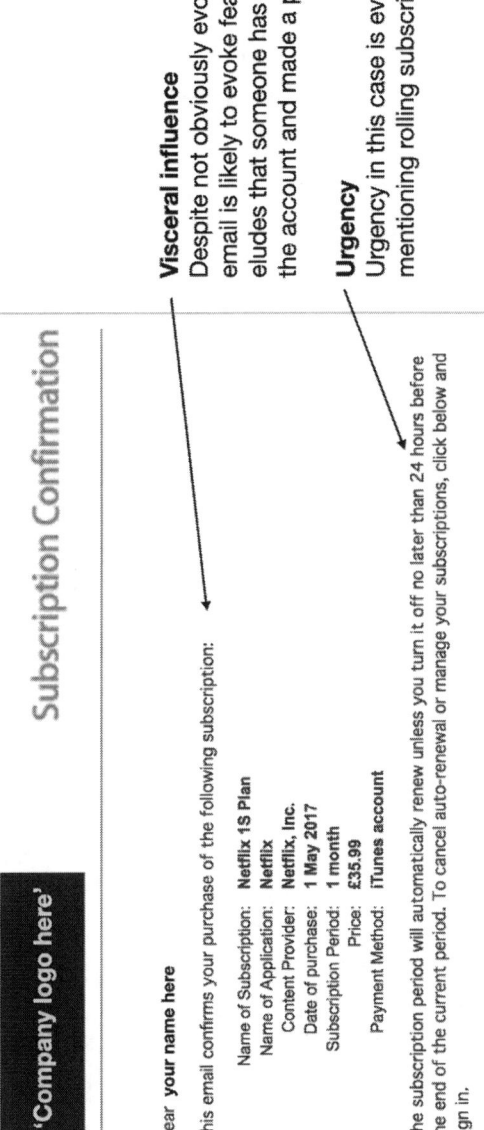

Figure 9.5 An example of a 'compromised account' scam that uses covert tactics.

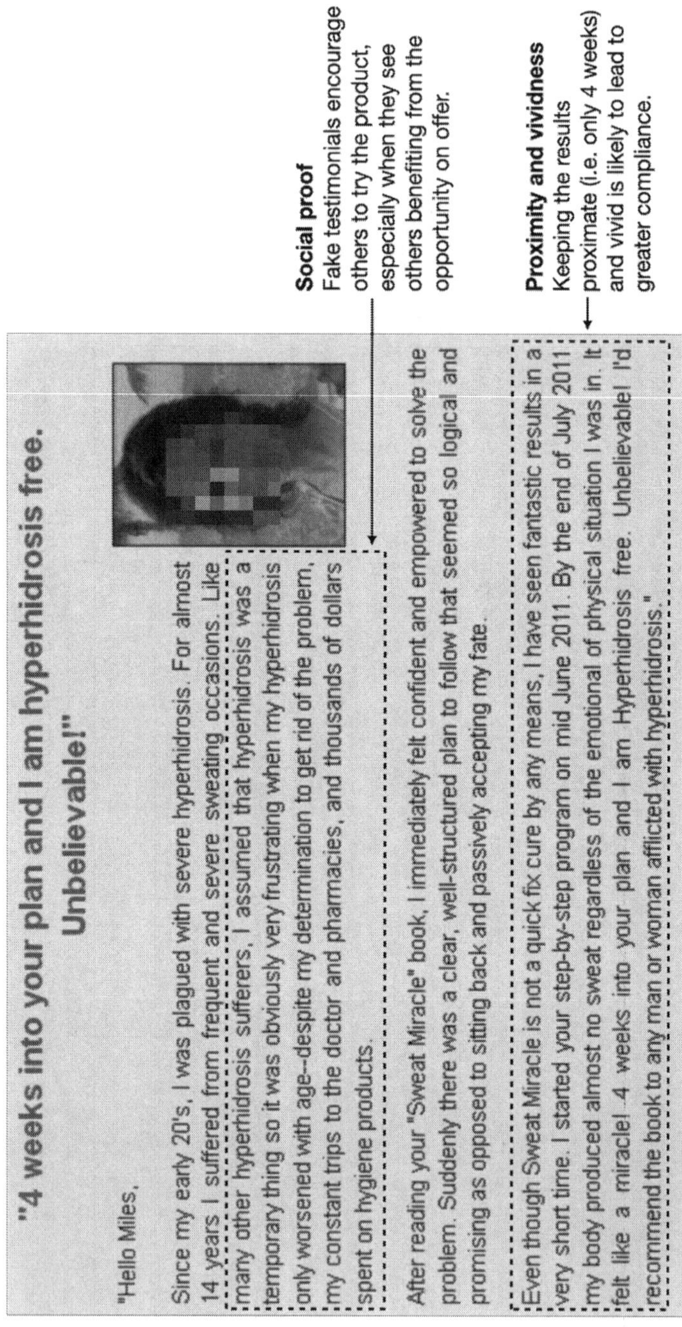

"4 weeks into your plan and I am hyperhidrosis free. Unbelievable!"

"Hello Miles,

Since my early 20's, I was plagued with severe hyperhidrosis. For almost 14 years I suffered from frequent and severe sweating occasions. Like many other hyperhidrosis sufferers, I assumed that hyperhidrosis was a temporary thing so it was obviously very frustrating when my hyperhidrosis only worsened with age--despite my determination to get rid of the problem, my constant trips to the doctor and pharmacies, and thousands of dollars spent on hygiene products.

After reading your "Sweat Miracle" book, I immediately felt confident and empowered to solve the problem. Suddenly there was a clear, well-structured plan to follow that seemed so logical and promising as opposed to sitting back and passively accepting my fate.

Even though Sweat Miracle is not a quick fix cure by any means, I have seen fantastic results in a very short time. I started your step-by-step program on mid June 2011. By the end of July 2011 my body produced almost no sweat regardless of the emotional of physical situation I was in. It felt like a miracle! 4 weeks into your plan and I am Hyperhidrosis free. Unbelievable! I'd recommend the book to any man or woman afflicted with hyperhidrosis."

-- Tanya Shearer, (Auckland, New Zealand)

Social proof
Fake testimonials encourage others to try the product, especially when they see others benefiting from the opportunity on offer.

Proximity and vividness
Keeping the results proximate (i.e. only 4 weeks) and vivid is likely to lead to greater compliance.

Figure 9.6 An example of a 'miracle cure' scam.

Figure 9.7 is an example of a scam targeting very specific personal circumstances. The more specific and personal the scam appears, the more likely it is that it will be found intriguing, leading to a response. This one targets gamblers, who may be more likely to have debts, therefore may consider this offer, however silly it seems to appears.

Figure 9.8 is an example of a job scam. Typically, job scams tend to be vague and are advertised as 'work from home', which will appeal to many people. They persuade by evoking visceral influence (greed), similar to business opportunities, which offer large returns.

Figures 9.9 and 9.10 are examples of phishing emails offering refunds. Some of them may use some form of visceral influence (either positive emotions due to getting money or slight fear because the account was overcharged); however, they are often designed to get the victim to act in order to benefit from the refund. Other popular examples include tax returns.

Figure 9.11 is quite interesting. I am noticing that phishing scams are becoming more sophisticated and less obvious. For example, look at how urgency is evoked by gently mentioning the expiry date, but then also repeating the message again so it sticks. There is no usual alarming wording and there is additional information added to appear as if this was just an informational email. However, there is a prominent button calling the recipient to proceed, demanding attention. It is likely that this email will not raise suspicions as it is so nicely designed. I think we are likely to see more scams designed in this way as people get more savvy about scams.

Finally, a nice giveaway – everyone likes those. There are many variants of this fraud, such as free flights, phones, etc. At best, they phish personal information, but they may also ask for delivery fees for items being sent. These types of frauds are often delivered via the post too, usually stating the recipient has won a lottery or other expensive items, such as a TV, and they tend to target elderly people. Lottery win or prize correspondence frequently has authority cues (fake approval seals, signatures, etc.). Some examples of those can be found in Lea et al.'s (2009) report on scams.

These examples are not exhaustive but I tried to cover different techniques. Hopefully, they will be helpful in learning to spot persuasive elements that most phishing scams contain. As you can see, often scam techniques repeat but sometimes they can be more sophisticated in how these techniques appear on the correspondence, so try not to just look for the obvious, look for what it is making you want to do.

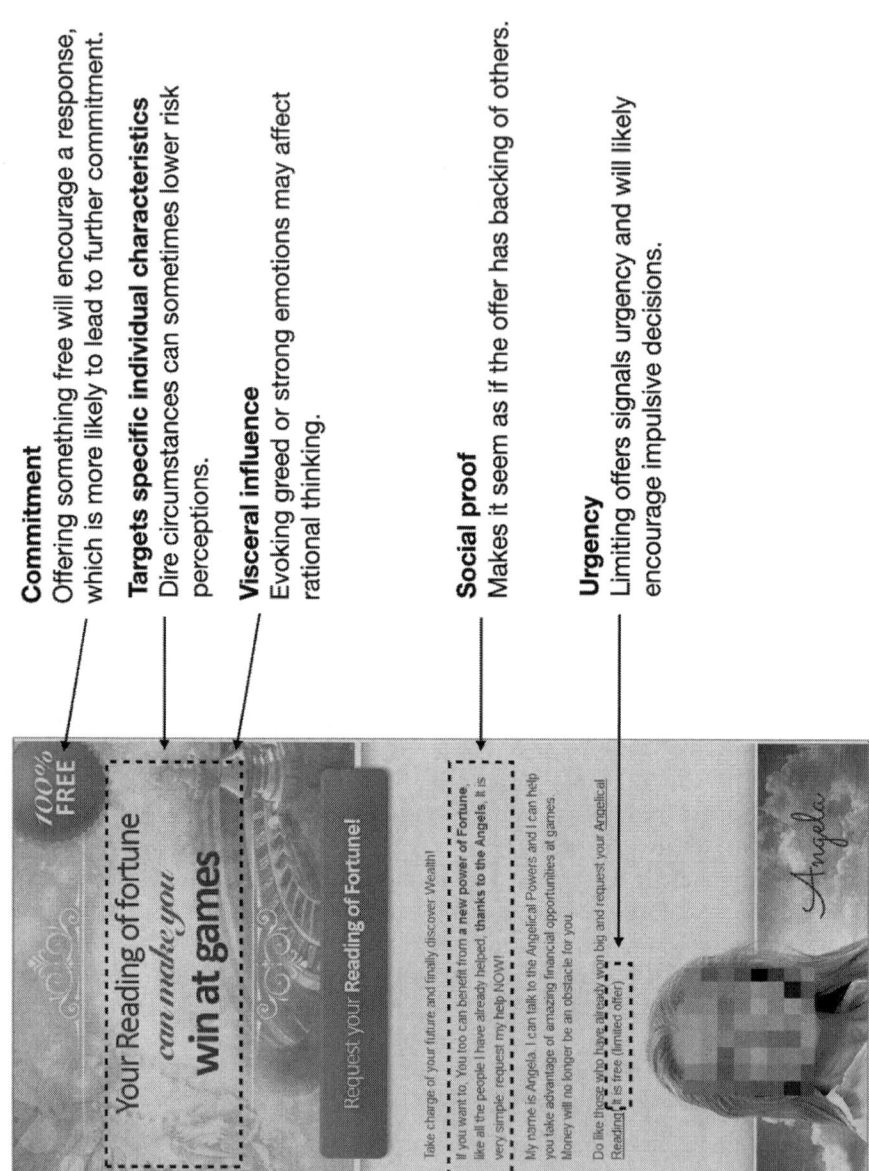

Figure 9.7 An example of a scam targeting people's circumstances.

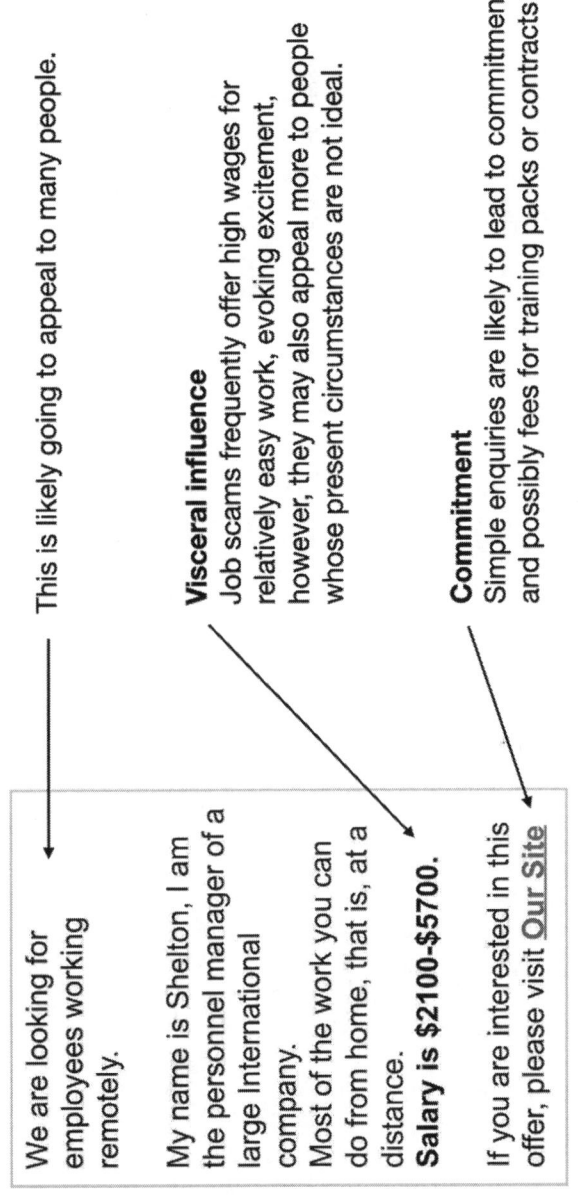

Figure 9.8 An example of a job scam.

116 Learning to spot scams and fraud

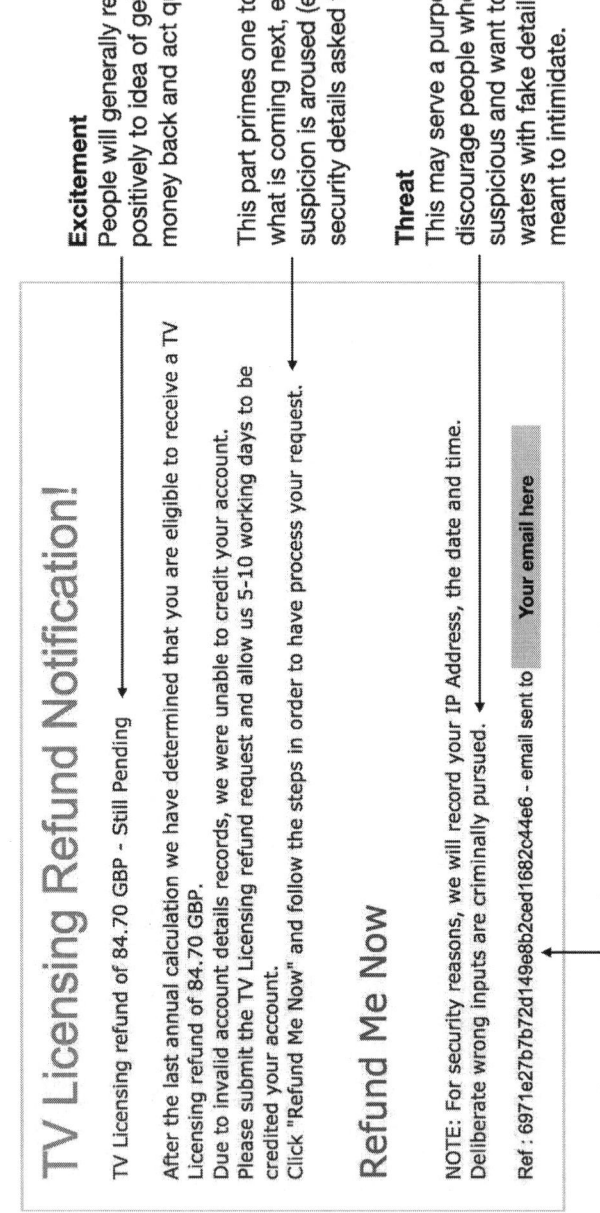

Figure 9.9 An example of a 'refund' phishing scam for TV licence.

Learning to spot scams and fraud 117

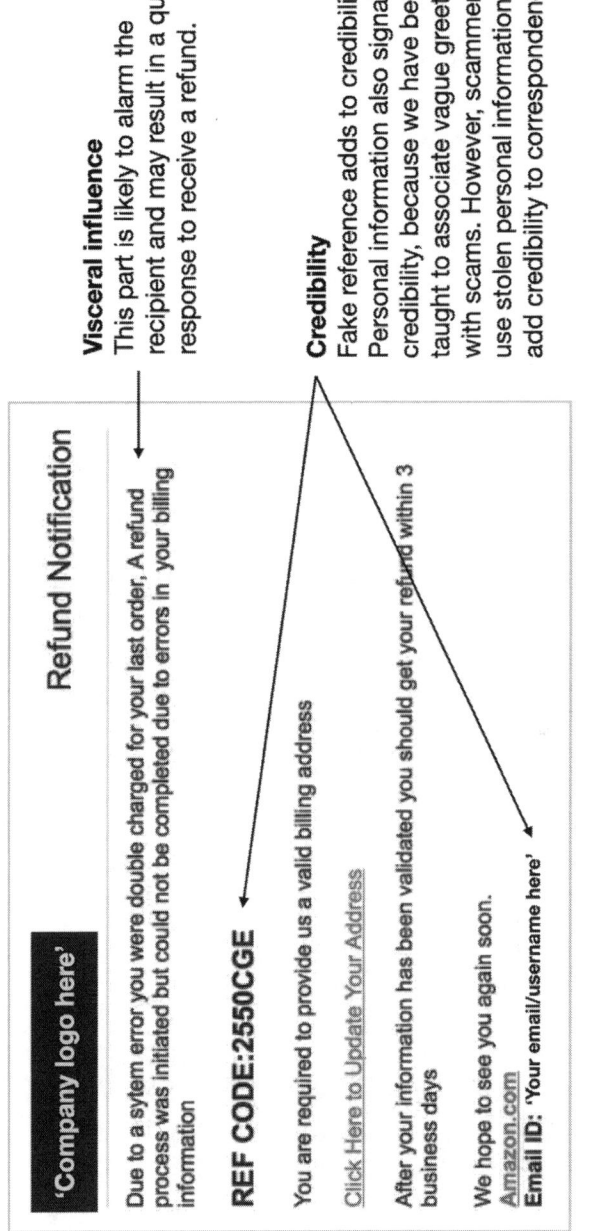

Visceral influence
This part is likely to alarm the recipient and may result in a quick response to receive a refund.

Credibility
Fake reference adds to credibility. Personal information also signals credibility, because we have been taught to associate vague greetings with scams. However, scammers now use stolen personal information to add credibility to correspondence.

Figure 9.10 An example of a 'refund' phishing scam for Amazon.

118 Learning to spot scams and fraud

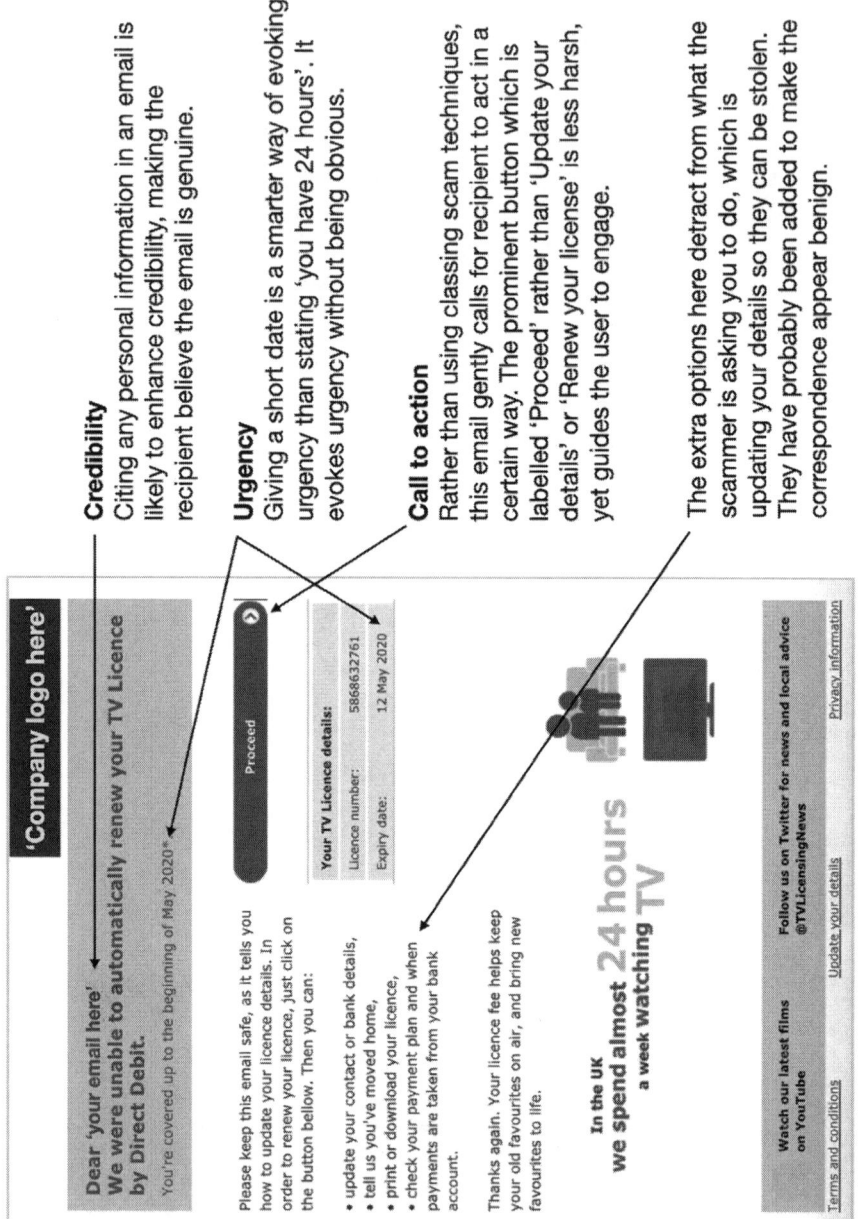

Figure 9.11 A more sophisticated example of a 'renew your account' phishing scam.

Learning to spot scams and fraud 119

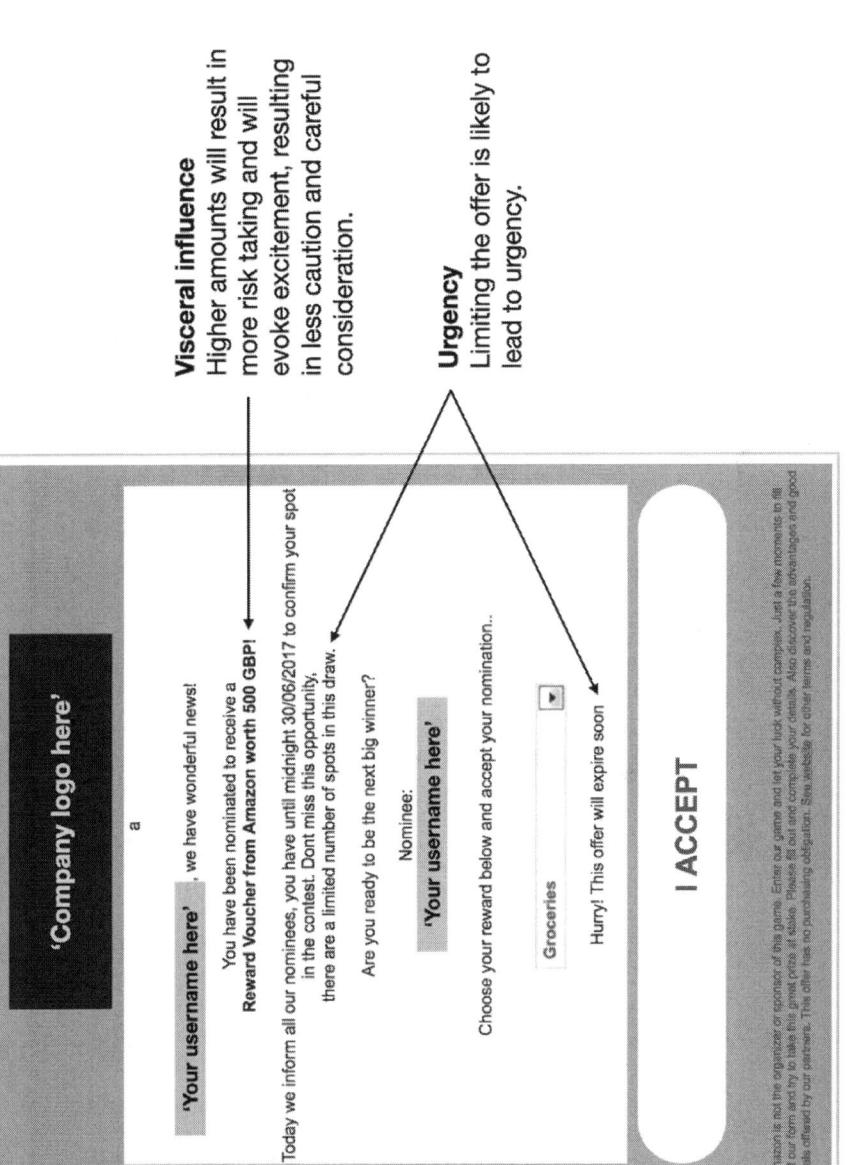

Figure 9.12 An example of a 'free giveaway' phishing scam.

Chapter 10

SCAMS checklist
Advice for reflection and protection

I want to summarise this book by saying that, with scams, there will always be an element of surprise and some scammers will be smarter, better and more skilled than anyone can ever imagine. However, there are things people can do to protect themselves when they encounter any unsolicited correspondence that invites or compels them to act, be that an amazing offer or a threatening or worrying email. Therefore, I developed a 'SCAMS checklist', a handy technique you can apply each time you are not sure if the correspondence is genuine, and I will explain in detail each of its components. However, I offer a few caveats. I am not going to concentrate on the 'common sense' advice, like creating good passwords, guarding personal details and social media accounts, updating your software, being careful using public Wi-Fi, etc. I am not going to list every single scam in detail and offer advice on what you should do when you encounter it either. This type of advice is prevalent online, on governmental websites or those of local authorities, as well as forums and various blogs. There are also great books out there, which break down different frauds and victim targeting, if you want to find out about different scams and how they work (e.g. Abagnale, 2019; Button & Cross, 2017).

I also want to say that I am often against issuing warnings that feature microscopic fraud advice. Detailed fraud advice that concentrates on every tiny characteristic dates quickly, as scammers change narratives, and can make you even more vulnerable. For example, if you concentrate only on very specific components of the scams you hear about, you will be on the lookout for those specifics and you may miss something else. I interviewed a participant who was defrauded on the phone once. He told me that since the scam, he refuses to deal with anybody he does not know on the phone, and insists on other modes of communication (e.g. mail). On the surface, this decision is a good idea; however, scams can be perpetrated via post, email, phone, on websites or face-to-face. In stark contrast, another participant, defrauded online, told me he regrets not insisting on speaking to the scammer over the

Scrutinise the correspondence
Consider scam techniques
Assess emotional state
Moderate the response
Share your experience with others

Figure 10.1 SCAMS checklist.

phone, because he felt this would allow him to make a better judgement whether the person is trustworthy (Dove, 2018). As humans, we naturally shield away from painful experiences once we encounter them, but sometimes we erroneously concentrate on the wrong cues.

I want to put a new spin on fraud prevention by highlighting what happens to our emotions and cognitive processes when we encounter scams and what you should do to make sure any eventual decision comes from a more rational perspective. A lot of frauds are very good but can give you small warnings if you dig a bit deeper, concentrate on the right things or check a few facts. So, hopefully, some of the things that I will mention in this chapter will come in handy for any correspondence that you receive and you are not sure about. For example, you can apply a 'SCAMS checklist' (see Figure 10.1). I explain these components further below.

Scrutinise the correspondence

When you receive any type of unsolicited correspondence, however benign it seems at first, that you find interesting or that panics you, take the time to scrutinise the correspondence. This also goes for getting correspondence from a friend that seems a little bit unusual or that alludes to an urgent problem of some sort (e.g. scammers can hack emails and social media accounts belonging to friends and family).

Take the time to double check the facts stated in the correspondence. Google a few things. I am an avid fan of Googling everything – names, numbers, emails, images. Often, you can find out in seconds if something is a hoax or a scam. If you have any images, such as before and after photos or, in the case of online romance, pictures of the person you are messaging, consider running them through a reverse image search online. For example, see what happened when I took some time to search the images of a nice man who sent me a friend request on Facebook (see Figure 10.2). First of all, the photos were connected to fraudulent activities and his likes on Facebook

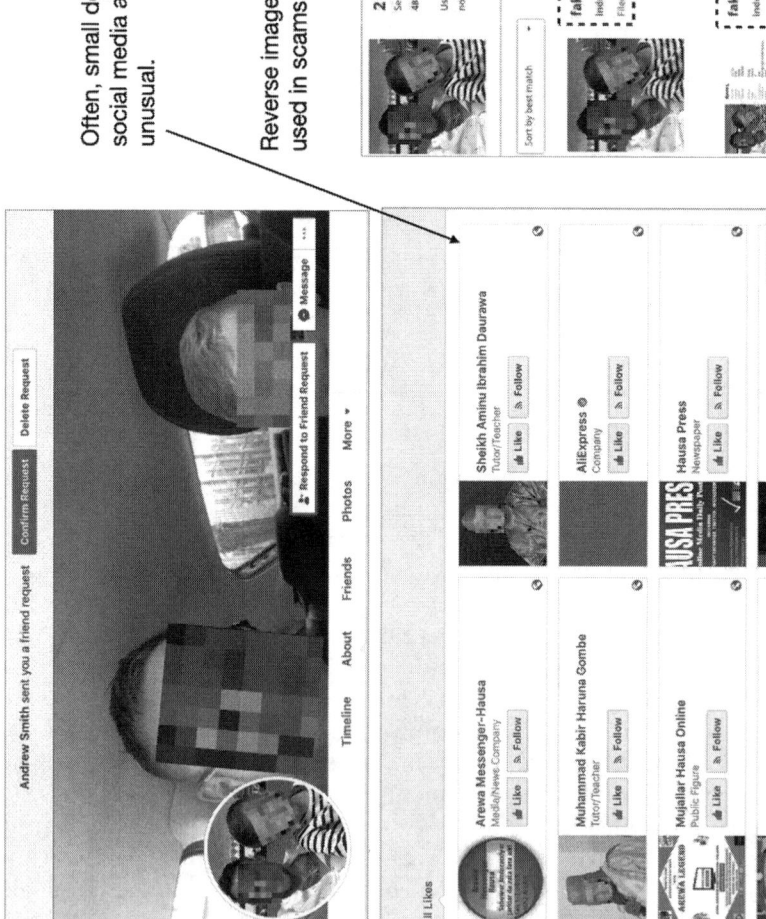

Figure 10.2 Cross-referenced information and the warning signs revealed by the search.

were also interesting because they seemed a bit unusual. It is often hard to stop communicating with someone who quickly becomes a love interest, therefore a few preliminary searches, raising red flags can greatly reduce the likelihood of engaging with a scammer.

However, I want to highlight that relying on the results of the online search completely is not prudent. Scammers will change emails frequently so not finding any results does not automatically mean the correspondence is legitimate, or the person who emailed you is trustworthy. Good scammers seize opportunities, adapting their narratives and modus operandi as needed. They may also use photographs that do not return anything and will appear genuine. Additionally, I have heard of cases where scammers went to great lengths to appear credible online, aligning different social media accounts so any search would come back consistent. Often, professional romance scammers steal whole collections of consistent photographs (e.g. pictures of the same person with family friends etc.), so that the fraud they are perpetrating appears genuine. You will not always see them coming no matter how hard you try; however, in most cases this is a good way to find out if someone is genuine.

If it is an offer to purchase a product, read product reviews, read them everywhere you can find them, cross reference if you can and do not believe testimonials offered to you. Organisations that sell various products will be under pressure from suppliers to remove negative reviews while those that sell their own products will probably not publish all the negative reviews they receive. This is not only done by fraudulent websites but also by the legitimate ones. They may not even see it as fraud but it is highly unethical. My advice, when seeking reviews online, is to be a detective and seek reviews for the same product on independent review sites. Often, the reviews will be totally different and you can spot discrepancies. Scammers definitely do this. And they will go an extra mile, posting fake reviews on public forums, which can easily be found if someone Googles the product so do not always take reviews you find online as honest recommendations. Check out the profile of the person posting the review to see what else they posted. If this is their only post on the social forum, they may be a shill reviewer (i.e. someone who posts fake reviews in order to persuade others).

I found Facebook to also be very good for detective work. Put the email and a phone number you have into search and see what happens, it may give you some clues. However, also be aware that this will only return results if the details are public. A good scammer might hide these details and make it private, so you may not find anything, but it is worth trying.

I will tell you a little story of how this helped me once. When I was conducting research and advertising on social media for fraud victims to talk to me, I was contacted by a guy who told me he was a victim of a job scam. He was applying for a job on a cruise ship and was told he was accepted but needed to send money for a work permit and a visa to be arranged. After sending the money, he never heard back. He was from an African country and gave me a different name in the correspondence than what his email suggested. This immediately intrigued me, so I ran the email through Facebook and found an account registered with that email. It belonged to a very good-looking male model who is also an Oxford University graduate and just happens to be lonely and looking for the love of his life. His Facebook friends were all middle-aged women. Therefore, looking at Facebook friends, likes and groups the person follows can also give you some clues. Scammers will lie but often leave a little bit of truth in their lies, so you may be able to see their genuine interests or the fact that their friends are of particular age or gender, which could be a warning. For example, when I saw that Facebook profile, I realised that my fraud victim was also possibly a romance scammer trying to befriend unsuspecting women on social media. Was he a genuine fraud victim? He probably was, just outsmarted by someone better than him. So, my advice on how to protect yourself from fraud is to be more curious and scrutinise everything by default.

Consider scam techniques

Even when the correspondence seems genuine (such as when it contains legitimate logos and is well written), try looking for the scam techniques mentioned in this book. Is the email trying to get you to click a link or an attachment (links are frequently clickable words that take you away from the email)? Are there urgency cues? Is the correspondence asking you to make a decision quickly because the deal will expire or you have only a limited time to deal with the problem (such as in fake invoices or tax returns)? Is the correspondence alluding to an excellent deal, win or a prize? Are there authority cues in it (e.g. is from the police, a government body, doctor or a lawyer)? Is the correspondence (both written or spoken, such as on the phone or in person) evoking some sort of panic or fear (e.g. compromised or deleted accounts, stolen details or money, etc.)? Is the correspondence vague and merely asking you to reply for more details? Doing a quick scan for common scam techniques will make you notice often very small details that distinguish real correspondence from the fake one.

In face-to-face situations, or to some degree on the phone, techniques may be slightly different. Focus on what the scammer is telling you and how they act. Do they appear likeable and friendly? Are they projecting that they like you and mentioning they value similar things to you (liking and similarity)? Are they offering you a personal discount or a mention that they are doing you a favour (reciprocity)? Are they putting pressure on you to make an instant decision or making you feel as if you owe them something? Are they mentioning urgent matters that you need to deal with (urgency)? All of this should raise red flags. Question motivations of others, especially if they approach you out of the blue.

Also, try to be aware of things that might appear a bit weird but you are not sure why. It is likely that on some level you are processing information that you do not quite know how to categorise. You can always walk away from it and seek advice if needed.

It is important to remember that like individuals vary in intelligence, ability and skills, so do scammers. The more charming ones will undoubtedly be more successful. The ones that have studied human nature and persuasion are charming and personable and can compromise someone's computer or security system will be extremely successful. I often have people coming up to me victoriously telling me how they outsmarted or baited a fraudster that called them or emailed them and I always say to them that a good scammer will not engage in nonsense. At the first sign of non-compliance, a good fraudster will cut their losses and move on. Underestimating what professional fraudsters would be able to do is your biggest vulnerability. They do this for a living and can be extremely successful (see Abagnale & Redding, 2000).

Assess emotional state

So many scams affect our emotional state. Either they evoke intense excitement (such as when an offer is a good deal or a prize has been won), sexual desire (romance), greed (investments) or fear (compromised accounts). They do so for a reason. Strong emotions compromise careful thinking and let us concentrate on our emotions and on what we need to do to deal with those emotions. Sometimes, we also may be dealing with strong emotions in our lives (e.g. bereavement, breakdown of a relationship, financial struggles) and this will also make us more vulnerable to fraud.

Upon receiving correspondence that appears to be interesting, it is good to do a quick scan of thoughts and emotions. How do you feel? Do you feel excited and hopeful? Or do you feel scared, anxious and ashamed? What makes the offer attractive right now? Does it satisfy a particular need (e.g. new job, investment opportunity, new partner, cure for an illness, etc.)? Does it promise to alleviate a problem you have? Are the feelings that you are having making you feel like acting straight away? Why do you think you need to act straight away? What would happen if you did nothing about it? How would that make you feel? Does something feel out of place but you cannot put your finger on it?

All of these questions are a good starting questions to ask yourself in order to assess how you feel about the offer and how this is likely to influence your thoughts. For example, so many scam offers lure potential victims with one-time deals, which evoke excitement. Urgency cues make potential victims act quickly but there also may be a feeling of regret that the good offer will slip out of our grasp if we fail to respond instantly. In reality, even legitimate offers repeat and these urgency cues only serve to make us feel that we may miss out on something. Other scams evoke fear, which can be extremely powerful. Fear is a visceral influence and consists of two components: biochemical (e.g. physical reactions such as increased adrenalin levels) and emotion (Adolphs, 2013). Emotional reaction to fear is usually unique to each person so it is difficult to know what effect fear will have on people.

Some people will react to it more adversely. If you are afraid of something, it is always good to talk to someone about it and get a new perspective on things. Doing a quick assessment of your emotions and connecting these emotions to what is being said in the correspondence can hopefully make you realise that most legitimate correspondence is not designed to evoke such strong feelings.

Sometimes, fraudsters do not have to evoke strong emotional responses, because we may already be in such a state. Are your circumstances making you anxious, worried or fearful? This is a perfect opportunity for fraudsters. For example, with recent Corona virus news, it is normal that people are extremely worried, and this may make them more likely to act on offers or emails that offer to fulfil specific needs (e.g. purchasing masks and gloves), mimic what is going on in the news to put a new spin on old scams or offer miracle cures (Better Business Bureau, 2020b; Bogle & Heanue, 2020; Ortiz, 2020; Penner, 2020).

I also want to address feelings and doubts that sometimes arise in the middle of the scam. I had many fraud victims tell me that they felt something was not right but they continued with the conversation or an interaction with the scammer. We often get a bad feeling about something, which we cannot explain, just a feeling of unease. Frequently, these suspicions are quashed because we feel it would be rude to say something or accuse someone (social norms at play here) or because we do not understand what it means in the moment. Only later, upon reflection, can we put all the pieces together and we realise it was a warning.

For example, some romance scams may evoke fear when a victim refuses to comply and this typically happens after months of correspondence. The scammer may threaten to end the relationship and the victim will comply under the influence of strong emotions.

There are also other scams that mimic regular products and services, where you may not be able to spot the warning signs or any scam techniques straight away. However, somewhere along the line, you may realise that something is not right and start feeling anxious about it as the scam gets a bit deeper. For example, in one of my studies, a participant who was a victim of an investment scam told me how when he started to feel uneasy as his investment was not forthcoming, he was put in touch with someone who would reassure him daily. His worries did not go away but he started feeling as if he could no longer get angry about his investment because the scammer had an answer for every question about the delay. What I am trying to say with this is that scammers may have ways of getting you to disregard your feelings. You can still do a quick assessment of what you are feeling and try to question why these feelings are present. Is the other party making you feel guilty or anxious in some way and this is why you are acting the way you are? Are they making you feel good and you feel it would not be fair to report them? Prioritise your doubts and, if you struggle with that, try seeking advice from a friend. Often, this can offer another perspective.

The presence of strong emotions evoked by relative strangers should always signal a warning sign. Take the time to consider how you are feeling as your emotions arise, whether this is as you are reading the correspondence you received, while on the phone with your bank or in the middle of your online relationship. Be aware of your circumstances and how they can influence emotional state as this can also make you an ideal fraud target. Strong emotions can influence how we think and act and traditional fraud warnings often fail because they forget to consider the influence of the strong emotions.

Moderate the response

Whenever we are under the influence of strong emotions, we are likely to make irrational decisions that are based on superficial information processing (Greenspan, 2009; Williams et al., 2017). Whenever we feel excitement or fear and panic, we are likely to want to act in the moment. However, the best thing to do in such a moment would be to try not to respond. Suppose you have already assessed your emotions and you realise that you are upset because you fear that your bank account has been compromised. All you naturally want to do is follow the link in the email you received to sort it out. This is a natural response to such a scenario. However, it is also a response that is most likely to lead to fraud vulnerability.

We have been around phishing scams for a long time and people can generally recognise and avoid them. However, when one breaks them down, it becomes clear that they serve a purpose. First the scammer introduces either an attractive proposition or a problem that has occurred, which stirs up emotions. These emotions compromise careful thinking, so the victim does not concentrate on the facts, which could alert to danger. The potential victim is usually presented with a solution at the end of the correspondence, usually brightly coloured words saying 'Update your payment', 'Claim here' or 'Issue my refund', etc. The process is designed this way so that at the end of the message, while the victim is still under the influence of the strong emotion, there is an invitation to respond immediately. Sometimes, urgency cues are used to make sure this response happens as planned. This happens in other scams also, even face-to-face ones and phone ones, where there may be an expectation to act in the moment, or a potential victim is put under pressure to make an instant decisions (e.g. phone tech support scams will typically encourage instant decisions).

In such situations, the urge to act will be pretty strong and it will be hard to moderate the response that comes naturally but you need to try. Most strong emotions wane relatively quickly and, once they do, our reactions change and that is the point. The best advice I can give you on this one is to always try to assess emotions and remember they are designed to evoke a response and moderating that response can lead to better decisions. Perhaps make a rule that you will not make decisions when you are extremely excited or upset. Even making a rule to just not react the way you want to is better. What I mean by that is, if you have received a message from your bank that someone has compromised your account, not clicking that link but, instead, calling your bank would be a moderated response to a phishing email. If you are looking for love and come across a perfect partner who cannot meet because they are living abroad, a moderated response would be to tell them to contact you once they are in the country, rather than engage in a lengthy conversation that can lead to strong emotions. Sometimes, asking people not to act on something when they want to will be too much for them (I am a realist). This is also, in my opinion, why those authoritarian Do and Don't warnings never seem to work. So instead of saying 'ignore and delete the message', we need to understand this is not always easy due to the emotional state we are in. Therefore, when you receive an unsolicited offer, think about what seems to be a natural reaction that seems the most obvious. Then, if you still feel strongly about doing something about the correspondence, such as sorting out your bank account, try to think of other ways to deal with it. For example, you could call the bank, log into your account independently of the email or tell the salesman at your door to come back tomorrow. This one is quite important because many people, especially elderly people, who often get scammers coming to their residence, told me that sometimes saying no to someone is uncomfortable because it seems impolite. Saying not today is a half way to no. You can always choose not to open the door the next day if you feel something is not right. However, small changes to your reactions can make a big difference.

My rule is always to delay any decisions by at least a day or more. I am pretty impulsive and having this rule helps me a great deal to not even have to have debates in my head whether I am making the right decision when trying to decide on the spot. Having strategies like this can be extremely protective. Remember Greg from the previous chapter? Be like Greg. Delay allows strong emotions to subside so any eventual decisions will be more rational (e.g. based on facts) than emotional. You may also find that you no longer want the thing that you thought you wanted with some time passing and being away from the source of the message (e.g. website, email, or a fraudster). Time also allows you to research the offer or a subject, which can raise warning signs and make you realise it may be a scam.

You also have the opportunity to discuss the offer with friends and family, who may offer advice, or you could seek professional help in the area. This is especially important if you are investing money as some investment scams can result in significant losses, which can have life-altering effects for the victim.

Share your experience with others

Finally, share your experience with others. So many scams prosper because people are ashamed to talk about what happened to them (Cross, 2013; Titus & Gover, 2001; Walsh & Schram, 1980). Some victims think they were greedy and this greatly impacts their self-esteem, which may be the reason why the majority of fraud victims refrain from reporting fraud (Citizen Advice, 2017; Cross, 2013; Dove, 2018). Victim shaming is common for certain types of crimes and fraud is one of them, but we must change this. This also happens for sex crimes. In their study, Niemi and Young (2016) looked at victim blaming and found that victims of sexual crimes were seen as tainted rather than injured. These views were stronger in individuals with binding moral values (those that value group loyalty, authority and purity) than in individuals with individualising moral values (those that value fairness and caring). By the same token, fraud victims are often seen as stupid or greedy and, therefore, deserving of the lesson they have been dealt and even victims themselves believe this to be true (Cross, 2013). However, the only lesson we should be learning is that some people commit fraud and this is not OK. It should be reported and punished.

Victim blaming and a general negative view when it comes to fraud victimisation is not only harmful but can affect the likelihood of reporting. I remember asking one of the fraud victims I spoke with if she reported it to the police. She said no because she expected the police to tell her she was stupid. This broke my heart. How many victims feel this way? As a result, this huge problem that is personal fraud, which harms people in more ways than one, is swept under the carpet. Yet, awareness and knowledge is the only way to tackle fraud. We need to break down the stigma around fraud victimisation and raise awareness of sophisticated fraud practices and the only way to do that is for people to have open conversations around frauds they encounter. If fraud victimisation is kept a secret, this not only allows the scammers to get away with it but also gives the skewed view of the problem (i.e. that only small number of naïve people fall for scams). This may also lead to confirmation of typical beliefs around fraud victimisation, such as that it only happens to people who somehow deserved it because they were foolish and that this is a good way to learn from mistakes. In reality, fraud can lead to financial hardship, psychological distress, health problems, relationship breakdown, anxiety and even suicide (Button et al., 2009a, 2010, 2013, 2014; Citizens Advice, 2017; Cross et al., 2014). Talking about fraud allows us to appreciate the scope of the problem and unite against fraudsters, instead of blaming the victims.

However, talking about fraud is not enough, fraud needs to be reported. Fraud reporting figures are shockingly low, often due to the humiliation and embarrassment fraud victims feel. In one of my studies (see Dove, 2018), I found that individuals who were more susceptible to fraud were also less likely to report fraud. This means that, potentially, the most vulnerable victims are often keeping fraud victimisation a secret, thus cutting themselves off from getting the help and information they may need in order to become less vulnerable and avoid repeat victimization. This is also consistent with other research. For example, Van Dijk (2001) found that repeat victims are the least likely to report crimes, while Kerley and Copes (2002) found that only 5 pe cent of repeat fraud victims report it to the police. Reporting rates for fraud are low anyway, but specifically low for repeat fraud victims.

Some fraud victims feel that nothing will be done about their experience and reporting it would, therefore, not be worth their time and this is particularly true of repeat victims and those with acute vulnerabilities, who often may not even realise they have been defrauded (Button et al., 2013; Day, 2019; Dove, 2018; J. J. Van Dijk, 2001). Sometimes that is true, nothing is done about reported fraud and this is extremely distressing to victims. Many victims express dissatisfaction with the authorities when they reported the crime. Either nothing was done, or they were being passed between different fraud reporting agencies (see Dove, 2018). This is frustrating and heart breaking. Fraud can be increasingly complex in terms of investigation and prosecution, especially when it involves different countries. Often, the victim and the perpetrator are located in different countries and establishing who should prosecute becomes difficult (Button, 2012; Cross, 2019). Additionally, not all reported cases are recorded by police, with some reports closed prior to being added to the crime database (Day, 2019). Such facts are discouraging, but I believe we should still persevere with reporting because there is a bigger picture here. Reporting fraud leads to a better understanding of the scope of the problem. Fraud reporting statistics often determine what resources will be allocated to fraud prevention efforts and guide the development of fraud prevention strategies by governments, including collaboration between different countries when it comes to prosecuting criminals.

There is one more reason to report any fraud, even when only an insignificant amount of money is lost and this is because fraudsters sometimes strategically keep the amount low to avoid detection. People are less likely to report a small loss than a large one and typically authorities do not prosecute smaller amounts (Button et al., 2012, 2015). However, reporting small losses sometimes leads the authorities to connect the dots and prosecute organised fraud networks, which purposely target large number of people whilst keeping the amount low to avoid being detected.

Sharing fraud stories also adds to collective knowledge and understanding we have on fraud victimisation and tactics and techniques that fraudsters use. These techniques often change slightly to adapt to current events so keeping the discourse around frauds and how they managed to persuade us is important. In the past two decades, fraud has increased sharply and it is unrealistic to believe that we can solve the problem by relying on conventional methods of investigating and prosecuting those responsible. With increased complexities, such as lack of data privacy and frequent data breaches, frauds are likely to evolve and become more sophisticated and convincing. My shot in the dark on the issue of fraud is that collectively we can make a huge difference in preventing fraud if we talk openly about it, encourage sharing of knowledge and try to understand what factors make us vulnerable to fraud. This includes continuous research in this area.

I also want to say that large businesses and organisations should encourage discourse around fraud and data breaches, instead of trying to hide it. I know that this is not always easy as there is stigma around this too; however, having transparency may actually increase public confidence rather than damage it. Frequently, data breaches are kept hidden from the public, which can put customers in danger (BBC News, 2019; Holmes, 2019). Having a swift, honest and transparent approach to company data breach, with clear guidance for customers, may help warn customers before they are targeted by fraudsters who get hold of their details. This is important because personal information can greatly influence the perceptions of legitimacy, making potential victims believe they are talking to the legitimate source (e.g. phone service provider, bank, etc.). Disclosing vulnerabilities is not easy; however, keeping fraud swept under the carpet has allowed fraudsters to proliferate their operations and gain momentum. It is time we fight back and the first step is admitting that we have a problem.

References

Abagnale, F. W. (2019). *Scam Me If You Can: Simple Strategies to Outsmart Today's Rip-off Artists*. Portfolio.
Abagnale, F. W. & Redding, S. (2000). *Catch Me If You Can: The True Story of a Real Fake*. Broadway Books.
Adolphs, R. (2013). The biology of fear. *Current Biology*, 23(2), R79–R93.
Albanese, J. S. (2008). White collar crimes and casino gambling: Looking for empirical links to forgery, embezzlement, and fraud. *Crime, Law and Social Change*, 49(5), 333–347.
Albrecht, W. S., Romney, M. B. & Howe, K. R. (1984). *Deterring Fraud: The Internal Auditor's Perspective* (1st edition). Inst of Internal Auditors.
Alseadoon, I., Othman, M. F. I., Foo, E. & Chan, T. (2013). Typology of phishing email victims based on their behavioural response. *Proceedings of the 19th Americas Conference on Information Systems*, 5, 3716–3624.
Anderson, C. T. (1989). *Operational Deception Doctrine Melding the Air, Ground, and Naval Effort*. Army Command and General Staff Coll Fort Leavenworth KS School of Advanced Military Studies. https://apps.dtic.mil/sti/citations/ADA215564
Andrews-Hanna, J. R., Snyder, A. Z., Vincent, J. L., Lustig, C., Head, D., Raichle, M. E. & Buckner, R. L. (2007). Disruption of large-scale brain systems in advanced aging. *Neuron*, 56(5), 924–935. https://doi.org/10.1016/j.neuron.2007.10.038
Barnum, P. T. (2014). *Humbugs of the World: An Account of Humbugs, Delusions, Impositions, Quackeries, Deceits and Deceivers Generally, in All Ages*. The Floating Press.
Baumer, E. P., Arnio, A. N. & Wolff, K. T. (2013). Assessing the role of mortgage fraud, confluence, and spillover in the contemporary foreclosure crisis. *Housing Policy Debate*, 23(2), 299–327. https://doi.org/10.1080/10511482.2012.727843
Bayard, S., Raffard, S., & Gely-Nargeot, M. C. (2011). Do facets of self-reported impulsivity predict decision-making under ambiguity and risk? Evidence from a community sample. *Psychiatry Research*, 190(2), 322–326. https://doi.org/10.1016/j.psychres.2011.06.013
BBC News. (2013, February 7). Findus lasagne beef '100% horsemeat'. *BBC News*. www.bbc.com/news/uk-21375594
BBC News. (2019, May 22). TalkTalk customer details found online. *BBC News*. www.bbc.com/news/business-48351900

Beals, M., DeLiema, M., & Deevy, M. (2015). *Framework for a Taxonomy of Fraud*. Stanford Longevity Center/FINRA Financial Investor Education Foundation/Fraud Research Center. http://longevity3.stanford.edu/wp-content/uploads/2015/11/Full-Taxonomy-report.pdf

Bénabou, R. & Tirole, J. (2003). Intrinsic and extrinsic motivation. *The Review of Economic Studies*, 70(3), 489–520. https://doi.org/10.1111/1467-937X.00253

Benton, A. a., Kelley, H. H. & Liebling, B. (1972). Effects of extremity of offers and concession rate on the outcomes of bargaining. *Journal of Personality and Social Psychology*, 24(1), 73–83. https://doi.org/10.1037/h0033368

Berlo, D. K. (1960). *The Process of Communication: An Introduction to Theory and Practice*. Holt, Rinehart and Winston, Inc.

Better Business Bureau. (2020a, February). *Online Romance Scams: A BBB Study on "How Scammers Use Impersonation, Blackmail, and Trickery to Steal from Unsuspecting Daters"*. www.bbb.org/central-georgia/news-events/news-releases/2020/02/online-romance-scams-a-bbb-study-on-how-scammers-use-impersonation-blackmail-and-trickery-to-steal-from-unsuspecting-daters/

Better Business Bureau. (2020b, April 15). *BBB Scam Alert: Puppy Scams Take COVID Twist*. Better Business Bureau. www.bbb.org/article/news-releases/22113-bbb-alert-puppy-scams-take-covid-twist

Blythe, M., Petrie, H. & Clark, J. A. (2011). F for fake: Four studies on how we fall for phish. *Proceedings of the SIGCHI Conference on Human Factors in Computing Systems*, 3469–3478. https://doi.org/10.1145/1978942.1979459

Bogle, A. & Heanue, S. (2020, March 22). Coronavirus is changing how we work. Online scammers are taking advantage. ABC News. www.abc.net.au/news/science/2020-03-23/coronavirus-phishing-scams-emails-texts-australians-vulnerable/12079486

Bok, S. (1999). *Lying: Moral Choice in Public and Private Life*. Vintage Books.

Bond, C. F., & Atoum, A. O. (2000). International Deception. *Personality and Social Psychology Bulletin*, 26(3), 385–395. https://doi.org/10.1177/0146167200265010

Bond, C. F., & DePaulo, B. M. (2006). Accuracy of deception judgments. *Personality and Social Psychology Review*, 10(3), 214–234. https://doi.org/10.1207/s15327957pspr1003_2

Brody, R. G., Kern, S., & Ogunade, K. (2020). An insider's look at the rise of Nigerian 419 scams. *Journal of Financial Crime* (ahead-of-print). https://doi.org/10.1108/JFC-12-2019-0162

Buchanan, T., & Whitty, M. T. (2014). The online dating romance scam: Causes and consequences of victimhood. *Psychology, Crime & Law*, 20(3), 261–283. https://doi.org/10.1080/1068316X.2013.772180

Buller, D. B., & Burgoon, J. K. (1996). Interpersonal deception theory. *Communication Theory*, 6(3), 203–242. https://doi.org/10.1111/j.1468-2885.1996.tb00127.x

Button, M., & Cross, C. (2017). *Cyber Frauds, Scams and their Victims* (1st edition). Routledge.

Button, M., Gee, J., Lewis, C., & Tapley, J. (2010). *The Human Cost of Fraud: A Vox Populi*. Institute of Criminal Justice Studies. Retrieved 22 April, 2020 from: https://researchportal.port.ac.uk/portal/en/publications/the-human-cost-of-fraud(14db9b58-b3bb-4c47-9398-bf4aef57ee37).html

Button, M., Lewis, C., Shepherd, D., Brooks, G., & Wakefield, A. (2012). *Fraud and Punishment: Enhancing Deterrence through More Effective Sanctions*. University of Portsmouth. Retrieved 22 April, 2020 from: https://researchportal.port.ac.uk/portal/files/1925554/filetodownload,161060,en.tmp.pdf

Button, M., Lewis, C., & Tapley, J. (2009a). *Fraud Typologies and Victims of fFraud* (p. 40). National Fraud Authority. Retrieved 22 April, 2020 from: https://researchportal.port.ac.uk/portal/files/1926122/NFA_report3_16.12.09.pdf

Button, M., Lewis, C., & Tapley, J. (2009b). *Support for the Victims of Fraud: An Assessment of the Current Infrastructure in England and Wales.* University of Portsmouth. Retrieved 22 April, 2020 from: https://researchportal.port.ac.uk/portal/files/1926164/support-for-victims-of-fraud.pdf

Button, M., Lewis, C., & Tapley, J. (2014). Not a victimless crime: The impact of fraud on individual victims and their families. *Security Journal*, 27(1), 36–54. https://doi.org/10.1057/sj.2012.11

Button, M., McNaughton Nicholls, C., Kerr, J., & Owen, R. (2015). Online fraud victims in England and Wales: Victims' views on sentencing and the opportunity for restorative justice? *The Howard Journal of Criminal Justice*, 54(2), 193–211. https://doi.org/10.1111/hojo.12123

Button, M., Shepherd, D., & Blackbourn, D. (2018). 'The iceberg beneath the sea', fraudsters and their punishment through non-criminal justice in the 'fraud justice network' in England and Wales. *International Journal of Law, Crime and Justice*, 53, 56–66. https://doi.org/10.1016/j.ijlcj.2018.03.001

Button, M., Tapley, J., & Lewis, C. (2013). The 'fraud justice network' and the infra-structure of support for individual fraud victims in England and Wales. *Criminology & Criminal Justice*, 13(1), 37–61. https://doi.org/10.1177/1748895812448085

Button, M. (2012). Cross-border fraud and the case for an "interfraud". *Policing: An International Journal of Police Strategies & Management*, 35(2), 285–303. https://doi.org/10.1108/13639511211230057

Button, M., Shepherd, D. W. . J., & Blackbourn, D. (2017). *Annual Fraud Indicator 2017: Identifying the Cost of Fraud to the UK Economy.* Centre for Counter Fraud Studies. Retrieved 22 April, 2020 from: https://researchportal.port.ac.uk/portal/files/18878333/Annual_Fraud_Indicator_report_1_2017.pdf

Cacciottolo, M., & Rees, N. (23 January 2017). Online dating fraud reaches record high. *BBC News.* www.bbc.com/news/uk-38678089

Cacioppo, John T., Petty, R. E., Kao, C. F., & Rodriguez, R. (1986). Central and peripheral routes to persuasion: An individual difference perspective. *Journal of Personality and Social Psychology*, 51(5), 1032–1043. https://doi.org/10.1037/0022-3514.51.5.1032

Cacioppo, J.T., & Petty, R. E. (1982). The need for cognition. *Journal of Personality and Social Psychology*, 42(1), 116–131. https://doi.org/10.1037/0022-3514.42.1.116

Callahan, C. M., Unverzagt, F. W., Hui, S. L., Perkins, A. J., & Hendrie, H. C. (2002). Six-item screener to identify cognitive impairment among potential subjects for clinical research. *Medical Care*, 40(9), 771–781. JSTOR.

Camden, C., Motley, M. T., & Wilson, A. (1984). White lies in interpersonal communication: A taxonomy and preliminary investigation of social motivations. *Western Journal of Speech Communication*, 48(4), 309–325. https://doi.org/10.1080/10570318409374167

Carswell, A. T., & Bachtel, D. C. (2007). Mortgage fraud: White-collar crime with long-standing community effects. *Public Administration & Management*, *12*(4), 39–69.

Carswell, A.T., & Bachtel, D. C. (2009). Mortgage fraud: A risk factor analysis of affected communities. *Crime, Law and Social Change*, *52*(4), 347–364. https://doi.org/10.1007/s10611-008-9186-5

Chang, J. H., & Lee, K. H. (2010). Voice phishing detection technique based on minimum classification error method incorporating codec parameters. *IET Signal Processing*, *4*(5), 502–509. https://doi.org/10.1049/iet-spr.2009.0066

Chang, J. J. S., & Chong, M. D. (2010). Psychological influences in e-mail fraud. *Journal of Financial Crime*, *17*(3), 337–350. https://doi.org/10.1108/13590791011056309

Cheng, P. Y., & Chiou, W. B. (2008). Framing effects in group investment decision making: Role of group polarization. *Psychological Reports*, *102*(1), 283–292. https://doi.org/10.2466/pr0.102.1.283-292

Cialdini, R. B. (2006). *Influence: The Psychology Of Persuasion, Revised Edition*. William Morrow.

Cialdini, R. B. (2014). *Influence: Science and Practice*. Pearson Education Limited.

Cialdini, R. B. & Goldstein, N. J. (2004). Social influence: Compliance and conformity. *Annual Review of Psychology*, *55*(1), 591–621. https://doi.org/10.1146/annurev.psych.55.090902.142015

CIFAS. (2019). *Fraudscape*. CIFAS. Retrieved on 9 June 2020 from: www.cifas.org.uk/insight/reports-trends/fraudscape-2019

Citizen Advice. (2017, March 8). *Changing the Story on Scams*. Citizen Advice. Retrieved on 13 May, 2020 from: www.citizensadvice.org.uk/about-us/policy/policy-research-topics/consumer-policy-research/consumer-policy-research/changing-the-story-on-scams/

Cohen, N. J., Deeds, J. R., Wong, E. S., Hanner, R. H., Yancy, H. F., White, K. D., Thompson, T. M., Wahl, I., Pham, T. D., Guichard, F. M., Huh, I., Austin, C., Dizikes, G., & Gerber, S. I. (2009). Public health response to puffer fish (tetrodotoxin) poisoning from mislabeled product. *Journal of Food Protection*, *72*(4), 810–817. https://doi.org/10.4315/0362-028X-72.4.810

Collodi, C. (2002). *Pinocchio* (M. A. Murray, Trans.). Penguin Classics.

Corritore, C. L., Kracher, B., & Wiedenbeck, S. (2003). On-line trust: Concepts, evolving themes, a model. *International Journal of Human-Computer Studies*, *58*(6), 737–758. https://doi.org/10.1016/S1071-5819(03)00041-7

Cowley, E., Farrell, C., & Edwardson, M. (2006). Strategies to improve the probability of winning a lottery: Gamblers and their illusions of control. *European Advances in Consumer Research*, *7*(597–601).

Cox, E. B., Zhu, Q., & Balcetis, E. (2020). Stuck on a phishing lure: Differential use of base rates in self and social judgments of susceptibility to cyber risk. *Comprehensive Results in Social Psychology*, *0*(0), 1–28. https://doi.org/10.1080/23743603.2020.1756240

Cramer, R. J., Brodsky, S. L., & DeCoster, J. (2009). Expert witness confidence and juror personality: Their impact on credibility and persuasion in the courtroom. *The Journal of the American Academy of Psychiatry and the Law*, *37*(1), 13.

Cressey, D. R. (1953). *Other People's Money: A Study of the Social Psychology of Embezzlement*. Free Press.

Cross, C. (2013). 'Nobody's holding a gun to your head ...': Examining current discourses surrounding victims of online fraud. In J. Tauri & K. Richards (Eds), *Crime, Justice and Social Democracy: Proceedings of the 2nd International Conference, 2013, Volume 1* (pp. 25–32). Crime and Justice Research Centre, Queensland University of Technology.

Cross, C., Smith, R., & Richards, K. (2014). Challenges of responding to online fraud victimisation in Australia. *Trends and Issues in Crime and Criminal Justice*, 474, 1–6.

Cross, C. (2015). No laughing matter: Blaming the victim of online fraud. *International Review of Victimology*, 21(2), 187–204. https://doi.org/10.1177/0269758015571471

Cross, C., Richards, K., & Smith, R. (2016). The reporting experiences and support needs of victims of online fraud. *Trends and Issues in Crime and Criminal Justice*, 518, 1–14.

Cross, C. (2019). 'Oh we can't actually do anything about that': The problematic nature of jurisdiction for online fraud victims. *Criminology & Criminal Justice*, 1748895819835910. https://doi.org/10.1177/1748895819835910

Cukier, W. L., Nesselroth, E. J., & Cody, S. (2007). Genre, Narrative and the 'Nigerian Letter' in Electronic Mail. 2007 40th Annual Hawaii International Conference on System Sciences (HICSS'07), 70–70. https://doi.org/10.1109/HICSS.2007.238

Cumming, D. J., Hornuf, L., Karami, M., & Schweizer, D. (2020). *Disentangling Crowdfunding from Fraudfunding* (SSRN Scholarly Paper ID 2828919). Social Science Research Network. https://doi.org/10.2139/ssrn.2828919

Da Silva, C. S., & Leach, A. M. (2013). Detecting deception in second-language speakers. *Legal and Criminological Psychology*, 18(1), 115–127. https://doi.org/10.1111/j.2044-8333.2011.02030.x

Daigle, R. J., Morris, P. W., & Hayes, D. C. (2009). Small businesses: Know thy enemy and their methods. *The CPA Journal*, 79(10), 30–37.

Dalbert, C. (1998). Belief in a just world, well-being, and coping with an unjust fate. In L. Montada & M. J. Lerner (Eds.), *Responses to Victimizations and Belief in a Just World* (pp. 87–105). Springer US. https://doi.org/10.1007/978-1-4757-6418-5_6

Dalbert, C. (1999). The world is more just for me than generally: About the personal belief in a just world scale's validity. *Social Justice Research*, 12(2), 79–98. https://doi.org/10.1023/A:1022091609047

Dana, R. H., & Fouke, H. P. (1979). Barnum statements in reports of psychological assessment. *Psychological Reports*, 44(3_suppl), 1215–1221. https://doi.org/10.2466/pr0.1979.44.3c.1215

Day, T. (2019). *'What's Going on 'ere, Then?': An Empirical Exploration of the Anatomy of Rogue Trading Incidents* [Ph.D., University of Portsmouth]. Retrieved on 10 July 2020 from: https://researchportal.port.ac.uk/portal/en/theses/whats-going-on-ere-then(8d321777-f482-44d4-82e1-d31b3ab27d88).html

DePaulo, B. M., Lindsay, J. J., Malone, B. E., Muhlenbruck, L., Charlton, K., & Cooper, H. (2003). Cues to deception. *Psychological Bulletin*, 129(1), 74. https://doi.org/10.1037/0033-2909.129.1.74

Doig, A., Johnson, S., & Levi, M. (2001). New public management, old populism and the policing of fraud. *Public Policy and Administration*, 16(1), 91–113. https://doi.org/10.1177/095207670101600106

Dove, M. (2018). *Predicting individual differences in vulnerability to fraud* [Ph.D., University of Portsmouth]. Retrieved on 10 July 2020 from: https://researchportal.port.ac.uk/portal/en/theses/predicting-individual-differences-in-vulnerability-to-fraud(cad05d23-5626-478c-975c-764cf41ce683).html

Dove, M. (2019). *Persuasive Elements in (S)extortion Correspondence Demanding Cryptocurrency (SSRN Scholarly Paper ID 3616205)*. Social Science Research Network. Retrieved on 20 July 2020 from: https://papers.ssrn.com/abstract=3616205

Driver, M. J., Brousseau, K. R., & Hunsaker, P. L. (1998). *The Dynamic Decision Maker: Five Decision Styles for Executive and Business Success*. iUniverse.

Druckman, J. N. (2001). Evaluating framing effects. *Journal of Economic Psychology*, 22(1), 91–101. https://doi.org/10.1016/S0167-4870(00)00032-5

Druckman, J.N. (2001). Using credible advice to overcome framing effects. *The Journal of Law, Economics, and Organization*, 17(1), 62–82. https://doi.org/10.1093/jleo/17.1.62

Duffield, G. M., Grabosky, P. N., & Australian Institute of Criminology. (2001). *The Psychology of Fraud* (Vol. 199). Australian Institute of Criminology. Retrieved 26 June 2020 from: www.anatomyfacts.com/Research/fraud.pdf

Dyrud, M. A. (2005). I brought you a good news: An analysis of Nigerian 419 letters. *Proceedings of the 2005 Association for Business Communication*, 20–25.

Egelman, S., & Peer, E. (2015). The myth of the average user: Improving privacy and security systems through individualization. *Proceedings of the 2015 New Security Paradigms Workshop*, 16–28. https://doi.org/10.1145/2841113.2841115

Ekman, P., & Friesen, W. V. (1969). Nonverbal leakage and clues to deception. *Psychiatry*, 32(1), 88–106. https://doi.org/10.1080/00332747.1969.11023575

Evans, A. D. & Lee, K. (2014). The relation between 8- to 17-year-olds' judgments of other's honesty and their own past honest behaviors. *International Journal of Behavioral Development*. https://doi.org/10.1177/0165025413517580

Evans, A. M. & Revelle, W. (2008). Survey and behavioral measurements of interpersonal trust. *Journal of Research in Personality*, 42(6), 1585–1593. https://doi.org/10.1016/j.jrp.2008.07.011

Experian. (2010). *The Insight Report. Victims of Fraud Survey*. Experian. Retrieved 16 March, 2020 from: www.experian.co.uk/assets/insight-reports/brochures/The-Insight-Report-Victims-of-fraud-survey-March-2010.pdf

Experian. (2017). *Synthetic Identities: Getting Real with Customers*. Experian. Retrieved 11 May 2020 from: www.experian.com/assets/decision-analytics/white-papers/synthetic-id-white-paper.pdf

Fischer, P., Jonas, E., Frey, D. & Kastenmüller, A. (2008). Selective exposure and decision framing: The impact of gain and loss framing on confirmatory information search after decisions. *Journal of Experimental Social Psychology*, 44(2), 312–320. https://doi.org/10.1016/j.jesp.2007.06.001

Fischer, P., Lea, S. E. G. & Evans, K. M. (2013). Why do individuals respond to fraudulent scam communications and lose money? The psychological determinants of scam compliance. *Journal of Applied Social Psychology*, 43(10), 2060–2072. https://doi.org/10.1111/jasp.12158

Fisher, K. (2015). *The Psychology of Fraud: What Motivates Fraudsters to Commit Crime?* (SSRN Scholarly Paper ID 2596825). Social Science Research Network. https://doi.org/10.2139/ssrn.2596825

Foozy, C. F., Ahmad, R. & Abdollah, M. F. (2013). Phishing detection taxonomy for mobile device. *International Journal of Computer Science Issues, 10*(1), 338–344.

Forer, B. R. (1949). The fallacy of personal validation: A classroom demonstration of gullibility. *The Journal of Abnormal and Social Psychology, 44*(1), 118–123. https://doi.org/10.1037/h0059240

Fraud Act. (2006). *Fraud Act 2006.* Accessed 11 July 2020 from: www.legislation.gov.uk/ukpga/2006/35/pdfs/ukpga_20060035_en.pdf

Fraudster's Diary. (15 November 2019). A little bit about me. *Fraudster's Diary.* Accessed 24 May 2020 from: www.fraudstersdiary.co.uk/post/a-little-bit-about-me

Frauenstein, E. D. & Flowerday, S. V. (2016). Social network phishing: Becoming habituated to clicks and ignorant to threats? *2016 Information Security for South Africa (ISSA),* 98–105. https://doi.org/10.1109/ISSA.2016.7802935

Frederick, S. (2005). Cognitive reflection and decision making. *Journal of Economic Perspectives, 19*(4), 25–42. https://doi.org/10.1257/089533005775196732

Frisch, D. (1993). Reasons for framing effects. *Organizational Behavior and Human Decision Processes, 54*(3), 399–429. https://doi.org/10.1006/obhd.1993.1017

Furnell, S. & Thomson, K.-L. (2009). Recognising and addressing 'security fatigue'. *Computer Fraud & Security, 2009*(11), 7–11. https://doi.org/10.1016/S1361-3723(09)70139-3

Furnham, A. & Boo, H. C. (2011). A literature review of the anchoring effect. *The Journal of Socio-Economics, 40*(1), 35–42. https://doi.org/10.1016/j.socec.2010.10.008

Furnham, A. & Varian, C. (1988). Predicting and accepting personality test scores. *Personality and Individual Differences, 9*(4), 735–748. https://doi.org/10.1016/0191-8869(88)90063-3

Gee, J., & Button, M. (2019). *The Financial Cost of Fraud 2019.* Crowe and Centre for Counter Fraud Studies. Accessed 21 July 2020 from: www.crowe.ie/wp-content/uploads/2019/08/The-Financial-Cost-of-Fraud-2019.pdf

Glickman, H. (2005). The Nigerian "419" advance fee scams: Prank or peril? *Canadian Journal of African Studies / Revue Canadienne Des Études Africaines, 39*(3), 460–489. https://doi.org/10.1080/00083968.2005.10751326

Global Deception Research Team. (2006). A world of lies. *Journal of Cross-Cultural Psychology, 37*(1), 60–74. https://doi.org/10.1177/0022022105282295

Goffman, E. (1952). On cooling the mark out. *Psychiatry, 15*(4), 451–463. https://doi.org/10.1080/00332747.1952.11022896

Gossner, C. M. E., Schlundt, J., Embarek, B. P., Hird, S., Lo-Fo-Wong, D., Beltran, J. J. O., Keng, N. T., & Tritscher., A. (2009). The melamine incident: Implications for international food and feed safety. *Environmental Health Perspectives, 117*(12), 1803–1808. https://doi.org/10.1289/ehp.0900949

Grabosky, P., & Duffield, G. (2001). *Red Flags of Fraud.* Australian Institute of Criminology. Accessed 22 May 2020 from: http://citeseerx.ist.psu.edu/viewdoc/download?doi=10.1.1.490.3589&rep=rep1&type=pdf

Gray, C. M., Kou, Y., Battles, B., Hoggatt, J., & Toombs, A. L. (2018). The dark (patterns) side of UX design. *Proceedings of the 2018 CHI Conference on Human Factors in Computing Systems,* 1–14. https://doi.org/10.1145/3173574.3174108

Grazioli, S., & Jarvenpaa, S. L. (2000). Perils of Internet fraud: An empirical investigation of deception and trust with experienced Internet consumers. *IEEE Transactions on Systems, Man, and Cybernetics – Part A: Systems and Humans*, 30(4), 395–410. https://doi.org/10.1109/3468.852434

Greenspan, S. (2008). Foolish action in adults with intellectual disabilities: The forgotten problem of risk-unawareness. In *International Review of Research in Mental Retardation* (Vol. 36, pp. 147–194). Academic Press. https://doi.org/10.1016/S0074-7750(08)00005-0

Greenspan, S. (2009). *Annals of Gullibility: Why We Get Duped and How to Avoid It*. Praeger Publishers.

Griffiths, M. A., & Harmon, T. R. (2011). Aging consumer vulnerabilities influencing factors of acquiescence to informed consent. *Journal of Consumer Affairs*, 45(3), 445–466. https://doi.org/10.1111/j.1745-6606.2011.01212.x

Gudjonsson, G. H., Sigurdsson, J. F., Brynjólfsdóttir, B., & Hreinsdóttir, H. (2002). The relationship of compliance with anxiety, self-esteem, paranoid thinking and anger. *Psychology, Crime & Law*, 8(2), 145–153. https://doi.org/10.1080/10683160208415003

Haddock, G., Maio, G. R., Arnold, K., & Huskinson, T. (2008). Should persuasion be affective or cognitive? The moderating effects of need for affect and need for cognition. *Personality and Social Psychology Bulletin*, 34(6), 769–778. https://doi.org/10.1177/0146167208314871

Hadlington, L., & Chivers, S. (2018). *Segmentation Analysis of Susceptibility to Cybercrime: Exploring Individual Differences in Information Security Awareness and Personality Factors*. https://doi.org/10.1093/police/pay027

Hadlington, L., & Parsons, K. (2017). Can cyberloafing and internet addiction affect organizational information security? *Cyberpsychology, Behavior, and Social Networking*, 20(9), 567–571. https://doi.org/10.1089/cyber.2017.0239

Hadlington, L. (2017). Human factors in cybersecurity: Examining the link between Internet addiction, impulsivity, attitudes towards cybersecurity, and risky cybersecurity behaviours. *Heliyon*, 3(7), e00346. https://doi.org/10.1016/j.heliyon.2017.e00346

Harren, V. A. (1979). A model of career decision making for college students. *Journal of Vocational Behavior*, 14(2), 119–133. https://doi.org/10.1016/0001-8791(79)90065-4

Harries, P. L., Davies, M. L., Gilhooly, K. J., Gilhooly, M. M. L., & Cairns, D. (2014). Detection and prevention of financial abuse against elders. *Journal of Financial Crime*, 21(1), 84–99. https://doi.org/10.1108/JFC-05-2013-0040

Herath, T., & Rao, H. R. (2009). Encouraging information security behaviors in organizations: Role of penalties, pressures and perceived effectiveness. *Decision Support Systems*, 47(2), 154–165. https://doi.org/10.1016/j.dss.2009.02.005

Herley, C. (2012). Why do Nigerian scammers say they are from Nigeria?. Proceedings of the Workshop on the Economics of Information Security. http://infosecon.net/workshop/downloads/2012/pdf/Why_do_Nigerian_Scammers_Say_They_are_From_Nigeria.pdf

Hernandez-Miranda, L. R., Ruffault, P., Bouvier, J. C., Murray, A. J., Morin-Surun, M. P., Zampieri, N., Cholewa-Waclaw, J. B., Ey, E., Brunet, J.-F., Champagnat, J., Fortin, G., & Birchmeier, C. (2017). Genetic identification of a hindbrain nucleus essential for innate vocalization. *Proceedings of the National Academy of Sciences*, *114*(30), 8095–8100. https://doi.org/10.1073/pnas.1702893114

Higgins, E. T., Rholes, W. S., & Jones, C. R. (1977). Category accessibility and impression formation. *Journal of Experimental Social Psychology*, *13*(2), 141–154. https://doi.org/10.1016/S0022-1031(77)80007-3

Hiß, F. (2015). Fraud and fairy tales: Storytelling and linguistic indexicals in scam e-mails. *International Journal of Literary Linguistics*, *4*(1), Article 1. https://doi.org/10.15462/ijll.v4i1.26

Holmes, A. (2019, November 22). T-Mobile just told some customers that there was a data breach of their personal information. Here's how to check if you're affected. *Business Insider*. www.businessinsider.com/t-mobile-data-breach-am-i-affected-2019-11

Holtfreter, K., Reisig, M. D., Leeper Piquero, N., & Piquero, A. R. (2010). Low self-control and fraud: Offending, victimization, and their overlap. *Criminal Justice and Behavior*, *37*(2), 188–203. https://doi.org/10.1177/0093854809354977

Holtfreter, K., Reisig, M. D., & Pratt, T. C. (2008). Low self-control, routine activities, and fraud victimization. *Criminology*, *46*(1), 189–220. https://doi.org/10.1111/j.1745-9125.2008.00101.x

Holtfreter, K., Reisig, M. D., Pratt, T. C., & Holtfreter, R. E. (2015). Risky remote purchasing and identity theft victimization among older Internet users. *Psychology, Crime & Law*, *21*(7), 681–698. https://doi.org/10.1080/1068316X.2015.1028545

Hong, Y. Y., Chiu, C. Y., & Kung, T. M. (1997). Bringing culture out in front: Effects of cultural meaning system activation on social cognition. *Progress in Asian Social Psychology*, *1*, 135–146.

Hunt, R. G., Krzystofiak, F. J., Meindl, J. R., & Yousry, A. M. (1989). Cognitive style and decision making. *Organizational Behavior and Human Decision Processes*, *44*(3), 436–453. https://doi.org/10.1016/0749-5978(89)90018-6

Isen, A. M., & Patrick, R. (1983). The effect of positive feelings on risk taking: When the chips are down. *Organizational Behavior and Human Performance*, *31*(2), 194–202. https://doi.org/10.1016/0030-5073(83)90120-4

Iuga, C., Nurse, J. R. C., & Erola, A. (2016). Baiting the hook: Factors impacting susceptibility to phishing attacks. *Human-Centric Computing and Information Sciences*, *6*(1), 8. https://doi.org/10.1186/s13673-016-0065-2

Jagatic, T. N., Johnson, N. A., Jakobsson, M., & Menczer, F. (2007). Social phishing. *Communications of the ACM*, *50*(10), 94–100.

James, B. D., Boyle, P. A., & Bennett, D. A. (2014). Correlates of susceptibility to scams in older adults without dementia. *Journal of Elder Abuse & Neglect*, *26*(2), 107–122. https://doi.org/10.1080/08946566.2013.821809

Jeon, W., Kim, J., Lee, Y., & Won, D. (2011). A practical analysis of smart-phone security. In M. J. Smith & G. Salvendy (Eds.), *Human Interface and the Management of Information. Interacting with Information* (pp. 311–320). Springer. https://doi.org/10.1007/978-3-642-21793-7_35

Jiang, L. C., Bazarova, N. N., & Hancock, J. T. (2011). The disclosure–intimacy link in computer-mediated communication: An attributional extension of the hyperpersonal model. *Human Communication Research*, *37*(1), 58–77. https://doi.org/10.1111/j.1468-2958.2010.01393.x

Johnson, J. T., Cain, L. M., Falke, T. L., Hayman, J., & Perillo, E. (1985). The 'Barnum effect' revisited: Cognitive and motivational factors in the acceptance of personality descriptions. *Journal of Personality and Social Psychology*, 49(5), 1378–1391. https://doi.org/10.1037/0022-3514.49.5.1378

Judges, R. A., Gallant, S. N., Yang, L., & Lee, K. (2017). The role of cognition, personality, and trust in fraud victimization in older adults. *Frontiers in Psychology*, 8. https://doi.org/10.3389/fpsyg.2017.00588

Kahneman, D. (2011). *Thinking, Fast and Slow*. Farar, Straus and Giroux.

Kaufman, D. Q., Stasson, M. F., & Hart, J. W. (1999). Are the tabloids always wrong or is that just what we think? Need for cognition and perceptions of articles in print media. *Journal of Applied Social Psychology*, 29(9), 1984–2000. https://doi.org/10.1111/j.1559-1816.1999.tb00160.x

Kendall, P. S., Scott, M., & Jolivette, K. (2018). "Well, you can't force them": Altercasting in the home health care context. *Communication Studies*, 70(1), 99–113. https://doi.org/10.1080/10510974.2018.1462838

Kerley, K. R., & Copes, H. (2002). Personal fraud victims and their official responses to victimization. *Journal of Police and Criminal Psychology*, 17(1), 19–35. https://doi.org/10.1007/BF02802859

Kerr, J., Owen, R., Nicholls McNaughton, C., & Button, M. (2013). *Research on Sentencing Online Fraud Offences*. Sentencing Council. http://rgdoi.net/10.13140/RG.2.1.1059.7528

Kim, D. J., Ferrin, D. L., & Rao, H. R. (2008). A trust-based consumer decision-making model in electronic commerce: The role of trust, perceived risk, and their antecedents. *Decision Support Systems*, 44(2), 544–564. https://doi.org/10.1016/j.dss.2007.07.001

Kim, H., & Markus, H. R. (1999). Deviance or uniqueness, harmony or conformity? A cultural analysis. *Journal of Personality and Social Psychology*, 77(4), 785–800. https://doi.org/10.1037/0022-3514.77.4.785

Knutson, B., & Samanez-Larkin, G. (2014). *Individual Differences in Susceptibility to Investment Fraud*. Stanford University. Working Paper.

Kramer, R. M. (1999). Trust and distrust in organizations: Emerging perspectives, enduring questions. *Annual Review of Psychology*, 50(1), 569–598. https://doi.org/10.1146/annurev.psych.50.1.569

Kranacher, M.J., & Riley, R. (2019). *Forensic accounting and fraud examination*. John Wiley & Sons.

Kühberger, A. (1998). The influence of framing on risky decisions: A meta-analysis. *Organizational Behavior and Human Decision Processes*, 75(1), 23–55. https://doi.org/10.1006/obhd.1998.2781

Kunwar, R. S., & Sharma, P. (2016). Social media: A new vector for cyber attack. *2016 International Conference on Advances in Computing, Communication, Automation (ICACCA) (Spring)*, 1–5. https://doi.org/10.1109/ICACCA.2016.7578896

Lake, L. (2019, May 6). *Avoid crowdfunding scams*. Consumer Information. Retrieved on 5 May 2020 from: www.consumer.ftc.gov/blog/2019/05/avoid-crowdfunding-scams

Langenderfer, J., & Shimp, T. A. (2001). Consumer vulnerability to scams, swindles, and fraud: A new theory of visceral influences on persuasion. *Psychology & Marketing*, 18(7), 763–783. https://doi.org/10.1002/mar.1029

Langer, E. J. (1975). The illusion of control. *Journal of Personality and Social Psychology, 32*(2), 311–328. https://doi.org/10.1037/0022-3514.32.2.311

Layne, C. (1978). Relationship between the "Barnum effect" and personality inventory responses. *Journal of Clinical Psychology, 34*(1), 94–97. https://doi.org/10.1002/1097-4679(197801)34:1<94::AID-JCLP2270340122>3.0.CO;2-T

Lea, S. E. G., Fischer, P., & Evans, K. M. (2009). *The Psychology of Scams: Provoking and Committing Errors of Judgement*. Office of Fair Trading. Retrieved on 22 May 2020 from: https://ore.exeter.ac.uk/repository/handle/10871/20958

Leal, S., Vrij, A., Deeb, H., & Jupe, L. (2018). Using the model statement to elicit verbal differences between truth tellers and liars: The benefit of examining core and peripheral details. *Journal of Applied Research in Memory and Cognition, 7*(4), 610–617. https://doi.org/10.1016/j.jarmac.2018.07.001

Lerner, M. J. (1965). Evaluation of performance as a function of performer's reward and attractiveness. *Journal of Personality and Social Psychology, 1*(4), 355–360. https://doi.org/10.1037/h0021806

Lerner, M. J., & Miller, D. T. (1978). Just world research and the attribution process: Looking back and ahead. *Psychological Bulletin, 85*(5), 1030–1051. https://doi.org/10.1037/0033-2909.85.5.1030

Levin, I. P., Schneider, S. L., & Gaeth, G. J. (1998). All frames are not created equal: A typology and critical analysis of framing effects. *Organizational Behavior and Human Decision Processes, 76*(2), 149–188. https://doi.org/10.1006/obhd.1998.2804

Lewis, C. C. (2009). *To Catch a Liar: A Cross-cultural Comparison of Computer-mediated Deceptive Communication*. [Doctoral thesis, Florida State University]. Retrieved on 12 July 2020 from: https://diginole.lib.fsu.edu/islandora/object/fsu:181283/datastream/PDF/view

Lim, I.K., Kim, Y.H., Lee, J.G., Lee, J.P., Nam-Gung, H., & Lee, J.K. (2014). The analysis and countermeasures on security breach of bitcoin. *Computational Science and Its Applications – ICCSA 2014*, 720–732. https://doi.org/10.1007/978-3-319-09147-1_52

Lippard, P. V. (1988). "Ask me no questions, I'll tell you no lies": Situational exigencies for interpersonal deception. *Western Journal of Speech Communication, 52*(1), 91–103. https://doi.org/10.1080/10570318809389627

Loewenstein, G. (1996). Out of control: Visceral influences on behavior. *Organizational Behavior and Human Decision Processes, 65*(3), 272–292. https://doi.org/10.1006/obhd.1996.0028

Lonsdale, J., Schweppenstedde, D., Strang, L., Stepanek, M., & Stewart, K. (2016). *National Trading Standards—Scams Team Review*. RAND Corporation. Retrieved on 11 July 2020 from: www.rand.org/pubs/research_reports/RR1510.html

Loveday, B. (2017). Still plodding along? The police response to the changing profile of crime in England and Wales. *International Journal of Police Science & Management, 19*(2), 101–109. https://doi.org/10.1177/1461355717699634

Luhmann, N. (2000). Familiarity, confidence, trust: Problems and alternatives. *Trust: Making and BREAKING COOPERATIVE RELATIONs* (Electronic edition, Department of Sociology, pp. 94–107). University of Oxford.

Macdonald, D. J., & Standing, L. G. (2002). Does self-serving bias cancel the Barnum Effect? *Social Behavior and Personality: An International Journal, 30*(6), 625–630. https://doi.org/info:doi/10.2224/sbp.2002.30.6.625

Maggi, F. (2010). Are the con artists back? A preliminary analysis of modern phone frauds. *2010 10th IEEE International Conference on Computer and Information Technology*, 824–831. https://doi.org/10.1109/CIT.2010.156

Manning, L. (2016). Food fraud: Policy and food chain. *Current Opinion in Food Science, 10,* 16–21. https://doi.org/10.1016/j.cofs.2016.07.001

Markoczy, L. (2003). Trust but verify: Distinguishing distrust from vigilance. *Academy of Management Conference.*

Martin, N. (2009). Consumer scams and the elderly: Preserving independence through shifting default rules. *Elder Law Journal, 17,* 1.

Mason, K. A., & Benson, M. L. (1996). The effect of social support on fraud victims' reporting behavior: A research note. *Justice Quarterly, 13*(3), 511–524. https://doi.org/10.1080/07418829600093071

Mayer, R. C., Davis, J. H., & Schoorman, F. D. (1995). An integrative model of organizational trust. *Academy of Management Review, 20*(3), 709–734. https://doi.org/10.5465/amr.1995.9508080335

Mazar, N., Amir, O., & Ariely, D. (2008). The dishonesty of honest people: A theory of self-concept maintenance. *Journal of Marketing Research, 45*(6), 633–644. https://doi.org/10.1509/jmkr.45.6.633

McCornack, S. A., & Levine, T. R. (1990). When lovers become leery: The relationship between suspicion and accuracy in detecting deception. *Communication Monographs, 57*(3), 219–230. https://doi.org/10.1080/03637759009376197

McKenna, F. P. (1993). It won't happen to me: Unrealistic optimism or illusion of control? *British Journal of Psychology, 84*(1), 39–50. https://doi.org/10.1111/j.2044-8295.1993.tb02461.x

McKenney, J. L., & Keen, P. G. (1974). How managers' minds work. *Harvard Business Review, 52*(3), 79–90.

Milch, K. F., Weber, E. U., Appelt, K. C., Handgraaf, M. J. J., & Krantz, D. H. (2009). From individual preference construction to group decisions: Framing effects and group processes. *Organizational Behavior and Human Decision Processes, 108*(2), 242–255. https://doi.org/10.1016/j.obhdp.2008.11.003

Misztal, B. (2013). *Trust in Modern Societies: The Search for the Bases of Social Order.* John Wiley & Sons.

Mitchell, R. W. (1996). The psychology of human deception. *Social Research, 63*(3), 819–861. JSTOR.

Modic, D., & Anderson, R. (2014). Reading this may harm your computer: The psychology of malware warnings. *Computers in Human Behavior, 41,* 71–79. https://doi.org/10.1016/j.chb.2014.09.014

Modic, D., & Lea, S. E. G. (2012). *How Neurotic are Scam Victims, Really? The Big Five and Internet Scams* (SSRN Scholarly Paper ID 2448130). Social Science Research Network. https://doi.org/10.2139/ssrn.2448130

Modic, D., & Lea, S. E. G. (2013). *Scam Compliance and the Psychology of Persuasion* (SSRN Scholarly Paper ID 2364464). Social Science Research Network. https://doi.org/10.2139/ssrn.2364464

Mohapatra, S. (2012).Stateless babies & adoption scams: A bioethical analysis of international commercial surrogacy. *Berkeley Journal of International Law*, *30*, 412.

Molden, D. C. (2014). Understanding priming effects in social psychology: What is "social priming" and how does it occur? *Social Cognition*, *32*(Supplement), 1–11. https://doi.org/10.1521/soco.2014.32.supp.1

Molloy, M. (2016, February 16). Astronaut stranded in space email scam sweeps the internet. *The Telegraph* www.telegraph.co.uk/news/newstopics/howaboutthat/12160621/Nigerian-astronaut-lost-in-space-email-419-scam-sweeps-the-internet.html

Morales-Vives, F., & Vigil-Colet, A. (2012). Are old people so gentle? Functional and dysfunctional impulsivity in the elderly. *International Psychogeriatrics*, *24*(3), 465–471. https://doi.org/10.1017/S104161021100161X

Morgan-Bentley, P., & Good, A. (2019, August). Action Fraud investigation: Victims misled and mocked as police fail to investigate. *The Times* www.thetimes.co.uk/article/action-fraud-investigation-victims-misled-and-mocked-as-police-fail-to-investigate-wlh8c6rs6

Morley, N. J., Ball, D. L. J., & Ormerod, T. C. (2006). How the detection of insurance fraud succeeds and fails. *Psychology, Crime & Law*, *12*(2), 163–180. https://doi.org/10.1080/10683160512331316325

Mouton, F., Leenen, L., Malan, M. M., & Venter, H. S. (2014). Towards an Ontological Model Defining the Social Engineering Domain. *ICT and Society*, 266–279. https://doi.org/10.1007/978-3-662-44208-1_22

Muscat, G., James, M., & Graycar, A. (2002). Older people and consumer fraud. Australian Institute of Criminology. Retrieved on 20 May, 2020 from: http://citeseerx.ist.psu.edu/viewdoc/download?doi=10.1.1.454.6309&rep=rep1&type=pdf

Nguyen, T. H., & Pontell, H. N. (2010). Mortgage origination fraud and the global economic crisis. *Criminology & Public Policy*, *9*(3), 591–612. https://doi.org/10.1111/j.1745-9133.2010.00653.x

Nickerson, R. S. (1998). Confirmation bias: A ubiquitous phenomenon in many guises. *Review of General Psychology*, *2*(2), 175–220. https://doi.org/10.1037/1089-2680.2.2.175

Niemi, L., & Young, L. (2016). When and why we see victims as responsible: The impact of ideology on attitudes toward victims. *Personality and Social Psychology Bulletin*, *42*(9), 1227–1242. https://doi.org/10.1177/0146167216653933

Nikiforova, B., & Gregory, W. D. (2013). Globalization of trust and internet confidence emails. *Journal of Financial Crime*, *20*(4), 393–405. https://doi.org/10.1108/JFC-05-2013-0038

Nisbett, R. E., & Wilson, T. D. (1977). The halo effect: Evidence for unconscious alteration of judgments. *Journal of Personality and Social Psychology*, *35*(4), 250–256. https://doi.org/10.1037/0022-3514.35.4.250

Norris, G., Brookes, A., & Dowell, D. (2019). The psychology of internet fraud victimisation: A systematic review. *Journal of Police and Criminal Psychology*, *34*(3), 231–245. https://doi.org/10.1007/s11896-019-09334-5

Norton, M. I., Mochon, D., & Ariely, D. (2012). The IKEA effect: When labor leads to love. *Journal of Consumer Psychology*, *22*(3), 453–460. https://doi.org/10.1016/j.jcps.2011.08.002

O'Connell, B. (18 April 2018). Here's everything you need to know about the risks of mortgage fraud. *Experian*. Retrieved on 29 April, 2020 from: www.experian.com/blogs/ask-experian/heres-everything-you-need-to-know-about-the-risks-of-mortgage-fraud/

O'Dell, J. W. (1972). P. T. Barnum explores the computer. *Journal of Consulting and Clinical Psychology*, 38(2), 270–273. https://doi.org/10.1037/h0032619

Oliver, P. (1980). Rewards and punishments as selective incentives for collective action: Theoretical investigations. *American Journal of Sociology*, 85(6), 1356–1375. https://doi.org/10.1086/227168

Olivier, S., Burls, T., Fenge, L.-A., & Brown, K. (2015). "Winning and losing": Vulnerability to mass marketing fraud. *The Journal of Adult Protection*, 17(6), 360–370. https://doi.org/10.1108/JAP-02-2015-0002

Oracle Mind. (May 2016). *This Is How Hackers Hack You Using Simple Social Engineering*. Retrieved on 29 April 2020 from: www.youtube.com/watch?v=lc7scxvKQOo

Orman, H. (2013). The compleat story of phish. *IEEE Internet Computing*, 17(1), 87–91. https://doi.org/10.1109/MIC.2013.16

Ortiz, A. (17 April 2020). Doctor Charged with fraud after U.S. Says he sold treatment as '100 percent' cure for Covid-19. *The New York Times*. www.nytimes.com/2020/04/17/us/coronavirus-treatment-pack-jennings-ryan-staley.html

Paese, P. W., Bieser, M., & Tubbs, M. E. (1993). Framing effects and choice shifts in group decision making. *Organizational Behavior and Human Decision Processes*, 56(1), 149–165. https://doi.org/10.1006/obhd.1993.1049

Pahnila, S., Siponen, M., & Mahmood, A. (2007). Employees' behavior towards IS security policy compliance. *2007 40th Annual Hawaii International Conference on System Sciences (HICSS'07)*, 156b–156b. https://doi.org/10.1109/HICSS.2007.206

Park, H. S., & Ahn, J. Y. (2007). Cultural differences in judgment of truthful and deceptive messages. *Western Journal of Communication*, 71(4), 294–315. https://doi.org/10.1080/10570310701672877

Parker, L. (2015, April). Crowdfunding or crowdfrauding? *Fraud Magazine*. Retrieved on 5 May 2020 from: www.fraud-magazine.com/article.aspx?id=4294987201

Parmar, B. (2012). Protecting against spear-phishing. *Computer Fraud & Security*, 2012(1), 8–11. https://doi.org/10.1016/S1361-3723(12)70007-6

Parrish, J. L., Bailey, J. L., & Courtney, J. F. (2009). *A Personality Based Model for Determining Susceptibility to Phishing Attacks*. University of Arkansas. Retrieved on 12 July 2020 from: www.swdsi.org/swdsi2009/Papers/9J05.pdf

Parsons, C. E., Stark, E. A., Young, K. S., Stein, A., & Kringelbach, M. L. (2013). Understanding the human parental brain: A critical role of the orbitofrontal cortex. *Social Neuroscience*, 8(6), 525–543. https://doi.org/10.1080/17470919.2013.842610

Penner, P. (2020, March 25). Local realtor's naturopathy company sending out ads for phony COVID-19 treatment. *Abbotsford News*. www.abbynews.com/news/local-realtors-naturopathy-company-sending-out-ads-for-phony-covid-19-treatment/

Petty, R. E., & Cacioppo, J. T. (1986). *Communication and Persuasion: Central and Peripheral Routes to Attitude Change*. Springer.

Pratt, T. C., Turanovic, J. J., Fox, K. A., & Wright, K. A. (2014). Self-control and victimization: A meta-analysis. *Criminology*, 52(1), 87–116. https://doi.org/10.1111/1745-9125.12030

Regge, A. (2009). What's love got to do with it? Exploring online dating scams and identity fraud. *International Journal of Cyber Criminology*, 3(2), 494.

Reisig, M. D., & Holtfreter, K. (2013). Shopping fraud victimization among the elderly. *Journal of Financial Crime*, 20(3), 324–337. https://doi.org/10.1108/JFC-03-2013-0014

Rich, T. (2018). You can trust me: A multimethod analysis of the Nigerian email scam. *Security Journal*, 31(1), 208–225. https://doi.org/10.1057/s41284-017-0095-0

Robson, K., Dean, M., Brooks, S., Haughey, S., & Elliott, C. (2020). A 20-year analysis of reported food fraud in the global beef supply chain. *Food Control*, 107310. https://doi.org/10.1016/j.foodcont.2020.107310

Rotter, J. B. (1966). Generalized expectancies for internal versus external control of reinforcement. *Psychological Monographs: General and Applied*, 80(1), 1–28. https://doi.org/10.1037/h0092976

Rotter, J. B. (1980). Interpersonal trust, trustworthiness, and gullibility. *American Psychologist*, 35(1), 1–7. https://doi.org/10.1037/0003-066X.35.1.1

Rousseau, D. M., Sitkin, S. B., Burt, R. S., & Camerer, C. (1998). Not so different after all: A cross-discipline view of trust. *Academy of Management Review*, 23(3), 393–404. https://doi.org/10.5465/amr.1998.926617

Salthouse, T. A. (2009). When does age-related cognitive decline begin? *Neurobiology of Aging*, 30(4), 507–514. https://doi.org/10.1016/j.neurobiolaging.2008.09.023

Sapp, S. G., & Harrod, W. J. (1993). Reliability and validity of a brief version of Levenson's locus of control scale. *Psychological Reports*, 72(2), 539–550. https://doi.org/10.2466/pr0.1993.72.2.539

Saunders, K. M., & Zucker, B. (1999). Counteracting identity fraud in the information age: the identity theft and assumption deterrence act. *International Review of Law, Computers & Technology*, 13(2), 183–192. https://doi.org/10.1080/13600869955134

Schreck, C. J. (1999). Criminal victimization and low self-control: An extension and test of a general theory of crime. *Justice Quarterly*, 16(3), 633–654. https://doi.org/10.1080/07418829900094291

Schreck, C. J., Stewart, E. A., & Fisher, B. S. (2006). Self-control, victimization, and their influence on risky lifestyles: A longitudinal analysis using panel data. *Journal of Quantitative Criminology*, 22(4), 319–340. https://doi.org/10.1007/s10940-006-9014-y

Scott, S. G., & Bruce, R. A. (1995). Decision-making style: The development and assessment of a new measure. *Educational and Psychological Measurement*, 55(5), 818–831. https://doi.org/10.1177/0013164495055005017

Seiter, J. S., Bruschke, J., & Bai, C. (2002). The acceptability of deception as a function of perceivers' culture, deceiver's intention, and deceiver-deceived relationship. *Western Journal of Communication*, 66(2), 158–180. https://doi.org/10.1080/10570310209374731

Shears, P. (2010). Food fraud – a current issue but an old problem. *British Food Journal*, 112(2), 198–213. https://doi.org/10.1108/00070701011018879

Sherman, J. W., Gawronski, B., & Trope, Y. (Eds.). (2014). *Dual-process theories of the social mind*. Guilford Publications.

Shleifer, A. (2012). Psychologists at the gate: A review of Daniel Kahneman's thinking, fast and slow. *Journal of Economic Literature*, *50*(4), 1080–1091. https://doi.org/10.1257/jel.50.4.1080

Silvia, P. J. (2005). Deflecting reactance: The role of similarity in increasing compliance and reducing resistance. *Basic and Applied Social Psychology*, *27*(3), 277–284. https://doi.org/10.1207/s15324834basp2703_9

Sims, R. L. (2002). Support for the use of deception within the work environment: A Comparison of Israeli and United States employee attitudes. *Journal of Business Ethics*, *35*(1), 27–34. https://doi.org/10.1023/A:1012755801190

Skagerberg, E. M., & Wright, D. B. (2009). Susceptibility to postidentification feedback is affected by source credibility. *Applied Cognitive Psychology*, *23*(4), 506–523. https://doi.org/10.1002/acp.1470

Slovic, P., & Peters, E. (2006). Risk perception and affect. *Current Directions in Psychological Science*, *15*(6), 322–325. https://doi.org/10.1111/j.1467-8721.2006.00461.x

Smith, R. G. (2000). Fraud and financial abuse of older persons. *Current Issues in Criminal Justice:*, *11*(3). https://doi.org/10.1080/10345329.2000.12036165

Smith, R. G. (2010). Identity theft and fraud. In *Handbook of Internet Crime* (pp. 273–301). Routledge.

Snyder, C. R., & Larson, G. R. (1972). A further look at student acceptance of general personality interpretations. *Journal of Consulting and Clinical Psychology*, *38*(3), 384–388. https://doi.org/10.1037/h0032899

Soman, D. (2004). Framing, loss aversion, and mental accounting. In *Blackwell Handbook of Judgment and Decision Making* (1st ed., pp. 379–398). Blackwell.

Speer, D. L. (2000). Redefining borders: The challenges of cybercrime. *Crime, Law and Social Change*, *34*(3), 259–273. https://doi.org/10.1023/A:1008332132218

Speights, D., & Hilinski, M. (2005). Return fraud and abuse: How to protect profits. *Retailing Issues Letter*, *17*(1), 1–6.

Spink, J., Ortega, D. L., Chen, C., & Wu, F. (2017). Food fraud prevention shifts the food risk focus to vulnerability. *Trends in Food Science & Technology*, *62*, 215–220. https://doi.org/10.1016/j.tifs.2017.02.012

Stajano, F., & Wilson, P. (2011). Understanding scam victims: Seven principles for systems security. *Communications of the ACM*, *54*(3), 70–75. https://doi.org/10.1145/1897852.1897872

Stanovich, K.E., West, R. F., & Toplak, M. E. (2014). Rationality, intelligence, and the defining features or Type I and Type 2 processing. In *Dual-Process Theories of the Social Mind* (pp. 80–91). The Guildford Press.

Stanovich, K. E., & West, R. F. (2000). Individual differences in reasoning: Implications for the rationality debate? *Behavioral and Brain Sciences*, *23*(5), 645–665. https://doi.org/10.1017/S0140525X00003435

Stanton, B., Theofanos, M. F., Prettyman, S. S., & Furman, S. (2016). Security fatigue. *IT Professional*, *18*(5), 26–32. https://doi.org/10.1109/MITP.2016.84

Stotland, E. (1977). White collar criminals. *Journal of Social Issues*, *33*(4), 179–196. https://doi.org/10.1111/j.1540-4560.1977.tb02531.x

Strough, J., Mehta, C. M., McFall, J. P., & Schuller, K. L. (2008). Are older adults less subject to the sunk-cost fallacy than younger adults? *Psychological Science*, *19*(7), 650–652. https://doi.org/10.1111/j.1467-9280.2008.02138.x

Taylor, P. J., Lamer, S., & Conchie, S. M. (2015). Cross-cultural deception detection. *Detecting Deception: Current Challenges and Cognitive Approaches*, 175–201.

Taylor, S. E., & Brown, J. D. (1988). Illusion and well-being: A social psychological perspective on mental health. *Psychological Bulletin, 103*(2), 193.

Teasdale, K., & Kent, G. (1995). The use of deception in nursing. *Journal of Medical Ethics, 21*(2), 77–81. https://doi.org/10.1136/jme.21.2.77

Thorndike, E. L. (1920). A constant error in psychological ratings. *Journal of Applied Psychology, 4*(1), 25–29.

Titus, R.M., Heinzelmann, F., & Boyle, J. M. (1995). Victimization of persons by fraud. *Crime & Delinquency, 41*(1), 54–72. https://doi.org/10.1177/0011128795041001004

Titus, R.M., & Gover, A. R. (2001). Personal fraud: The victims and the scams. *Crime Prevention Studies, 12*, 133–152.

Turner, M. M., Banas, J. A., Rains, S. A., Jang, S., Moore, J. L., & Morrison, D. (2010). The effects of altercasting and counterattitudinal behavior on compliance: A lost letter technique investigation. *Communication Reports, 23*(1), 1–13. https://doi.org/10.1080/08934211003598759

Turner, R. E., Edgley, C., & Olmstead, G. (1975). Information control in conversations: Honesty is not always the best policy. *The Kansas Journal of Sociology, 11*(1), 69–89. JSTOR.

Twersky, A., & Kahneman, D. (1979). Prospect theory: An analysis of decision under risk. *Econometrica, 47*(2), 263–291.

Twersky, A., & Kahneman, D. (1981). The framing of decisions and the psychology of choice. *Science, 211*(4481), 453–458.

Van de Weijer, S. G. A., & Leukfeldt, E. R. (2017). Big five personality traits of cybercrime victims. *Cyberpsychology, Behavior, and Social Networking, 20*(7), 407–412. https://doi.org/10.1089/cyber.2017.0028

Van Dijk, E., & Zeelenberg, M. (2003). The discounting of ambiguous information in economic decision making. *Journal of Behavioral Decision Making, 16*(5), 341–352. https://doi.org/10.1002/bdm.450

Van Dijk, J. J. (2001). Attitudes of victims and repeat victims toward the police: Results of the International Crime Victims Survey. *Crime Prevention Studies, 12*, 27–52.

Van Putten, M., Zeelenberg, M., & Van Dijk, E. (2010). Who throws good money after bad? Action vs. state orientation moderates the sunk cost fallacy. *Judgment and Decision Making, 5*(1), 33.

Victor, D. (7 March 2019). Woman and homeless man plead guilty in $400,000 GoFundMe scam. *The New York Times*. www.nytimes.com/2019/03/07/us/gofundme-homeless-scam-guilty.html

Vishwanath, A., Harrison, B., & Ng, Y. J. (2018). Suspicion, cognition, and automaticity model of phishing susceptibility. *Communication Research, 45*(8), 1146–1166. https://doi.org/10.1177/0093650215627483

Walsh, M. E., & Schram, D. D. (1980). The victims of white collar crime: Accuser or accused. In *White-Collar Crime – Theory and Research*. Sage. Retrieved 12 July 2020 from: www.ncjrs.gov/App/Publications/abstract.aspx?ID=65757

Weber, E. U., & Hsee, C. (1998). Cross-cultural differences in risk perception, but cross-cultural similarities in attitudes towards perceived risk. *Management Science, 44*(9), 1205–1217. https://doi.org/10.1287/mnsc.44.9.1205

Weinstein, E. A., & Deutschberger, P. (1963). Some dimensions of altercasting. *Sociometry*, 26(4), 454–466. JSTOR. https://doi.org/10.2307/2786148

Whitty, M.T. (2013). The scammers persuasive techniques model: Development of a stage model to explain the online dating romance scam. *The British Journal of Criminology*, 53(4), 665–684. https://doi.org/10.1093/bjc/azt009

Whitty, M.T. (2017). Do you love me? Psychological characteristics of romance scam victims. *Cyberpsychology, Behavior, and Social Networking*, 21(2), 105–109. https://doi.org/10.1089/cyber.2016.0729

Whitty, M.T., & Buchanan, T. (2012a). The online romance scam: A Serious cybercrime. *Cyberpsychology, Behavior, and Social Networking*, 15(3), 181–183. https://doi.org/10.1089/cyber.2011.0352

Whitty, M.T., & Buchanan, T. (2012b). *The Psychology of the Online Dating Romance Scam*. University of Leicester. Retrieved on 12 July 2020 from: https://fido.nrk.no/d6f57fd73b9898b42c8c322c961c8255f370677fbac5272b71d86047a5359b66/Whitty_romance_scam_report.pdf

Whitty, M.T., & Buchanan, T. (2016). The online dating romance scam: The psychological impact on victims – both financial and non-financial. *Criminology & Criminal Justice*, 16(2), 176–194. https://doi.org/10.1177/1748895815603773

Williams, E. J., Beardmore, A., & Joinson, A. N. (2017). Individual differences in susceptibility to online influence: A theoretical review. *Computers in Human Behavior*, 72, 412–421. https://doi.org/10.1016/j.chb.2017.03.002

Wilson, J. (2017). There is no silver bullet to stop fraudsters. *The Conversation*. http://theconversation.com/there-is-no-silver-bullet-to-stop-fraudsters-70416

Wilson, J. (2018, October). The unusual suspects. *Accounting and Business*. https://abinternational.accaglobal.com/2018/09/24/18oct_int_i_fraudsters/pugpig_index.html

Wittes, B., Poplin, C., Jurecic, Q., & Spera, C. (2016). *Sextortion: Cybersecurity, Teenagers, and Remote Sexual Assault* (p. 47). Center for Technology Innovation. Retrieved on 12 July 2020 from: www.brookings.edu/wp-content/uploads/2016/05/sextortion1-1.pdf

Wolak, J., & Finkelhor, D. (2016). *Sextortion: Findings from a Survey of 1,631 Victims* (p. 81). University of New Hampshire. Retrieved on 12th July, 2020 from: www.unh.edu/ccrc/pdf/Sextortion_RPT_FNL_rev0803.pdf

Wolfe, D., & Hermanson, D. (2004). The fraud diamond: Considering the four elements of fraud. *CPA Journal*, 74(12), 38–42.

Workman, M. (2008). Wisecrackers: A theory-grounded investigation of phishing and pretext social engineering threats to information security. *Journal of the American Society for Information Science and Technology*, 59(4), 662–674. https://doi.org/10.1002/asi.20779

Wright, R. T., & Marett, K. (2010). The influence of experiential and dispositional factors in phishing: An empirical investigation of the deceived. *Journal of Management Information Systems*, 27(1), 273–303. https://doi.org/10.2753/MIS0742-1222270111

Yamagishi, T., & Kakiuchi, R. (2000). It takes venturing into a tiger's cave to steal a baby tiger: Experiments on the development of trust relationships. *The Management of Durable Relations: Theoretical Models and Empirical Studies of Households and Organizations*, 121–123.

Yamagishi, T., Kikuchi, M., & Kosugi, M. (1999). Trust, gullibility, and social intelligence. *Asian Journal of Social Psychology*, *2*(1), 145–161. https://doi.org/10.1111/1467-839X.00030

Yamagishi, T., & Yamagishi, M. (1994). Trust and commitment in the United States and Japan. *Motivation and Emotion*, *18*(2), 129–166. https://doi.org/10.1007/BF02249397

Yan, G., Eidenbenz, S., & Galli, E. (2009). SMS-Watchdog: Profiling social behaviors of SMS users for anomaly detection. In E. Kirda, S. Jha, & D. Balzarotti (Eds.), *Recent Advances in Intrusion Detection* (pp. 202–223). Springer. https://doi.org/10.1007/978-3-642-04342-0_11

Yang, J., Hauser, R., & Goldman, R. H. (2013). Taiwan food scandal: The illegal use of phthalates as a clouding agent and their contribution to maternal exposure. *Food and Chemical Toxicology*, *58*, 362–368. https://doi.org/10.1016/j.fct.2013.05.010

Yuki, M., Maddux, W. W., Brewer, M. B., & Takemura, K. (2005). Cross-cultural differences in relationship- and group-based trust. *Personality and Social Psychology Bulletin*, *31*(1), 48–62. https://doi.org/10.1177/0146167204271305

Zenone, M., & Snyder, J. (2019). Fraud in medical crowdfunding: A typology of publicized cases and policy recommendations. *Policy & Internet*, *11*(2), 215–234. https://doi.org/10.1002/poi3.188

Zuckoff, M. (2005). Annals of crime: The perfect mark. *The New Yorker*, *82*, 36–42.

Index

Note: References to figures are in *italics*.

Action Fraud 15
advance fee fraud 6, 16–17, 39, 53; and examples *107*, *108–9*
affinity groups 56–57
age 85–86
ageing 76–77
agreeableness 85–86
alcohol addiction 10
altercasting 64, 65, 83, 98
anchoring effect 50–51
attitudes 31–2
auctions 6, 93–4
authority 58–59, 69–70, 82, 99
automacity 87–88
awareness 74–75

background knowledge 74–75, 82–83; and case studies 92, 94, 96, 99, 100, 101, 103
banking 20–21, 106, *110*
Barnum effect 49–50
behaviours 78–79
beliefs 78–79
bereavement 21, 76, 97–98, 100
bitcoin 24
boiler room fraud 23
business opportunities 23–24

capability 9–10
case studies 92–105
central route of processing 45, 83
channel of communication 30–31, 33
charities 5, 6, 22, 58

CIFAS 9
circumstances 76–77, 88, *114*; and case studies 92, 93, 101
clairvoyant scams 21, 49–50
coercion 10
cognition 72, 85, 87–88
cognitive biases 47–53
cold readings 21, 49–50
commitment 59, 82
communication 29–33; and deceptive 33–35
companies 23; and case studies 102–4; and imitating 64, 106, *110–111*, *117*, *119*
compliance 3, 69–70, 91–105
compromised accounts *110–111*
conscientiousness 85
consistency 59, 82
control 51–52, 68–70
correspondence scrutiny 121, 123
credibility 57–58, 99, 103, 105
crowdfunding 22
crying 60–61
cryptocurrency 24
cues and leakage 34; and deception 34, 38, 78; and visual 37, 94; and peripheral 45; and authority 59, 70, 113, 124; and scarcity 60; and urgency 124–127
cultural differences 35–36, 77, 85
cultural norms 32; and deception 35–36, 40
cybersecurity 58, 60, 80, 95

deception 6, 7–8, 35–36; and communication 33–35; and detection 36–38; and fraudsters 38–40; and societal conventions 35–36
decision-making styles 46–53
delaying decisions 74–75, 89
dementia 76–77
demographics 76–77
disability 92
dishonesty 7–8; *see also* deception; lying
dishonesty and distraction 61–62
doorstep scams 6
drug addiction 10
drug smuggling 19

eBay 1–2, 93
ego 10
Elaboration Likelihood Model (ELM) 45–46, 71–72, 83–84
elderly 76–7, 85–86
email 6, 24, 74–75; and Nigerian fraud 16, 17; *see also* phishing
embarrassment 13, 22, 62–64, 123, 121, 126–128, 130
emotion 3, 26, 64, 68, 91; and advance fee fraud 16–17; and emotional state 51, 73, 76, 79, 125; and crowdfunding 22; and romance scams 19–20, 65, 101; and vulnerability 76, 100
employment *see* jobs
errors in judgment 47, 82–3, 91
extortion 24, 25, 71
extraversion 85–86

Facebook 95, 121, *122*, 123–4
false consensus 83
false representation 5
fear 21, 24–5, 55, 60, 64, 71, 124–126, *110*; and case studies 102
finance *see* investment opportunities
flattery 50, 71
food fraud 27
foolish action 84–85
framing effects 47–9
fraud 1–4; and authority 58–59; and case studies 91–105; and charities 22; and checklist 120–121, 123–124; and communication 31; and control 51–52; and correspondence 121, 123; and culture 35; and definition 5–8; and emotion 125–127; and extortion 24–26, *25*; and food 27; and grooming 65–66; and health 21–22; and identity 18–19; and investments 23–24; and likeability 56; and mortgages 26–27; and reporting 13–14, 130–131; and responding 127–129; and romance 19–20; and sanctions 13–15; and similarity 57; and social influence 61; and susceptibility 67, 88–90; and taxonomy 11–13; and techniques 46, 124–125; and vulnerability 68–81, 83–84; *see also* phishing; fraud victims
fraud against individuals 5–7, 9, 12, 14
'Fraud triangle' 9–10
Fraud victims 2–3, 5–8, 13–14, 67, 80; and authority 70; and beliefs 78; and charity and crowdfunding 21; and deception 39–41; and elderly 85–86; and errors in judgment 83; and flattery 50; and fraud reporting 13, 129–131; and fraud sanctions 14–15; and grooming 65–66; and gullibility 73; and identity fraud 18–19; and illusion of control and just world hypothesis 51–52; and impulsivity 68–69; and jobs and investments 23–24; and miracle cures 21–22; and Nigerian fraud 16–17; and phishing 20–21, 74; and psychic scams 21; and risk assessment 71; and romance scams 19–20, 77; and rushing decisions 75; and sextortion 24–26; and sharing 129–131; and suspicions 126
fraud warnings 3, 79, 120–121, 127–128
fraudsters 3, 8–11, 37–41
funds *see* money

gambling addiction 10, 113
gender 19–20, 77, 85
giveaways 23, *119*
goals and visceral influence 24
GoFundMe 6, 22
greed 10, 16–17, 55, 82, 125; and victims 52, 129; and case study 97
grooming 19, 65–66; and case study 101
gullibility 72–74, 84–85

Index 153

halo effect 56
health 14, 129; and scams 5, 21–22, 27; and vulnerability 77
helplessness 102
holiday scams 5; and case study 104–105
hook 87

identity fraud 18–19, 41, 69
ideology 10
Ikea effect 47
illusion of control 51–52, 78
impulsivity 68–69, 73, 77, 80, 86, 89
information 5, 7, 82; and beliefs 78; and communication 33–34; and cross referencing 121–123; and decisions 43, 46; and mortgage fraud 26–27; and processing 3, 45, 71–73, 82–84, 87–88; and risk assessment 71; and phishing 20–21; and security 78–79; and synthetic fraud 18–19; and taxonomy 11–13
inheritance fraud 6
insurance fraud 5, 27, 75
Internet 6
intimidation 71
introversion 86
investment opportunities 23–24, 49, 53, 62, 125–127; and case study 96–7

job scams 6, 23–24; and deception 34; and example 113, *115*
judgment *see* errors in judgment
just world hypothesis 51–52

Kahneman, Daniel: *Thinking Fast and Slow* 43
kidnapping 17

language 36
legitimacy 57–58, 94, 103, 105
liking 31, 56–57, 82, 93, 100
loneliness 76–77
lottery scams 6, 23, 53, 59, 70–71
lure 87
lying 7, 34–38, 40

malware 3, 20
manipulation 49, 58–59, 73, 76
miracle cures 21–22, 49, 57, 76, 106, *112*
mobile phones 20–21, 79

'Model of Fraud Susceptibility' 88–90
moderating responses 127–129
money 10–11, 22, 28, 39, 52, 58–59, 91, 129; and case studies 95–96, 100–104; and extortion 24; and laundering 19, 62; and transfers 12, 16–17, 65
mortgage fraud 26–27
motivations 125; and deception 35–38; and errors in judgments 82; and information processing 45, 72, 85, 104; and perpetrating fraud 9–11; and security behaviour 79
murder 17

neuroticism 85–86
Nigerian scams 6, 16–17, 39, 53, 106 and altercasting 65; and examples *107–109*

obedience to authority 59, 69–70, 80, 99
occupational fraud 9
openness to experience 85–86

PayPal 1–2, 93–94
pension scams 5
peripheral route of processing 45, 72, 83–84
perpetrators *see* fraudsters
personality 49–50, 73, 85–87
personality feedback 49–50
persuasion 17, 20, 45, 91, 83; and techniques 7, 56–62, 80, 82, 106
pharming 20
phishing scams 17, 20–1, 24, 38, 41, 67, 106, 127–128; and anchoring effect 51; and beliefs 78; and case studies 93, 98–99; and compliance 69; and credibility 57–8; and examples *105–119*; and framing 49; and impulsivity 68; and priming 64; and obedience to authority 59, 80; and susceptibility 85–88; and techniques 105, 106, 113; and trust 80; and urgency 60; and vigilance 74–75; and visceral influence 55, 91
Pinocchio 5
police 40–41, 130; and case studied 99; and impersonating 5, 20, 58; and sanctions 13–14; positive illusions 82–83

pressure 23, 124, 128; and fraud offending 9; and case studies 104–105; and compliance 69; and framing 48
priming 62–64
prize draws 6, 23
prize proximity 39, 62, 84, 97, 106
prize vividness 62, 84, 106
prosecutions 13–15, 130
psychic scams 6, 16, 21, 49–50; and case studies 97–98
pyramid schemes 6, 24, 39, 61; and case studies 96–97

reciprocation 58, 73, 82; and case study 104–105
reciprocity 80, 124
refunds 113; and examples *116–17*
rental scams 6
response to a fraud 127–129
risk assessment 19, 23, 48, 56, 61, 70–71, 87–88, 103; and case studies 102–103; and fraud offending 8, 11, 13, 15
risk taking 68, 70, 73, 76, 79, 82
romance scams 19–20, 39–40, 55; and authority 59; and beliefs 78–79; and case studies 100–101; and emotion 126; and gender differences 77; and grooming 65; and impulsivity 69; and liking and similarity 57; and reciprocation 58; and risk assessment 70; and romantic beliefs 78

sanctions 13–14
scammers *see* fraudsters
scams *see* fraud
scam techniques 5, 14, 17, 19, 46, 50, 55–66, 73, 106; and case studies 92–105, 113, 124–125; and examples *107–119*
scarcity 59–61, 82; and case studies 102–103
scrutiny 23, 58, 121, 123
security 74, 79–81; and advice 86; and data 20, 60
self-control 45, 68–69, 75, 82, 84
self-esteem 2, 3, 14, 41, 129; and belief in just word 78; and compliance 70
sensation seeking 70–71, 82
sextortion 24–26, *25*, 57–8 and case studies 101–102; and intimidation 71; and priming 62, 64, *64*; and technology 87
sharing fraud experience 13, 129–131
similarity 56–57, 61–62; and case studies 92–93, 100
smartphones 21, 79
smishing 20
SMRC model of communication 30–31
social engineering 20–21, 59, 80
social influence 61, 96–97; *see also* social proof
social isolation 77
social media 79, 88, 91; *see also* Facebook
social norms 11, 22, 58, 77; and case studies 95, 102, 105; and communication 32
social proof 61, 82; and case study 96
spear phishing 20; and case study 98–99
stereotypes and fraud offending 8; and deception 37; and information processing 43
sunk-cost fallacy 52–53
surrogacy 28
susceptibility 67; and flattery 71; and interpersonal influence 84; and phishing 85–90
suspicion 45, 89, 95, 99, 113, 126–127; and deception 34, 36; and phishing 87–88
sweepstakes 23, *see also* giveaways
synthetic fraud 18–19
System 1 and System 2 of processing 43–45

tax frauds 6
tax returns 113, 124
technological savviness 10, 87
terrorism 10, 18
text messages 20–21
thought processes 43–53
ticket fraud 6
time limits 24, 46, 55; and case studies 96–97, 104–105
trust 2–3, 5, 15, 17, 20, 40, 50, 57, 72–75, 77, 86; and case studies 102–104

urgency 23, 59–61, 106, 113, 124–127; and case studies 93–94, 101–102; and examples *108*, *111*, *114*, *118–119*

victims' details sold by scammers 17
vigilance 69–70, 74–75, 88–89; and case studies 94, 96, 102–105
visceral influence 24–5, 55, 56, 62, 80, 82, 84; and case studies 97, 102

voice phishing 20–21
vulnerability 68–81, 83–85

warning signs 84
warranties 6–7, 57, 73
websites 6, 7, 18, 20, 65, 120, 123

9780367859565